THE
PETERBOROUGH
CHRONICLE

NUMBER XLIV OF THE
RECORDS OF CIVILIZATION, SOURCES AND STUDIES
AUSTIN P. EVANS, *Editor*

THE
PETERBOROUGH
CHRONICLE

Translated with an Introduction

By HARRY A. ROSITZKE

COLUMBIA UNIVERSITY PRESS

NEW YORK 1951

RECORDS OF CIVILIZATION, SOURCES AND STUDIES

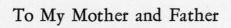

To My Mother and Father

PREFACE

NO ONE OF THE OLD ENGLISH CHRONICLES HAS EVER BEEN TRANSLATED AS A UNIT INTO MODERN ENGLISH. THE EXISTING translations, even where based on a reliable text, represent a conflation of four separate chronicles into a synthetic text whose composition lies pretty much at the will of the editor. The result is that four more or less independent traditions are fused into one—and generally according to the fullness of various sections of the narrative, rather than on the basis of the reliability of the separate traditions.

The historical importance of these documents, however, is more than sufficient to justify their being made independently accessible to the modern reader and to students of English history. They are the only documents to invest two vital phases of early English history—the Scandinavian and Norman conquests—with some clarity of outline, and in important ways they supplement Bede in the centuries after the coming of the Germans.

Since the Winchester Chronicle has recently appeared in a first-rate French version, by Marie Hoffmann-Hirtz, the logical second choice for translation is the Peterborough Chronicle. This is the longest—by seventy-five years—of all the chronicles; it is unique in giving a picture of the Norman period; and in the earlier annals it represents for the most part a totally new tradition—the Northern-Kentish—as opposed to the almost exclusively West Saxon character of the Winchester annals.

I am grateful to Professor Francis P. Magoun, Jr., of Harvard University, for various useful hints and suggestions.

H. A. R.

Fairfax, Virginia
January, 1951

CONTENTS

ABBREVIATIONS

EHR	*English Historical Review*
HE	Bede *Historia ecclesiastica gentis Anglorum*
OE	Old English
ON	Old Norse
p	part
Plummer	Charles Plummer, ed., *Two of the Saxon Chronicles Parallel*
Plummer's *Bede*	Charles Plummer, ed., *Venerabilis Baedae opera historica*

INTRODUCTION

INTRODUCTION

THE HISTORIANS OF ENGLAND, IRELAND, AND RUSSIA SHARE THE DISTINCTION OF BEING THE FIRST IN EUROPE TO EMploy their native tongue in place of Latin in recording the early stages of their national history. The Old English Chronicles (60 B. C.–A. D. 1154), various Irish writings, especially the Annals of Ulster (A. D. 431–1540),[1] and the Russian Nestor or Primary Chronicle (A. D. 852–1110) [2] are the only European historical compositions in the vernacular before 1200. The English and Russian documents, or rather sets of documents, are in particular built on very much the same plan. They are monastic compilations of anonymous or conjectural authorship; they are composed of a mixture of annalistic notation and historical narrative; and they employ foreign materials, early legends, local traditions, extraneous documents, and descriptions of natural and supernatural phenomena to fill out the brief catalogue of the local and national events it is their business to narrate. For the periods which they cover, both have been extensively and often exclusively employed by later historians, medieval and modern. Without them the history of the Germanic colonization—for both the English and Russian annals tell of clans or tribes from northern Germany and Scandinavia that left their homeland to conquer or rule a foreign country—would be marked by even more extensive gaps than it now displays.

Of the historical productions of pre-Conquest England in vernacular prose, seven manuscripts have survived.[3] The extent to which writings of this character have been destroyed or are still lost can hardly be estimated, but the existence of intermediate chronicles to be inferred from a comparison of the surviving texts, as well as references and borrowings in outside sources, indicates that their number is not inconsiderable. The burning of the monasteries during the Danish invasions, the advent of the Normans and the growing incomprehensibility of the older language, and the dissolution of the mon-

---

[1] See R. I. Best, *Bibliography of Irish Philology and of Printed Irish Literature* (Dublin, 1913), pp. 249–56; Charles Gross, *The Sources and Literature of English History*, 2d ed. (London, 1915), nos. 1377, 1380, 1705–13.

[2] Translated, with introduction, by Samuel H. Cross, "The Russian Primary Chronicle," *Harvard Studies and Notes in Philology and Literature*, XII (1930), 75–297.

[3] A single leaf of an eighth MS was first edited by J. Zupitza, "Fragment einer englischen Chronik aus den Jahren 1113 und 1114," *Anglia*, I (1877), 196–97.

asteries under Henry VIII are the factors mainly responsible for the failure to preserve more fully these oldest memorials of English prose and English historiography.

The surviving manuscripts of Old English vernacular history represent four more or less independent chronicles customarily and falsely labelled the Anglo-Saxon Chronicle. Not a single fact about the authorship, the origin, or the date of these documents is directly supplied by the chronicles themselves; nor, except in a few cases, can the contemporaneity of their entries be established with any certainty. Any description of the origin, relationship, or value of these chronicles must accordingly be based upon a comparative analysis of their contents—an analysis that was rigorously and, in all but a few details, definitively carried out by Plummer in his revision of Earle's edition of the two main chronicles.[4]

The starting point of all four chronicles is clearly a series of annals ending about 890 which was probably compiled in Wessex about that date at the direction of King Alfred. A copy of this original compilation became the prototype of a series of further copies which eventually developed into the four main chronicles as we now have them.

1. *The Winchester Chronicle.*[5] One of these copies remained at the foundation where the original source chronicle was compiled—Winchester or a place farther to the southwest—and was extended by a contemporary continuation from 894 to 924 and by a more meagre set of annals from 925 to 975, eked out by a few local notices and poems. During the tenth century the chronicle was at Winchester, where it was sporadically added to up to 1001, but for some time thereafter it lay untouched. Later, possibly about 1070, it was transferred to Christ Church, Canterbury, where a few local entries were appended, running down to 1070 and ending with a long Latin notice on the life of Lanfranc.

This chronicle, customarily designated by the siglum A or $\bar{A}$, survives in Corpus Christi College, Cambridge, MS 173, folios 1–32. The items to 891 are written in a single hand, apparently of that date, while the succeeding hands are approximately contemporary with the

---

[4] Plummer, *Two of the Saxon Chronicles Parallel,* II, xxxvii–cxxvii.
[5] The appropriateness of this designation is discussed by Smith, *The Parker Chronicle (832–900),* pp. 7–10. An account of this chronicle in sharp disagreement with Plummer's is given by H. H. Howorth, "Notes on the Anglo-Saxon Chronicle. I. The Value of Codex A.," *EHR,* XV (1900), 748–54.

events they describe. There are many interpolations, most of them by the final scribe, who is also the compiler and translator of *F* (see under 4, below).

The Winchester Chronicle survives also in an abbreviated form; for about 1025, before *A* left Winchester, it was copied by a local scribe to the year 1001 with only slight alteration of the original, the new chronicle remaining a barren stock. The small remains of this transcript (variously labelled *A, G, W*) is contained in British Museum, Cotton Otho MS B. xi, for the manuscript was reduced to a charred remnant of three leaves (giving snatches of the text from 823 to 871) [6] in the Cotton fire of 1731. The text is, however, fortunately preserved in an edition made almost a century earlier [7] and in two sixteenth-century transcripts.[8]

2. *The Abingdon Chronicle.* A second copy of the ninth-century compilation was sent to the monastery at Abingdon either shortly after 892 or about 915 with the first continuation up to 915 already entered. A miniature chronicle of Mercian events (the so-called Mercian Register or Wars of Æthelflæd) was incorporated into the chronicle, and the continuation from 934 to 975 and a few local notices were added.

Shortly after this the manuscript was copied at least twice. One copy was sent to St. Augustine's, Canterbury, where it found no continuator. This text, designated *B,* is preserved in British Museum, Cotton Tiberius MS A. vi, folios 1–34. It extends to 977 and is written in one hand of about the year 1000.

The second transcript remained at Abingdon and was continued down to 1066, partly from written sources utilized by other scriptoria, partly from independent materials. The extant *C*-text is a copy of this lost Abingdon chronicle made in the middle of the eleventh century. It is contained in British Museum, Cotton Tiberius MS B. i, folios 112–164*r*, and is written in several hands, all of about 1050.[9]

[6] Printed by K. Horst, "Die Reste der Handschrift G der altenglischen Annalen," *Englische Studien,* XXII (1896), 447–50.
[7] Abraham Wheelocke, "Chronologia Anglo-Saxonica," appended to *Historiæ ecclesiasticæ gentis Anglorum libri V. a venerabili Beda presbytero scripti* (Cambridge, 1643; reissued 1644), pp. 501–566.
[8] British Museum, MS Add. 43703; Trinity College, Dublin, MS E. 5. 19. On this latter transcript see H. H. Howorth, *op. cit.,* 748; A. Campbell, *The Battle of Brunanburh* (London, 1938), pp. 133 ff.
[9] The *B*-text was being edited before the war by Reinold Hoops, of the University of Innsbruck. An edition of the *C*-text by the present writer has appeared recently:

3. *The Worcester Chronicle.* A third transcript of the master copy of the original compilation came to a northern monastery, probably Ripon, where it was enlarged and continued by the use of various southern and northern materials ending with a group of Northumbrian annals running down to 966. At some time between this date and 1033 the chronicle, or a copy of it, came to a monastery in the diocese of Worcester, possibly Evesham, where it was actively continued until 1079. This chronicle, known as the *D*-text, is contained in British Museum, Cotton Tiberius MS B. iv, folios 3–86.[10] It is written in various hands of about the year 1100 and accordingly represents a very late transcript of the original chronicle. It is defaced by a lacuna extending from 262 to 693 inclusive, and the end is in a mutilated condition.

4. *The Peterborough Chronicle.*[11] Before the continuations had been added to the transcript at Ripon, a copy of it was made and sent to another monastery. This chronicle was continued for a time in the north, later in the south, coming eventually to St. Augustine's, Canterbury.

In Canterbury a bilingual (Latin and English) epitome, designated *F,* was made at Christ Church and is preserved in British Museum, Cotton Domitian MS A. viii. This hitherto unedited version [12] was written about 1100, principally by one hand, but with frequent marginal and interlinear insertions, and breaks off mutilated at 1058.

After leaving Canterbury, the manuscript was copied and redacted by a scribe of the abbey of Peterborough about 1121 and continued there until 1154. This, our *E*-text, is preserved in the Bodleian Library (Oxford), Laud Misc. 636. It is written in one hand to 1121 and in several further hands to 1154, where it ends. The manuscript has occasionally been described as ending in a mutilated condition, but enough of the rubbed script on the last page has been made out

---

The C-Text of the Old English Chronicles, Beiträge zur englischen Philologie, Heft XXXIV (Bochum-Langendreer, 1940).

[10] Reliably edited by E. Classen and F. E. Harmer, *An Anglo-Saxon Chronicle* (Manchester, 1926).

[11] Essentially, as will appear more clearly later, *E* is a Peterborough chronicle only as it now stands in its final form. More properly, it is a Northumbrian edition of a West Saxon chronicle extended by a southern (Augustinian) and a Peterborough continuation.

[12] It is now being jointly edited by Marie Hoffmann-Hirtz of Strasbourg and F. P. Magoun, Jr., of Harvard University.

to show that the final sentence is a commendation of the new abbot and is stopped by the usual triangular punctuation—a perfectly normal conclusion. The manuscript must accordingly be considered intact, with possibly the loss of a blank leaf at the end.

Even from this brief account of the Old English Chronicles it is plain that *E* has the most complicated structure of the four extant recensions. It was composed at five or six different foundations; it was, from start to finish, copied at least four and possibly seven or eight times; and especially in its later sections it displays, quite irregularly, connections with the other three chronicles. The extent of these relations and the successive stages in the growth of the Peterborough Chronicle itself will emerge most clearly from the following chronological analysis of its evolution. The sources of the individual entries supplied below (all annal references are to the numbering of *E*) and the probable place and time at which the various sections were composed will place in fairly clear perspective the rapidly shifting value and reliability of the information contained in this heterogeneous collection of historical materials.

I. PRIMARY COMPILATION. The so-called Alfredian Chronicle represents a West Saxon [13] compilation edited about 890 [14]—presumably under the supervision of King Alfred [15]—from a miscellaneous assortment of older materials. It seems likely that the basis of this compilation was a short chronicle that had been put together at the end of the reign of King Æthelwulf. This earlier chronicle was apparently composed of some local annals, covering roughly the cen-

[13] The traditional association of the Primary Compilation with Winchester has been challenged, on good grounds, by F. M. Stenton, "The Southwestern Element in the Old English Chronicle," *Essays in Medieval History Presented to T. F. Tout* (Manchester, 1925), pp. 15–24. Frequent local notices concerned with Dorset and Somerset in the text from 750 to 891 point to a southwestern locale for the original compilation. The central position of Winchester in West Saxon civil life developed only after the ninth century.

[14] The confused chronology of the four chronicles from 892 on and the change in reckoning the start of the year at 891 (see below) support 891–92 as the date of the final editing of the Primary Compilation before copies were made and sent to the various foundations.

[15] The *a priori* probability that Alfred had a hand in the compilation of an essentially West Saxon vernacular chronicle edited about the year 890 is only slightly strengthened by some phrasal parallelisms between Alfred's translation of Orosius and the Primary Chronicle (Plummer, II, cvi–cvii) and by its ascription to Alfred in the twelfth-century *L'Estorie des Engles* of Geoffrey Gaimar, edited by C. T. Martin, "Rolls Series" (London, 1888), I, 144.

tury after the end of Bede's *Historia ecclesiastica,* which were borrowed from a monastic chronicle kept at Canterbury, supplemented and extended for some twenty years from traditional oral recollections as well as from earlier, probably contemporaneous, memoranda of West Saxon and Mercian affairs.[16]

This section of the Primary Compilation (733–855), as it now stands intact in the *A* and *C* texts, comprises over fifty entries, all but three of which (entries for the years 755, 823, 827) are strictly annalistic. Though primarily ecclesiastical in content, they furnish considerable data on secular West Saxon and, less frequently, Mercian affairs. From 835 to 855 a short series of only slightly fuller annals narrates the chief events in the wars with the Danes—835–40 (*E* omits 838), 845, 851, 852*b*, 855.

To this earlier nucleus the Alfredian compilers added some thirty annals, most of them curt notices, which describe the conflicts with the Danes and are probably roughly contemporary with the events they recount. In addition, they prefixed to the Æthelwulfian chronicle a miscellany of independent and second-hand information which carried back their chronicle to the beginning of the Christian era, although some of this latter material may already have been incorporated into the older compilation.

The bulk of these supplementary annals was taken from Bede's *Historia ecclesiastica,* almost all of them having been drawn from the chronological epitome at the end of that work (v. 24). These notices extend, for the most part, from 596 to 731, though a few earlier items, mainly on Romano-British relations, were also taken over. The *E*-entries from Bede are listed in the next section. In addition, a series of short annals—*E*-entries for the years 1–46, 62–155 (non-Latin)— containing a few Roman and ecclesiastical *notitiae,* was extracted from a hitherto unidentified universal chronicle.

The most important additions, however, were two groups of independent annals apparently based upon oral traditions current in Alfred's time or upon written notices of some indefinitely earlier date [17]

---

[16] On the pre-Alfredian materials and compilation(s), see Grubitz, *Kritische Untersuchung über die angelsächsischen Annalen bis zum Jahre 893, passim;* Plummer, II, cix–cxiv.

[17] They were probably written down after Bede, who had little West Saxon data to draw upon, although it has been suggested by H. M. Chadwick, *Origin of the English Nation* (Cambridge, 1907), p. 26, that a set of contemporaneous annals ending in 754 was employed by the Alfredian compilers.

The first set of entries supplies a handful of dates, names, and battles for the otherwise almost completely vacant history of the Anglo-Saxon kingdoms from the coming of the English to the arrival of Augustine : the early history of the kingdoms of Kent (455, 456, 465, 473, 488), of Sussex (477, 485, 491), and of Wessex (495, 501, 508, 514, 519, 527, 530, 534, 544) ; the accessions and battles of the West Saxon kings from Cynric to Ceolric (552, 556, 560 part, 568, 571, 577, 584, 591, 592p, 593p) ; and the accessions of three Northumbrian kings (560p, 588, 593p).

For the period essentially covered by Bede's history, the independent entries are also concerned in the main with Wessex. Except for a few miscellaneous bits (653, 654p, 669, 671, 692p, 694p, 714), they recount the royal accessions, baptisms, battles, and episcopal affairs of the kings of Wessex from Ceolwulf to Æthelhard (597, 607, 611, 614, 628, 636p, 639, 648, 658p, 672, 674, 675p, 676p, 682, 686, 687, 715, 718, 722, 725p, 726, 730). A series of over a dozen genealogies, almost all of which were excised from E before it assumed its final form, were also inserted into the Primary Compilation.

The original manuscript of the Primary Compilation into which the above materials were incorporated was copied off, apparently almost at once; but in the process of copying, the scribe's failure to omit several eventless years produced a serious chronological displacement of two, later three, years from 754 to 845. Although a majority of the events in this section can be reliably dated two or three years after the annuary indications of the four chronicles, the existence of the true chronology in the original version of the Primary Chronicle is unequivocally attested by the existence of this earlier correct annuary numbering in the so-called *Annals of St. Neots* which are based upon an older lost chronicle related to *ACDE*.[18] It is a copy, perhaps even a copy of a copy, and not the original compilation itself that forms the prototype of the earlier sections of all four Old English Chronicles.

II. NORTHERN RECENSION. One of the several copies made of this transcribed Primary Chronicle and distributed to an undetermined

[18] The *Annals* have been edited by Stevenson, *Asser's Life of King Alfred,* pp. 117–45. The dislocation was first pointed out by William Stubbs, *Chronica magistri Rogeri de Hoveden* (London, 1868–71), I, xci–c, and subsequently analyzed in greater detail by Theopold, *Kritische Untersuchungen über die Quellen zur angelsächsischen Geschichte des achten Jahrhunderts,* pp. 9–90.

number of religious houses settled somewhere in the north, probably at Ripon, about 892 and was there revised and enlarged by the incorporation of two substantial groups of annals:

1. A series of passages was taken from the body of the *Historia ecclesiastica* to replace or expand most of the Bede citations from the Epitome which had been almost exclusively employed in the Primary Compilation. All the Bede annals in *E* and the passage of the *HE* on which they are based are contained in the following list. An asterisk marks the annals that did not exist in any form in the Primary Compilation.

E (year)	*HE* (book and section)	*E* (year)	*HE* (book and section)
Pref.	I. 1	635	III. 7
B.C. 60	I. 2	636p	III. 8
A.D. 47	I. 3	639*b*	III. 8
167	I. 4	641p	III. 9–14 *passim*
189	I. 5	643	III. 14
*286	I. 7(?)	644	III. 7
*379	I. 9(?)	645	III. 7
380	I. 9–10	649	III. 7
409	I. 11	650	III. 14
*423	I. 13	652	V. 24
430	I. 13	653p	III. 18, 20
*443	I. 13–14	654p	III. 24
449	I. 15	*655p	III. 20
538	V. 24	656	III. 24
540	V. 24	658p	III. 7
547p	V. 24	660	III. 7
565	III. 4	661p	IV. 13
*583	I. 23	664	III. 26–28, IV. 1
596	V. 24	*667	III. 29, IV. 1
601	V. 24	668	IV. 1
603p	I. 34	670	IV. 5, III. 7
604	II. 3	673	IV. 5, 19
605	II. 1–2	675p	V. 24
616	II. 5–8	676p	IV. 12
*617p	II. 12	678	IV. 12
*624	II. 7	679	IV. 21
625	II. 9	680	V. 24
626p	II. 9, 14	*681	IV. 12
627	II. 14, 16–19	*684	IV. 26
632	II. 15	685p	IV. 26–V. 6 *passim*
633	II. 20	688	V. 7
634	III. 1, 7	690	V. 8

E (year)	HE (book and section)	E (year)	HE (book and section)
692p	v. 8	709	v. 18–19
*693	v. 8	710p	v. 20, 24
694p	IV. 26	716p	v. 22–24
*697	v. 24	721p	v. 6
*699	v. 24	725p	v. 23
703	v. 18	*727	v. 23
704	v. 24	729	v. 22–23
705p	v. 18	731	v. 23

2. A series of Northumbrian annals (733–806) was introduced into the eighth-century section of the Primary Compilation to supplement its rather meagre and one-sided information for that century. From 733 [19] to 755 these northern additions (almost verbally identical in D and E) are rather sporadic, but for the next fifty years they bulk far larger in D and E than the original entries of the Primary Compilation, only half a dozen of which have been left intact. Most of this northern element is concerned with Northumbrian episcopal affairs and royal obits and successions. Easily identifiable by comparison with AC, it is represented in over thirty-five annals (733 part, 734p, 735, 737p, 741, 744p, 757, 759p, 760p, 761p, 762p, 765, 766, 768, 774p, 776, 777p, 778, 779p, 780, 782, 785p, 788, 789, 790p, 791, 792p, 793, 794p, 795, 796p, 797p, 798, 800p, 802p, 803p, 806).

The set of Latin Northumbrian annals upon which the northern redactor drew for these additions was also employed, though in a slightly shorter version, in a tenth-century compilation which Simeon of Durham incorporated into his Historia regum and in the twelfth-century Historia post Bedam, based upon Simeon, which was taken over by Roger of Howden to form the first section of his Chronica. These annals, apparently labelled Gesta veterum Northanhymbrorum according to the twelfth-century Richard of Hexham, were ostensibly compiled as a contemporary record at some northern foundation to continue the chronological epitome appended to Bede's Historia ecclesiastica and furnish virtually the only information about northern affairs between the deaths of Æthelstan and Edmund. Several indications within the Gesta that they were compiled at Ripon agree neatly with similar internal evidence that the Northern Recension was edited at the same spot.

[19] Northern additions in DE not derived from Bede at 702, 705, 710, 716 are probably derived from a separate source.

III. Northern Continuation. At least two copies were made of this Northern Recension. One remained at Ripon and eventually came to rest in the West Midlands, where it finally produced the *D* or Worcester Chronicle. A second copy was sent to some other northern monastery where it remained from 893 to 900 without receiving any additional entries: it did not get the rather full continuation to 915, common to the other three chronicles, or the Mercian Register incorporated into *C* and *D*. Even during the next quarter century *E* was added to only very sporadically—it has a mere handful of single-line general notices for the entire reign of Edward the Elder (901, 906, 910p, 918, 924, 925). During the next fifty years, however, there found its way into this copy an abbreviated version of the northern recension of the spotty continuation (934–975) found most fully in *A* and *C*. These national entries, as they now stand in *E*, comprise 934, 937, 940, 944, 945, 948, 955, 956, 959, 969, 970, 972, 975.

The northern continuator again eked out this sparse record with extracts from a second set of lost Northumbrian annals (901–966) which was also employed by the scribe of the Ripon copy, *D*, and is more fully represented in both parts of Simeon of Durham's *Gesta regum*. A few of these northern additions are common to *DE* (910p, 923, 927p, 954, 966), but others are peculiar to *E* (921, 942, 949, 952). Three further non-northern items (927p, 933, 963) appear in *E* alone in this section.

IV. Second Continuation. This extended Northern Recension, or a copy of it, was continued quite actively for the next fifty years, but it is impossible to determine from internal evidence where the manuscript was lodged. Down to 1022 *E* frequently draws upon the same sources as *D* and, less extensively, *C*, so that the three chronicles, or rather their predecessors, must have come into contact with each other or with some common source during this period. All that can be said with reasonable assurance is that at some time after 966 (the last of the Northumbrian annals) and before 1036 (where the southern point of view becomes unmistakable) the manuscript, or a copy of it, was transferred to the south.

After the meagre tenth-century entries of the Northern Continuation, four short annals of West Saxon affairs (978–81), identical in *DE,* lead into a longer, more or less unified set of annals (983–1018) which covers in detail the endless fighting of Æthelred the Unready and Edmund Ironside with the Danes. The account of Æthelred's reign from 983 on and of Edmund's reign becomes progressively fuller and more spirited, and marks the hand of a highly competent chronicler—ironic, independent, and graphic in description. But for a few sporadic additions and insertions these annals are almost verbally identical in *C, D,* and *E;* the large number of local Canterbury notices interspersed provides some ground for placing their *composition* at Canterbury. The annals 1019–22 are also closely related to the entries in *C* and *D.*

V. SOUTHERN CONTINUATION. By 1036, or possibly 1023, the manuscript, or a transcript of it, had found its way to St. Augustine's (Canterbury) where it was continued for some time—quite certainly up to the Conquest and possibly until as late as 1121. This Augustinian Continuation represents an essentially independent tradition, although its entries occasionally run very close to *D* (1028–31, 1059, 1064, 1071–76) and a few are peculiar to *CE* (1042, 1043).

In the pre-Conquest section (1023–66) a handful of short entries about Canute's reign prefaces a succession of long, detailed notices dealing primarily with southern affairs during the reigns of Canute's sons and of Edward the Confessor. The relationship of these entries in *E* to the materials of *C* and *D* is extremely complicated and shifting. In some annals all three employ a common source; in others two agree in one version with the third independent; and in almost all the entries details are added, omitted, shifted. Furthermore, even in annals where the accounts do not have a discernible common origin, a great deal of the material is common to all three. It is in this eleventh-century section that the customary conflation of the chronicles produces the maximum distortion of the genuine nature of the materials. *C, D,* and *E* are here distinct chronicles, and their information, often inconsistent or contradictory, must be handled on that basis. The narrative of *E* itself is characterized by a much more precise knowledge of southern events than appears in *C* or *D* (see especially 1036, 1041, 1046*b*, 1048) and, as in *D,* by a strongly pro-Godwine tone (see especially 1048, 1052, 1055) easily accounted for by the assumption that the chronicle was being written in Kent.[20]

At some time before the manuscript left Canterbury, two sets of Latin entries were interpolated into the chronicle: three notices (890, 892, 964) concerning English ecclesiastical affairs were probably copied from marginal annotations in the manuscript which the scribe copied; a longer series (876, 928, 942, 994, 1024, 1031, 1046, 1054, 1056, 1060, 1062) dealing with Norman affairs was taken from an unidentified Norman chronicle closely related to the *Annals of Rouen*. All but five of these Latin entries appear in the bilingual Canterbury epitome (*F*), which shows no trace whatever of the two other groups of Latin additions mentioned below.

The place where the Norman section of *E* up to 1121 was composed cannot be precisely ascertained, but the manuscript was apparently somewhere in the south—with its continuance at Canterbury always a likely possibility. The manuscript, or a copy of it, must have been at Canterbury circa 1100, when it was employed in the compilation of *F*.

The account of the Conqueror's reign in *E* (which at 1079, the virtual end of *D*, becomes the sole vernacular authority for Norman affairs) is marked by several valuable narratives (1075, 1083, 1085), but above all by the extremely individual first-hand portrait of William (1086). The stormy reign of William Rufus is very fully documented with over a dozen, for the most part quite detailed, entries. *E* here provides a particularly valuable complement to the relatively sparse treatments of the Latin chroniclers. The first twenty years of Henry's reign are more regularly covered by annual entries, but they are in general far less copious in detail than those of the preceding reign.

These later annals exhibit some unity of structure. From 1091 (and going on to 1127) the three annual royal courts are regularly mentioned as a preface to the national and foreign notices of the year. A general evaluation of the year, particularly in regard to the taxes and the weather, concludes the annals 1085b, 1086, 1090–1121. These latter exhibit also some uniformity of tone in their repeated com-

---

[20] The Augustinian Chronicle of this section forms the basis of *F*. A continuation of this lost chronicle to 1121 is attested by borrowings from it in the *Annals of Waverley* for the years 1000–1121 and in Henry of Huntingdon's *Historia Anglorum* from the beginning to 1121.

plaints about the hard times, in their frequent notice of strange mete-orological phenomena, and in the occasional intrusion of the chronicler's personality into his writing (1100, 1106, 1120).

VI. PETERBOROUGH RECENSION. This chronicle reaching to 1121 was copied about that date by a monk of Peterborough whose editing gave to it the conspicuously Peterborough character it now has.[21] The Peterborough copyist here and there incorporated into his transcript over a score of local notices and documents, generally at the end of annals (but see 870, 1014) and occasionally with little regard for chronology (see 1102). These interpolated materials are of three types: translations of abbey charters, short historical notices bearing directly on the history of the abbey, and two further sets of Latin entries.

1. The inserted charters, with a single exception (852), are based on spurious originals which may have been compiled at the instigation of Bishop Ernulf, who is also suspected of charter forgeries at Rochester and Canterbury.

654. The foundation of Peterborough (same source as the next insertion).

656. The foundation of Peterborough, Wulfhere's restoration of the monastery, his deed of gift, and an epitome of Pope Vitalian's confirmatory charter (a paraphrase and summary of a twelfth-century forged Latin charter preserved in two copies: Kemble 9841, Birch 22).

675. Confirmation of the preceding grant by Pope Agatho (based on a spurious Latin charter: Kemble 990, Birch 48).

686. Ceadwalla's grant of *Hoge* to Peterborough (condensed from a forged document: Kemble 40, Birch 89).

777. Lease of land (from the probably spurious Latin original: Birch 271) and a grant of exemptions to Woking (abstract of a suspicious document: Birch 275).

852. Lease of land (epitome of a bilingual twelfth-century copy of

---

[21] The southern chronicle was probably copied to replace a local compilation destroyed in the Peterborough fire of 1116 and may possibly have been procured through Bishop Ernulf of Rochester who had been abbot of Peterborough from 1107 to 1114 and previously prior of Canterbury. Hugo Candidus, author of a Latin history of Peterborough, has been put forward as the copyist and redactor: H. H. Howorth, "The Anglo-Saxon Chronicle, Its Origin and History," *Archaeological Journal*, LXV (1908), 141–204; see English, *Ancient History, English and French*, pp. 135–75.

an apparently valid original: Kemble 277, Birch 464, A. J. Robertson, *Anglo-Saxon Charters,* Cambridge, 1939, pp. 12 f.).

963. Restoration of Peterborough under Edgar (essentially an abstract of Peterborough history for sixty-two years based on several Latin originals: Birch 1280, spurious grant from Edgar; Birch 1258, corrupt copy of the preceding).

2. The second set of interpolations is a collection of abbey items probably preserved in a purely local chronicle or by oral tradition.

870. Razing of Peterborough by the Danes.

1013. Abbot Ælfsige's purchase of the head of St. Florentine.

1041. Death of Ælfsige and succession of Earnwig.

1052. Resignation of Earnwig and affairs under Leofric.

1070. Looting of the abbey.

1102. Looting of the abbey.

1107. Ernulf becomes abbot.

1114. Ernulf leaves and John of Sées becomes abbot.

1115. Abbot John brings over the Archbishop's pallium.

1116. Burning of the abbey.

The obits of Abbots Leofric (1066), Brand (1069), Turold (1098), and Matthias (1103) also belong to this group of insertions.

3. Two further groups of Latin annals were also added: of the first (114, 124, 134, 202, 254, 311, 379, 403, 425, 431, 433, 439, 449, 490, 528, 591, 625), all but one (425) are concerned with ecclesiastical affairs on the Continent and are close transcriptions from the *Annals of Rouen;* the second (769, 778, 788, 800, 810, 812) is a series of short items about Charles the Great and his wars, taken from the same source.

VII. Peterborough Continuation. The recension of 1121 was spasmodically added to at Peterborough by a number of different scribes for some thirty years. The ten annals from 1122 to 1131 were entered more or less contemporaneously (see especially the comment on Abbot Henry, who was expelled in 1135, in 1127 *ad fin.,* and the pious adjurations in 1128, 1129, 1130, 1131). They deal primarily with national affairs, the accounts of which may very possibly have been drawn from other scriptoria. A handful of local notices was also interspersed (1124-45, 1127-28, 1130-31).

The six remaining dated annals were entered by the last continuator, all of them probably about 1154. The first two are quite short, the first (1132) local, the second (1135) national. The four entries for Stephen's reign are muddled and patchwork history, but they are forcefully and often movingly written. The entry under 1137 is a disordered collection of primarily national items without chronological order, but in its graphic portrayal of the conditions of life under Stephen it furnishes an insight, rare for this period, into the common man's perspective. This long annal is followed, after a short notice of the Battle of the Standard (1138), by a second miscellaneous accumulation of isolated notices covering the main events of Stephen's reign from 1136 to 1153. The short concluding annal (1154) simply records the death of Stephen and the accession of Henry, and ends with a local notice of the death of Abbot Martin and the election of William.

Among the four major recensions of the Old English Chronicles *E* plainly occupies an exceptional position. In the first place, it illustrates most clearly the growth of these chronicles—the centuries-long process of copying, revision, interpolation, and critical editing that lies behind the final form of these documents as the historian now reads them. As a linguistic document, further, *E* is unique in illustrating the changes, for two and a half centuries, of the English language during one of the most vital periods of its history. So far as its contents are concerned, it has much of value to offer even where the other chronicles provide full materials, especially in its detailed narratives for the period before the Norman Conquest. Its primary value, however, is simply due to the fact that it was continued for almost seventy-five years longer than any of the other extant chronicles. *E*'s intelligent, forthright accounts of Norman affairs are in many details both of tone and content unapproached by any of the Latin chronicles.

According to the earliest information that we have about the Peterborough Chronicle subsequent to the history traced above, the manuscript of *E* was obtained in 1634, apparently from Peterborough, by William Lisle, who made several marginal notes, inserted a few annals from *A* on the blank leaves at the end, and made some further notes on interleaved sheets—chiefly collations from *A*. On Lisle's death in 1638 the manuscript came into the possession of Archbishop Laud, who is probably responsible for the underlinings in red. The first page of the manuscript now bears the inscription: *Liber Guil. Laud Archiep. Cant. et Cancellar. Universit. Oxon. 1638.* The manuscript was presented to Oxford University by Laud and is now in possession of the Bodleian Library (former shelf mark E 80, now Laud Misc. 636).

The first to make use of the Laud manuscript of the Peterborough Chronicle was Edmund Gibson (1692). Although Wheelocke was acquainted with the collations from *E* added by Joscelyn to *A,* which Wheelocke himself collated for his text of *G,* he made no use of the *E*-collations in the *editio princeps* appended to his edition of the *Historia ecclesiastica.* Gerard Langbaine, provost of Queen's College (Oxford), had apparently planned to publish *E,* but he gave up the idea when he learned that Wheelocke was working on his edition. The history of the employment of *E* in Gibson's and subsequent editions is outlined in the notes to section B of the Bibliography.

Translations, no less than editions, of the Old English Chronicles are comparatively numerous (see the Bibliography), but of the ten translations in which *E* is employed, not one gives a picture of the chronicle as it stands in the manuscript. This eclectic treatment has also been consistently applied to the other chronicles, and it was not until the publication in 1933 of *Une Chronique anglo-saxonne,* a French translation of *A* by Marie Hoffmann-Hirtz, that any one of these chronicles was completely and exactly available in a modern language.

The most recurrent and baffling cruxes in the interpretation of the Old English Chronicles, as of medieval chronicles generally, have to do with the chronology. Many sources of error have contributed to the chronological inaccuracies in these documents. Scribal slips in the copying of the easily misread Roman numerals, the accidental omission of eventless years in the manuscript before the copyist, miscopyings and careless repetitions of annuary numbers, the incorrect adaptation of regnal to calendar years, and the uncritical amalgamation of correct and false datings from different sources within the same annal have all conspired to produce countless datings in the Old English Chronicles which are at variance with reliable external evidence and often with other statements in the chronicles themselves as well.

No attempt has been made in the present translation to correct all known errors of chronology and to discuss, or even to point out, all suspicious or unlikely dates. The more important errors and corrections are treated in the notes, but for a more comprehensive analysis of chronological inaccuracies in *E* Plummer's notes to his edition of the two chronicles and, for the earlier years, to his edition of the *Historia ecclesiastica* should be consulted.

An equally important source of chronological confusion is the varying scribal practice in reckoning the start of the historical year. The medieval chronicler, once he had determined upon his era, had at least half a dozen New Year's days to choose from. Among those most commonly used were the Nativity (December 25), the Circumcision (January 1), the Annunciation (March 25), the movable feast of the Passion, and the Imperial or Caesarian Indiction (September 24).

Evidence for at least three methods of reckoning the first day of the year is visible in *E* as it now stands. The information taken from the *Historia ecclesiastica* is dated on the basis of the year beginning with September 24 according to the Caesarian Indiction adopted by Bede. There is little evidence to be obtained from the older independent entries of the Primary Compilation until the middle of the ninth century. Positive evidence for a Christmas or Indictional beginning is confined to two annals:

794 (796). Pope Adrian died on Dec. 27, 795.

827 (829). The Christmas Eve eclipse occurred at 2 a. m., Dec. 25, 828.

Negative proof that the year did not begin on March 25 can also be found in two early annals:

538. The eclipse of Feb. 16 occurred in 538.

762. "Jænbert was consecrated archbishop on the fortieth day after Christmas . . ."

In the more or less contemporary entries from 866 to 890, however, the West Saxon annalists who wrote this section clearly followed the same reckoning as Bede.[22]

[22] From an analysis of the chronological indications in the annals from 866 to 887 M. L. R. Beaven, "The Beginning of the Year in the Alfredian Chronicle (866–87)," *EHR*, XXXIII (1918), 328–42, fixed the beginning of the chronicler's year between Aug. 11 and Oct. 29, thus supporting an earlier suggestion of A. Anscombe, "The Date of the Council at Hertford," *Athenaeum* (Sept. 22, 1900), p. 380, that during these years the annalists began the year in September—probably on the 24th, according to the Caesarean Indiction, for there is no sign of the Sept. 1 Indiction in English writings. It was subsequently pointed out by R. H. Hodgkin, "The Beginning of the Year in the English Chronicle," *EHR*, XXXIX (1924), 497–510, that the indictional reckoning continued as far as the annal for 890.

For the century subsequent to the dispersion of copies of the Primary Compilation the reckoning from Christmas appears to be the common practice in *E,* as in the other chronicles.[23] Among the sparse entries of *E,* however, only the annal for 979 (also in *ACD*), which starts with the mention of March 18, speaks against the reckoning from March 25 that was shortly to come into favor.

In the eleventh century, during which the whereabouts of the progenitor of *E* is certain only for the Augustinian section, the practice of *E* is curiously irregular. It seems most likely that these inconsistencies were produced by the employment of materials originally written down at several scriptoria which reckoned the calendar year in varying fashion.

Some of these eleventh-century annals testify, positively or by implication, to the practice, gradually coming into favor about this time, of reckoning the year from the Annunciation: [24]

1006: "Christmas-tide" at end.

1009: Mid-Lent at end.

1010: "after Easter" at beginning.

1013: "after Christmas" at end.

1042: Easter at beginning.

1043*b:* December 26 at end.

1075: Christmas at end.

1077: February 20 at end.

1083: "after Christmas" at end.

1085: Christmas near end.

1085*b:* Easter at beginning.

1086: Christmas at end.

Interspersed in this same section of *E* are as many annals which clearly or presumably do not follow the Lady-Day reckoning and support a Christmas beginning:

1012: "before Easter" at beginning.

1014: February 3 at beginning.

---

[23] See Hodgkin, *op. cit.,* for evidence drawn from the Edwardian entries in all four chronicles. 901 and 913, however, may be exceptional in following the indictional reckoning.

[24] The evidence squares equally well with a commencement at Easter (*Monumenta historica Britannica,* p. 435, n. a; Plummer, II, cxxxix–cxli) or on March 25 (R. H. Poole, "The Beginning of the Year in the Anglo-Saxon Chronicles," *EHR,* XVI, (1901, 719–21). The Easter beginning, however, is not otherwise surely attested in England until about 1200.

1020: "and then at Easter" near beginning.

1039: March 17 at beginning.

1047: Mid-Lent at beginning.

1048: Mid-Lent at beginning.

1055: "seven days before Mid-Lent" at beginning.

1061: March 9 at beginning.

1066: December 28 at beginning.

1070: "in the following spring" at beginning.

1087: "as soon as Easter came" near beginning.

From 1091 the majority of the annals in *E* certify to a Christmas beginning. In addition to the annals which regularly start with a notice of the Christmas court—1094–1116 (except 1112), 1121–23, 1127— Christmas is mentioned at the beginning of 1091, January 6 at the beginning of 1118, and January 11 at the beginning of 1131. 1125 begins with "before Christmas," but the affair of the moneyers extended through Twelve Nights and has simply been treated as a unit.

Technical terms in the original which have no precise equivalent in modern English are retained in the translation. The principal of these social and military terms are: [25]

Alderman (OE *ealdorman*). A territorial official exercising both military and civil authority over a large district, often a county or former kingdom. In the time of Canute the title was generally supplanted by *eorl* "earl."

Atheling (OE *æþeling*). In a general sense, the member of a noble family, but more restrictedly, and more commonly, applied to a prince of the blood-royal.

Earl (OE *eorl*). An old native word, originally "a member of the nobility, a person of high estate," later under the influence of *jarl* (see below) applied to Danish officials or leaders; eventually superseded the native title of *alderman*. After the Norman Conquest the title was employed as the equivalent of the French title of count, and also specifically designated a particular rank in the peerage of England, Scotland, and Ireland implying the governorship or the feudal lord-

---

[25] For a more detailed analysis of what is known about the meaning of these and other technical terms which appear in the translation, consult H. Munro Chadwick, *Studies on Anglo-Saxon Institutions* (Cambridge, 1905) and, most recently, Jolliffe, *The Constitutional History of Medieval England*, pp. 1–303 *passim*. It may be pointed out here that the term "taxes" in the translation should generally be interpreted in its most inclusive sense of "any assessed (money) payment" and not in its more specialized modern signification.

ship of a county. French nobles designated *eorl* in the original are given their proper titles (*count, duke, earl*) in the translation.

Fyrd. The national army or militia, employed in contradistinction to *here* "army," which signifies the foreign army. The latter word has been translated "army," "Scandinavian army," or "Scandinavians."

Housecarl. A Scandinavian loan-word (ON *húskarl*) applied to members of the royal bodyguard as opposed to the militia.

Jarl (ON *jarl*). A Danish leader; also a viceroy or governor of one of the great divisions of the kingdom under Canute.

Reeve (OE *gerefa*). A high-ranking official exercising a local jurisdiction under the king (*king's reeve*), or simply a foreman on the estate of an important land-owner. The distinction between a king's reeve and a high-reeve (OE *héahgerefa*) cannot be made out with any certainty.

Thegn (OE *þegn*). Generally, one holding land of the king (*king's thegn*) or other superior with certain prescribed duties and privileges. The rank of thegn was partly inheritable, partly acquired.

Witan. The "wise men" or *seniores* who formed the council or assembly of a nation or smaller political unit. *Witenagemót* signifies the "meeting of the witan."

An attempt has been made to regularize the extreme orthographical inconsistencies in the traditional modern representation of the pre-Conquest English personal names by normalizing the hypocoristic names and the first and second elements of compound names according to the usual dictionary form of the words entering into the formation of these names. The following are the only exceptions:

1. Where the name exists in a modern form, this has been substituted for the Old English: *e. g.,* Alfred, Edgar, Edith, Edmund, and the like for Ælfred, Éadgár, etc.

2. The second elements of compound names have been normalized under their commonest forms: *e. g., briht, bryht, berht, beorht* under *bert,* and similarly under *bald, frith, gifu, hard, wald,* and *ward* the numerous forms in which these name elements appear.

3. Unaccented *u* in the second syllables of the first elements has been normalized to *o*.

Post-Conquest English and French names are given in their commonest orthography except where a modern form of the name can be employed. British (Welsh) and Scandinavian names are given under

the modern Welsh or Scandinavian form where the name has survived, otherwise under the Old Welsh or Old Scandinavian form,
except that in cases of doubtful names the Old English orthography has
been retained. The following names are treated exceptionally: Canute,
Hardecanute, Svein.

In the treatment of place names, the modern name of the site referred to in the original is given where the identification is certain.
Where the original name has been lost or the site is unknown or dubious, the Old English form is retained in italics, and the name, where
necessary, discussed in the Appendix. The untranslated place names,
though consisting of various significant words, have been arbitrarily
written as one OE compound; thus, *Ecgbrihtesstán* and not *Ecgbrihtes
stán,* "Egbert's stone."

"England" occasionally appears in the translation where it does not
appear in the original—*e. g., hiðer to land,* "hither to land," has been
translated "here to England." The Alps are referred to in the original
as "the mountain(s)." The word *here,* "foreign army," has frequently been translated "Scandinavians" or "Scandinavian army."

The present translation of *E* is based on the text printed by Plummer
in his *Two Saxon Chronicles Parallel.*[26] Its primary purpose is to give
an exact version of the sense of the original in current English. The
text is translated as it stands—except that obvious scribal slips in the
manuscript are noted only in exceptional cases.[27] All corrections and explanatory words or phrases, emendations or additions (generally on
the evidence of the other MSS), and words required to satisfy current syntax or to clarify the sense, but not represented in the original,
have been placed in square brackets. The translations of the Latin
entries are printed in italics, and the twelfth-century Peterborough
interpolations are set in reduced type.

[26] Plummer's text has been corrected in a few places from a collation of the MS for
1132–54 made by N. R. Ker, "Some Notes on the Peterborough Chronicle," *Medium
Aevum,* III (1934), 136–38. A few orthographic corrections are printed by Karl
Horst, *Zur Kritik der altenglischen Annalen* (Darmstadt, 1896), p. 38.
[27] The days of the month in the original are ordinarily computed according to the
Roman calendar or by religious festivals. In the translation these Roman dates have
been converted into the modern form. The festivals are retained and the dates of their
celebration added in square brackets; the dates of a few festivals fixed in relation to
Easter are not given.

THE
PETERBOROUGH
CHRONICLE

PREFACE TO THE CHRONICLE[1]

THE ISLAND OF BRITAIN IS EIGHT HUNDRED MILES LONG AND TWO HUNDRED MILES BROAD, AND HERE IN THIS ISland there are five languages: English and British and Welsh and Erse and Pictish and Latin.[2] The first inhabitants of this country were Britons; they came from Armenia [*for* Armorica] and first settled southern Britain. Then it happened that the Picts came from the south [3] from Scythia with long ships, not many, and they landed first in northern Ireland and there asked the Scots if they might live there. But they would not let them, for they [said that they could not all live there together, and then] [4] the Scots said: "We can nevertheless give you advice. We know another island here to the east where you may live if you wish, and if anyone resists you, we will help you to subdue it."

The Picts then went and conquered this country [Britain] in the north—and in the south the Britons possessed it, as we said before. And the Picts secured wives for themselves from the Scots on condition that they always choose their royal line on the woman's side; [5] they held to that for a long time afterwards. And then it happened after a number of years that some of the Scots withdrew from Ireland to Britain and conquered part of the country, and their leader was called Riada, after whom they are called Dalriadi.

[60 B. C.] Sixty years before Christ was born, Gaius Julius, emperor of the Romans, came to Britain with eighty ships [55 B. C.]. There he was first distressed by a fierce fight and lost a great part of

[1] This geographic-historical preface (summarizing Bede I. 1) appears also in *D*. *A* begins with a West Saxon genealogy, *C* with a metrical calendar and some gnomic verses.

[2] British (Welsh) and Welsh (Cornish) for Bede's *Brettonum* (1. 1) should be taken together; *D* has correctly *Brytwylsc* "Brito-Welsh." The *E*-scribe apparently wanted to make five secular languages out of Bede's list, but the names clearly refer to those employed in the church service.

[3] Bede applies the phrase *incipientes ab Austro* to the Britons (of the preceding sentence), not to the Picts, who are simply mentioned as having landed in northern Ireland. Scandinavia is probably the country meant by "Scythia."

[4] Supplied from *D* and probably omitted by the *E*-scribe because of the repetition of *cwædon* "said."

[5] The compiler from Bede omitted the important preceding phrase, *ubi res veniret in dubium* "in case of dispute." According to this old law of the Pictish succession, sons of the same mother succeeded each other, then sons of the sisters or of the nearest female relative.

his army. And then he left his army to remain among the Irish [6] and departed to Gaul and there gathered six hundred ships with which he again left for Britain [54 B. C.]. And when they first clashed, an officer of the emperor's called Labienus [*for* Laberius] [7] was killed. Then the Welsh took and drove great sharp stakes in the water right across the ford of a certain river—the river was called the Thames. When the Romans discovered this, they would not cross that ford. Then the Britons fled to the wood forts,[8] and the emperor conquered a great many of the chief towns with much fighting, and departed again to Gaul.

[6] This false statement was produced by the misreading *Hibernia* for *hiberna* "winter quarters" (I. 2) in several Bede MSS.

[7] This error for (Quintus) Laberius (Durus) (Caesar *De bello Gallico* v. 15) goes back through Bede (I. 2) to Orosius (VI. 9). Labienus had been left in charge on the continent (*De bello Gallico* v. 8). The MS *gerefa* "reeve" for Bede's *tribunus* has been rendered "officer."

[8] MS *wudu færstenum* (for *fæstenum*) "wood forts." The reading of *D, wudu westenum* "wild woodland," is perhaps preferable (Bede I. 2: *silvis*).

IN THE YEAR 1. OCTAVIAN REIGNED FIFTY-SIX YEARS, AND IN THE FORTY-SECOND YEAR OF HIS REIGN CHRIST WAS BORN.

2. The Magi came from the east to worship Christ, and the children in Bethlehem were killed because of the persecution by Herod. And he [Herod] died, stabbed by his own hand, and Archelaus, his son, succeeded to the throne.

11. From the beginning of the world to this year, five thousand and two hundred years had passed.

12. Philip and Herod divided Judea—they divided it into four tetrarchies.

16. Here Tiberius succeeded to the throne.

26. Here Pilate succeeded to the administration over the Jews.

30. Here Christ was baptized, and Peter and Andrew converted, and James and John and the twelve apostles.

33. Here Christ was hanged, five thousand two hundred and twenty-six years from the beginning of the world.

34. Here St. Paul was converted and St. Stephen stoned.

35. Here the holy apostle Peter established a bishop's see in Antioch.

39. Here Gaius succeeded to the throne.

45. Here the holy apostle Peter established a bishop's see in Rome.

46. Here Herod died who killed James one year before his own death.

47. Here Claudius, king of the Romans, departed with an army to Britain and conquered the island and subjected all the Picts and Welsh [1] to the Roman rule. He waged this war in the fourth year of his reign. In that year there was the great famine in Syria which was foretold in the Acts of the Apostles [11:28] by Agabus the prophet. Then Claudius was succeeded to the throne by Nero who, through his indolence, almost lost the island of Britain.

62. Here James, *the brother of the Lord,* suffered martyrdom.

62b.[2] Here Mark the Evangelist died.

69. Here Peter and Paul suffered martyrdom.

70. Here Vespasian succeeded to the throne.

[1] This phrase extends materially the compass of Bede's *plurimam insulae partem* (I. 3).

[2] Corrected to 63 by a later hand.

71. Here Titus, [son of] [3] Vespasian, killed one hundred and eleven thousand Jews in Jerusalem.

81. Here Titus succeeded to the throne, he who said that he lost the day on which he did no good.

84. Here Domitian, the brother of Titus, succeeded to the throne.

87. Here John the Evangelist wrote the Book of the Apocalypse in the island of Patmos.

100. Here Simon the apostle was hanged, and John the Evangelist rested in Ephesus.

101. Here Pope Clement died.

110. Here Bishop Ignatius suffered martyrdom.

114. *Here Alexander decreed that the water should be blessed.*[4]

124. *Here Pope Sixtus decreed that the Sanctus be sung in the office of the mass.*

134. *Here Pope Telesphorus decreed that the Hymnus angelicus, "Gloria in excelsis Deo," be sung on feast days.*

155. Here Marcus Antoninus and his brother, Aurelius, succeeded to the throne.

167. Here Eleutherius succeeded to the bishopric of Rome and held it honorably for fifteen years. Lucius, king of the Brito-Welsh, sent men to him and asked for baptism, and he sent to him at once; and they continued afterwards in the orthodox faith until the reign of Diocletian.[5]

189. Here Severus succeeded to the throne and went with an army to Britain and conquered a great part of the island by battle; and then for the protection of the Britons he built a rampart of sods with a board wall on top of it from sea to sea.[6] He reigned seventeen years, and then died at York. His son, Bassianus, succeeded to the throne. His other son, who died, was named Geta.

---

[3] From *D*.

[4] According to tradition, Pope Alexander I introduced the use of blessing water mixed with salt to protect Christian homes from evil influences.

[5] A curious and impossible story first found in the *Liber Pontificalis* I. 136, translated by L. R. Loomis, *The Book of the Popes* (New York, 1916), p. 17. It is very likely based upon a false identification of Lucius Abgar, king of Edessa in Mesopotamia, whose fortress was called Birtha (found written *Britium*): Adolf Harnack, "Der Brief des britischen Königs Lucius an den Papst Eleutherus," *Sitzungsberichte der königlich preussischen Akademie der Wissenschaften*, 1904, pp. 909–16.

[6] Severus' reconstruction of Hadrian's Wall very early gave rise to the tradition that he had actually built it. On the chronology of Severus' reign, see Collingwood and Myres, *Roman Britain*, pp. 155–60.

202. *Here Pope Victor, like his predecessor, Eleutherius, decreed that Easter be celebrated on a Sunday.*

254. *Here Pope Cornelius by night brought up the bodies of the apostles from the catacombs and placed Paul's in the Ostian Way, where he had been beheaded, but Peter's near the place where he had been crucified.*

286. Here St. Alban, the martyr, suffered martyrdom.

311. *The holy Silvester—twenty-third pope. In his time the Council of Nicaea [325] was held, also the first [Council] of Arles [314], at which Avitianus, archbishop of Rouen, was present.*

379. Here Gratian succeeded to the throne.

379b [380]. *In this year the Council of Constantinople [381], of a hundred and fifty fathers, was held under Damasus against Macedonius and Eunomius.*

380 [381]. Here Maximus succeeded to the throne. He was born in Britain [7] and went thence to Gaul, and there he killed Emperor Gratian and drove his brother, who was called Valentinian, out of the country; and this Valentinian later gathered an army and killed Maximus and succeeded to the throne. At that time the Pelagian heresy arose throughout the world.

403. *Here Pope Innocent sent a decretal to Victricius, archbishop of Rouen. Here he decreed that Sunday should be a fast day because the Lord lay in the sepulchre on that day.*

409. Here Rome was stormed by the Goths eleven hundred and ten years after it had been built. After that the kings of the Romans no longer ruled in Britain.[8] Altogether they had ruled there four hundred and seventy years since Gaius Julius first came to the country.

418. Here the Romans gathered all the hoards of gold that were in Britain and hid some in the earth,[9] so that no one could afterwards find them, and carried some with them into Gaul.

[7] This erroneous statement, common to all the chronicles, is based upon a mistranslation of Bede's *Maximus . . . in Brittania . . . imperator creatus* (1. 9).
[8] The traditional conception of the Roman evacuation of Britain circa 410 has again lately been challenged in favor of a continued or reestablished fifth-century occupation lasting into the twenties (Collingwood and Myres, *Roman Britain*, pp. 292–301, 476–77; cf. Oman, *England*, pp. 170, 176).
[9] Fifth-century coin finds (the "gold" of the Chronicle is not to be taken too literally) are sparse (Collingwood and Myres, *Roman Britain*, pp. 295, 299–300), though not non-existent; see Plummer, II, 8; F. Haverfield, *Romanization of Roman Britain* (Oxford, 1923), p. 78.

423. Here Theodosius the Younger succeeded to the throne.

425. *In this year the kings of the Franks began [to reign], the first [being] Faramundus.*

430. Here Patrick [10] was sent by Pope Celestine to preach baptism to the Irish.

431. *In this year the devil, appearing to the Jews in Crete in the form of Moses, promised to lead them dry-shod through the sea to the Promised Land. And so, after many had been killed, the rest were converted to the grace of Christ.*

433. *Pope Celestine. In his time a synod of two hundred bishops was assembled at Ephesus [431]. It was headed by Cyril of Alexandria against Nestorius, the bishop of Constantinople.*

439. *Pope Leo. Here he blessed the synod of Chalcedon [451].*

443. Here the Britons sent overseas to Rome and asked them for help against the Picts, but they got none there because they [the Romans] were fighting against Attila, king of the Huns; and then they sent to the Angles and made the same request of the athelings of the tribe of the Angles.

449. *In his [Pope Leo's] time the council of Chalcedon of three hundred bishops was held against Abbot Eutyches and Dioscorus.*

Here Martianus and Valentinian succeeded to the throne and reigned seven years, and in their days [11] Vortigern invited the tribe of the Angles here, and they came in three ships here to Britain at the place [called] *Heopwinesfleot.*[12] King Vortigern gave them land in the southeast of this country on condition that they fight against the Picts. Then they fought against the Picts and were victorious wherever they came. Then they sent to Angle, ordered more help sent, and let them [the Angles] know of the worthlessness of the Britons and the virtues of the land. Then they at once sent a larger force here to help the others.

Men then came from three tribes of Germany: from the Old Saxons,

[10] Bede (1. 13) and *ABCF* have correctly "Palladius" who was sent to the Irish to combat Pelagianism, for they were already Christian at this time, but he did not complete his mission. On the suggested identity of the two men, see Louis Gougaud, *Christianity in Celtic Lands* (London, 1932), pp. 29–31.

[11] "In their days" (Bede 1. 15 *tunc,* v. 24 *quorum tempore*) simply dates this invitation, allowing for Bede's own irregular chronology, between 446 and 457. For a discussion of the conflicting evidence on the dating of the first settlement, see Plummer's *Bede,* II, 27–28; Collingwood and Myres, *Roman Britain,* pp. 352–56; Hodgkin, *History,* pp. 66–68.

[12] Bede (1. 15) does not mention the name of the landing place of the "Angles."

from the Angles, from the Jutes.[13] From the Jutes came the men of
Kent and the men of the Isle of Wight, that is, the tribe which now
lives on the Isle of Wight, and that race among the West Saxons
which is still called the race of Jutes. From the Old Saxons came the
East Saxons and South Saxons and West Saxons. From Angle,
which has ever since stood waste between the Jutes and the Saxons,
came the East Angles, Middle Angles, Mercians, and all the Northumbrians. Their leaders were two brothers, Hengest and Horsa. They
were sons of Wihtgils. Wihtgils was the son of Witta, Witta of
Wecta, Wecta of Woden. From this Woden sprang all our [14] royal
line and [that] of the Southumbrians also.[15]

455. Here Hengest and Horsa fought against King Vortigern at
the place called Aylesford, and his brother Horsa was killed. And
after that Hengest and his son Oisc succeeded to the throne.

456. Here Hengest and Oisc fought against the Britons at the
place called *Crecganford* and there killed four bands, and the Britons
then abandoned the land of Kent and fled to London in great terror.

465. Here Hengest and Oisc fought against the Welsh near *Wip-
pedsfleot* and there killed twelve Welsh aldermen, and one of their
thegns whose name was Wipped was killed there.

473. Here Hengest and Oisc fought against the Welsh and seized
countless spoils, and the Welsh fled from the Angles as fast as they
could.

[13] On the still uncertain identification of the Jutes, see a convenient summing-up of
the evidence in Hodgkin, *History*, pp. 81–101, and, more particularly, J. E. A. Jolliffe,
Pre-Feudal England, the Jutes (Oxford, 1933).
[14] *I. e.*, the Northumbrian, representing the point of view of the expander of the
Bede annals in the Northern Recension from which *D* and *E* are ultimately derived.
[15] For critical examinations of this entry and of the original annals for the first
century after the coming of the Anglo-Saxons in the light of evidence furnished by
archeological remains, language, place names, terrain, etc., see Hodgkin, *History*,
pp. 74–183; Collingwood and Myres, *Roman Britain*, pp. 325–456, 478–88; Oman,
England, chaps. 11–12; H. M. Chadwick, *Origin of the English Nation* (Cambridge,
1907); E. Wadstein, *On the Origin of the English* (Uppsala, 1927); S. W. Wool-
dridge, "The Anglo-Saxon Settlement," in H. C. Darby, ed., *An Historical Geography of England before* A. D. *1800* (Cambridge, 1936), pp. 88–132; R. Lennard,
"The Character of the Anglo-Saxon Conquests: A Disputed Point," *History*, XVIII
(1933–34), 204–15. On more particular aspects, see K. Schreiner, *Die Saga von
Hengest und Horsa* (Berlin, 1921); C. W. C. Oman, "The Kingdom of Kent,"
Archaeological Journal, LXXXVI (1929), 1–19; E. T. Leeds, *Early Anglo-Saxon
Art and Archaeology* (Oxford, 1936), especially "The Kentish Problem," pp. 41–
78; G. H. Wheeler, "The Genealogy of the Early West Saxon Kings," *EHR*,
XXXVI (1921), 161–71; E. T. Leeds, "The West Saxon Invasion and the Icknield
Way," *History*, X (1925), 97–109; O. G. S. Crawford, "Cerdic and the Cloven
Way," *Antiquity*, V (1931), 441–58.

477. Here Ælle and his three sons, Cymen and Wlencing and Cissa, came to Britain with three ships at the place called *Cymenesora* and there killed many Welsh and chased some into the wood called the Weald.

485. Here Ælle fought against the Welsh near *Mearcredesburnansteð*.

488. Here Oisc succeeded to the throne and was king thirty-four [*for* twenty-four] years.[16]

490. *In this year the blessed Mamertus, bishop of Vienne, introduced the solemn litanies of the [Minor] Rogations [the three days before Ascension].*

491. Here Ælle and Cissa besieged Pevensey and killed all who lived there. Not even one Briton was left there.

495. Here two aldermen, Cerdic and his son, Cynric, came to Britain with five ships at the place called *Cerdicesora* and on the same day fought against the Welsh.

501. Here Port and his two sons, Bieda and Mægla, came to Britain with two ships at the place called Portsmouth and at once landed and killed a very noble young Briton.

508. Here Cerdic and Cynric killed a British king whose name was Nazaleod [*for* Natanleod] and five thousand men with him; and after that the land was named *Nazanleog* [for *Natanleag*] as far as Charford.

514. Here the West Saxons came to Britain with three ships at the place called *Cerdicesora,* and Stuf and Wihtgar fought against the Britons and routed them.

519. Here Cerdic and Cynric obtained the throne of Wessex; and that same year they fought against the Britons at a place now [17] called Charford, and from that day on the royal line of the West Saxons has reigned.

527. Here Cerdic and Cynric fought against the Britons at the place called Charford.[18]

---

[16] As in *AC*. For some regnal redatings of the fifth and sixth centuries, especially for Oisc's reign, see G. H. Wheeler, "Gildas de Excidio Britanniae, Chapter 26," *EHR,* XLI (1926), 500–503.

[17] *I. e.,* at the time of the Primary Compilation.

[18] MS *Certicesford; A* has *Cerdicesleaga, C Cerdicesleag,* an unidentified site, perhaps in Wiltshire. The false reading in *E* was apparently produced by a careless repetition of the battle site of 519.

528. *In this year Dionysius composed the Easter Cycle in Rome. Then Priscian sounded the depths of grammar.*

530. Here Cerdic and Cynric took the Isle of Wight and killed many men at Carisbrooke.

534. Here Cerdic died, and his son Cynric reigned on for twenty-six years, and they gave the whole Isle of Wight to their two nephews,[19] Stuf and Wihtgar.

538. Here the sun was eclipsed on February 16 from early morning until 9 a. m.

540. Here the sun was eclipsed on June 20, and the stars appeared almost half an hour after 9 a. m.

544. Here Wihtgar died, and he was buried in Carisbrooke.

547. Here Ida succeeded to the throne [of Bernicia]—from him sprang the royal line of the Northumbrians—and reigned twelve years. And he built Bamborough—it was first enclosed by a stockade, and later by a rampart.

552. Here Cynric fought against the Britons at the place called Old Sarum and routed the Britons.

556. Here Cynric and Ceawlin fought against the Britons at Barbury Camp.

560. Here Ceawlin succeeded to the throne of Wessex, and Ælle succeeded to the throne of Northumbria [*i. e.,* of Deira], Ida having died,[20] and each of them reigned thirty years.

565. Here Æthelbert succeeded to the throne of Kent and held it fifty-three years.[21] In his days Gregory sent us baptism, and the priest Columba came to the Picts and converted them to the faith of Christ —they live along the northern mountains. And their king gave him the island called Iona where there are five hides [of land], from what men say. There Columba built a monastery, and he was abbot there thirty-two years, and died there when he was seventy-seven years old. His successors still [22] have the place. The South Picts had been

[19] The meaning of OE *nefa* is broader than that of modern "nephew."

[20] This phrase, peculiar to *EF*, mistakenly implies that Ælle succeeded Ida, king of Bernicia.

[21] See 616 where his death and the length of his reign agree with Bede (II. 5) who places his accession in 560. *F* has fifty-three years under 565 and 616 as well. These discrepancies are impossible to resolve (see Plummer's *Bede*, II, 85; G. H. Wheeler, "Gildas de Excidio Britanniae," *EHR*, XLI [1926], 501-2).

[22] *I. e.,* at the time of the Primary Compilation. This sentence is not in Bede (III. 4).

baptized long before—Bishop Ninian, who had been taught at Rome, preached baptism to them. His church and monastery are at Whithorn, hallowed in Martin's name; there he rests with many holy men. Now there must always be an abbot in Iona, not a bishop, and all [23] the Irish bishops must [be] subject to him, because Columba was an abbot, not a bishop.[24]

568. Here Ceawlin and Cutha fought against Æthelbert and drove him into Kent, and killed two aldermen, Oslac and Cnebba, at *Wibbandun.*

571. Here Cutha fought against the Britons [25] at *Biedcanford* and took four villages: Limbury and Aylesbury and Bensington and Eynsham. And in the same year he died. This Cutha was the brother of Ceawlin.

577. Here Cuthwine and Ceawlin fought against the Britons, and they killed three kings, Cynfael and Condidan and Farinmail, at the placed called Dyrham, and took three towns: Gloucester and Cirencester and Bath.

583. Here Maurice succeeded to the throne of Rome.

584. Here Ceawlin and Cutha fought against the Britons at the place called *Feþanleah,* and Cutha was killed, and Ceawlin took many villages and countless spoils.

588. Here King Ælle died, and Æthelric reigned for five years after him.

591. Here Ceolric reigned six years.

Here Pope Gregory added "Diesque nostros in tua pace disponas" to the canon in the prayer.

592. Here Gregory succeeded to the papacy in Rome. And there was a great slaughter this year in Britain at *Wodnesbeorh,* and Ceawlin was driven out.

593. Here Ceawlin and Cwichelm and Crida perished; and Æthelfrith succeeded to the throne of Northumbria. He was the son of Æthelric, Æthelric [the son] of Ida.

[23] Bede (iii. 4) simply says that the whole province of his monastery *et ipsi etium episcopi* (*i. e.,* within the province) are subject to the abbot.

[24] On this and subsequent entries dealing with Scottish affairs, see A. O. Anderson, *Scottish Annals from English Chroniclers* (London, 1908).

[25] Though Oman (*England*, pp. 231 f.) considers "Britons" a scribal error, a victory over the Britons here is entirely feasible (see Hodgkin, *History*, pp. 188 f.; see also M. W. Hughes, "Grimsditch and Cuthwulf's Expedition to the Chilterns in A. D. 571," *Antiquity*, V [1931], 291–314).

596. *In this year the monastery of St. Benedict [at Norcia] was destroyed by the Lombards.*

Here Pope Gregory sent Augustine to Britain with a great many monks who preached God's word to the English.[26]

597. Here Ceolwulf began to reign in Wessex, and he constantly fought and won against both the Angles and the Welsh and the Picts and the Scots.[27]

601. Here Pope Gregory sent the pallium to Archbishop Augustine in Britain, and a great many religious teachers to help him. And Bishop Paulinus converted Edwin, king of Northumbria, to baptism.[28]

603. Here Aidan, king of the Scots, fought against the Dalriadi [29] and against Æthelfrith, king of Northumbria, at *Dægsanstan,* and nearly all his [Aidan's] army was killed. Theobald, Æthelfrith's brother, was killed there with his whole troop. After that no king of the Scots dared lead an army against this nation. Hering, son of Hussa, led the army there.[30]

604. Here Augustine consecrated two bishops, Mellitus and Justus. He sent Mellitus to preach baptism to the East Saxons; the king there was called Sæbert, son of Ricola, Æthelbert's sister, whom Æthelbert appointed king there; and Æthelbert gave Mellitus a bishop's see in London. And to Justus he gave Rochester which is twenty-four miles from Canterbury.

605. Here Pope Gregory died.[31] And here Æthelfrith led his fyrd to Chester and there killed countless Welshmen; [32] and so Augustine's prophecy was fulfilled when he said: "If the Welsh refuse peace with us, they shall perish at the hands of the Saxons." Two hundred

---

[26] The mission of St. Augustine and the history of the Conversion are best studied in the notes to Plummer's *Bede;* see also Wm. Bright, *Chapters on Early English Church History,* 3d ed. (Oxford, 1897), H. H. Howorth, *Saint Augustine of Canterbury* (London, 1913), and, for a good survey, Hodgkin, *History,* pp. 245–302.

[27] This statement should perhaps not be taken too literally. The geographical difficulties induce Oman (*England,* p. 249) to suspect that the entry should be connected with the Northumbrian Ceolwulf (729–37).

[28] This statement is a misconstruction based upon Bede's notice in the Epitome: *misit papa Gregorius pallium . . . et . . . ministros, in quibus et Paulinum.* Paulinus did not go to Northumbria until circa 626.

[29] Aidan, king of the Dalriadi (see Bede I. 34), is here erroneously said to have fought against them, a statement which appears only in *E.*

[30] This detail is not in Bede (I. 34), from which the rest of the annal is taken. Hussa is apparently the son of Ida found listed in several genealogies (see Plummer, II, 19).

[31] *A* dates Gregory's death 606, Bede (II. 1) 605; the correct date is 604.

[32] From the order of events in Bede (II. 2) the scribe falsely inferred 605 as the date of the battle of Chester. It is not dated in Bede, but probably took place in 613.

priests were also killed there [Chester] who came there to pray for the army of the Welsh—their leader was called Brochfael [33] who escaped from there with forty-nine others.

607. Here Ceolwulf fought against the South Saxons.

611. Here Cynegils succeeded to the throne of Wessex and held it thirty-one years.

614. Here Cynegils and Cwichelm fought at *Beandun* and killed two thousand and sixty-five Welshmen.

616. Here Æthelbert, king of Kent, died—he had reigned fifty-six [34] years; and he was succeeded to the throne by his son, Eadbald, who gave up his baptism and lived in heathen fashion, having his father's widow for his wife. Then Laurentius, who was archbishop in Kent, planned to go south over the sea and leave it all, but the Apostle Peter came to him at night and beat him severely because he planned to abandon God's flock in this fashion, and ordered him to go to the king and preach the true faith to him. And he did so, and the king was converted and baptized.

In the days of this king [Eadbald] Laurentius, who was archbishop in Kent after Augustine, died and was buried beside Augustine on February 2 [619].[35] Then Mellitus, who had previously been bishop of London, succeeded him to the archbishopric. At that time the men of London, where Mellitus had been before, were heathen. And in about five years, during the reign of Eadbald, Mellitus went to Christ. Then Justus succeeded him to the archbishopric, and he consecrated Romanus to Rochester where he [himself] had previously been bishop.

617. Here Æthelfrith, king of Northumbria, was killed by Redwald, king of East Anglia; and Edwin, son of Ælle, succeeded to the throne and conquered all Britain except Kent alone and drove out the athelings, the sons of Æthelfrith: the first was Eanfrith, [then] Oswald and Oswy, Oslac, Oswudu, Oslaf, and Offa.[36]

624. Here Archbishop Mellitus died.

625. Here Archbishop Justus consecrated Paulinus bishop on July 21.

---

[33] MS *Scromail* for *Brocmail* (Bede II. 2).
[34] Cf. 565 and note.
[35] According to Bede II. 7, where Mellitus' death is dated April 24, 624.
[36] This annal is peculiar to *E*. The names of Æthelfrith's sons do not appear in Bede (III. 1).

Here the cycle of Dionysius, composed of five [units of] nineteen years, that is, ninety-five years. . . .[37] *And it starts from* A. D. *30 and stops with the year 626. This nineteen-year cycle, which the Greeks call* ἐννεακαιδεκαετηρίδα, *was instituted by the holy fathers at the synod of Nicaea [325] in which [the Sunday following] the fourteenth day of the Paschal moon [was fixed] for each year without any uncertainty.*[38]

626. Here Eomer came from Cwichelm, king of Wessex. He planned to stab King Edwin, but he stabbed Lilla, his thegn, and Forthhere, and wounded the king. And that same night a daughter was born to Edwin who was named Eanflæd. Then the king promised Paulinus to give his daughter to God if he might obtain from God the power to kill his enemy who had sent the assassin there. And then he went against the West Saxons with a fyrd and there killed five kings and killed many of the people. And Paulinus baptized his daughter and eleven others at Pentecost; and within a year the king was baptized with all his nobles at Easter—that year Easter was on April 12. This was done in York where he had previously ordered a church to be built of wood—it was consecrated in the name of St. Peter. There the king gave Paulinus a bishop's see, and afterwards he ordered a larger church of stone to be built there.

And here Penda succeeded to the throne [of Mercia] and reigned thirty years.

627. Here King Edwin was baptized by Paulinus, and this Paulinus also preached baptism in Lindsey, where the first to believe was a certain powerful man called Blecca with all his followers. And at this time Honorius, who sent the pallium here to Paulinus, succeeded Boniface to the papacy. And Archbishop Justus died on November 10, and Honorius was consecrated by Paulinus at Lincoln. The pope also sent the pallium to Honorius, and he sent a letter to the Scots enjoining them to turn to the correct Easter.

628. Here Cynegils and Cwichelm fought against Penda at Cirencester and then came to terms.

[37] Bede gives an account of this nineteen-year cycle for the calculation of Easter in *HE* v. 21 and *De temporum ratione* chap. 44. On the introduction of the Dionysian cycle into England, see R. L. Poole, "The Earliest Use of the Cycle of Dionysius," *EHR*, XXXIII (1918), 57–62. The sentence has been left incomplete.

[38] The words, *Johannes papa*, from another entry (634) in the *Annals of Rouen*, have been by error inserted in the middle of the Greek word, presumably from a misunderstood marginal note. The last clause is also corrupt.

632. Here Eorpwald was baptized.[39]

633. Here King Edwin was killed by Cadwallon and Penda at Hatfield on October 14, and he had reigned seven [*for* seventeen] [40] years; and his son, Osfrith, was also killed with him. And then Cadwallon and Penda afterwards went and ravaged the whole of Northumbria. When Paulinus saw that, he took Æthelburg, Edwin's widow, and went by ship to Kent, and Eadbald and Honorius received him very honorably and gave him the bishop's see at Rochester, and he stayed there till his death.

634. Here Osric, whom Paulinus had previously baptized, succeeded to the throne of Deira—he was the son of Ælfric, the paternal uncle of Edwin. And Eanfrith, son of Æthelfrith, succeeded to the throne of Bernicia. And here also Birinus first preached baptism to the West Saxons under King Cynegils. This Birinus came there at the command of Pope Honorius, and he was bishop there until the end of his life. And here also Oswald succeeded to the throne of Northumbria, and he reigned nine years. The ninth was reckoned to him on account of the heathenism which they [Osric and Eanfrith] had practised who reigned the one year between him and Edwin.[41]

635. Here Cynegils was baptized by Bishop Birinus at Dorchester, and Oswald, king of Northumbria, sponsored him.

636. Here Cwichelm was baptized at Dorchester, and he died the same year; and Bishop Felix preached the faith of Christ to the East Angles.[42]

639. Here Birinus baptized Cuthred at Dorchester and received him as his [god-]son.

639*b* [640].[43] Here Eadbald, king of Kent, died—he had been

[39] Bede (II. 15) has no date for Eorpwald's succession or baptism. The latter probably took place in 628.
[40] Bede (II. 20) : *decem et septem*.
[41] Bede (III. 1) explains that earlier writers have agreed to obliterate the memory of these two *regum perfidorum* by assigning the year of their reign to Oswald, *viri Deo dilecti*.
[42] Bede does not record Cwichelm's baptism and death. Felix probably came to East Anglia not later than 631.
[43] The annuary markings of *E* for the next fifteen years are thoroughly confused. The careless repetition of 639 has antedated this and the next four entries by a year; the correct dates are found only in *A*, for *BC* are here also dated one year too early. The blank annal for 647 in the Primary Chronicle brings *E* back into line with *A* at 648, only to diverge again at 649, where *AF* have 650, *BC* 649, with the true date uncertain. In the Primary Chronicle entries for 650–56 (except 655, which is not in *AC*), *E* is again one year behind *A* except that Honorius' death (not in *A*) is rightly dated 653 (see Bede III. 20).

king twenty-four years. Then his son Eorconbert succeeded to the throne. He destroyed all idolatry in his kingdom, and—first of all English kings—he established [the observance of] Lent. His daughter was named Eorcongota, a holy virgin and a wonderful person, whose mother was Seaxburg, daughter of Anna, king of the Angles.

641 [642]. Here Oswald, king of Northumbria, was killed by Penda, the Southumbrian, at *Maserfeld* on August 5, and his body was buried at Bardney. His holiness and miracles were afterwards manifested in many ways throughout this island, and his hands are at Bamborough uncorrupted. And here Cenwalh succeeded to the throne of Wessex and he held it twenty-one [*for* thirty-one] [44] years. This Cenwalh ordered the church built at Winchester, and he was son of Cynegils. And the same year that Oswald was killed, his brother Oswy succeeded to the throne of Northumbria, and he reigned twenty-eight years.

643 [644]. Here Paulinus, archbishop of York, died on October 10—he had been bishop nineteen years and two months and twenty-one days. And here Oswine, son of Osric [who was Edwin's] [45] cousin on his father's side, succeeded to the throne of Deira and reigned seven years.

644 [645]. Here Cenwalh was driven out of his kingdom by King Penda.[46]

645 [646]. Here Cenwalh was baptized.

648. Here Cenwalh gave Eadred [*for* Cuthred],[47] his kinsman, three thousand [hides] [48] of land near Ashdown.

649. Here Ægelbert of Gaul succeeded Birinus, the Roman bishop, to the Saxon bishopric.

650 [651]. Here King Oswy ordered King Oswine killed on August 20; and about twelve days later Bishop Aidan died on August 31.

652 [653]. Here the Middle Angles received the true faith under Alderman Penda [*for* Peada].[49]

653. Here King Anna was killed, and Botwulf began to build a church at *Icanho*. And here Archbishop Honorius died on September 30.

[44] As in *A;* see 672, where *ACE* all agree in placing Cenwalh's death.
[45] MS *Oswines* emended to *Oswine Edwines* (Plummer); see 634, 650.
[46] Cf. 658.
[47] As in *AC.*
[48] *BC* insert the *hida*, though the ellipsis is common.
[49] *A Peada*, as in Bede's Epitome.

654 [655]. Here Oswy killed Penda at *Winwidfeld* and thirty of royal blood with him, and some of them were kings—one of them was Æthelhere, brother of Anna, [both] kings of East Anglia. At that time five thousand eight hundred years had passed from the beginning of the world. And Peada, son of Penda, succeeded to the throne of Mercia.

In his [Peada's] time they came together, he and Oswy, brother of King Oswald, and determined to build a monastery to the glory of Christ and to the honor of St. Peter. And they did so, and gave it the name of *Medeshamsted* [*i. e.,* Peterborough] because there is a well there called *Medeswæl.* And then they began the foundations and worked on them. They then entrusted it to a monk called Seaxwulf. He was a sincere friend of God, and all people loved him, and he was very nobly born in the world and rich. He is now much richer with Christ.[50]

And King Peada did not reign a long time, for he was betrayed by his own wife at Easter time.[51]

655. Here Ithamar, bishop of Rochester, consecrated Deusdedit to Canterbury on March 26.

656 [657]. Here Peada was killed, and Wulfhere, son of Penda, succeeded to the throne of Mercia.

In his [Wulfhere's] time the abbacy of Peterborough, which his brother [Peada] had founded, grew very rich. The king [Wulfhere] loved it very much for love of his brother, Peada, and for love of Oswy, his[52] sworn brother, and for love of Abbot Seaxwulf. He said that he would honor and exalt it by the counsel of Æthelred and Merewald, his brother, and by the counsel of Cyneburg and Cyneswith, his sisters, and by the counsel of the archbishop, who was named Deusdedit, and by the counsel of all his witan, ordained and lay, who were in his kingdom. And he did so.

Then the king sent for the abbot to come quickly to him, and he did so. Then the king said to the abbot: "Lo, I have sent for you, beloved Seaxwulf, for the need of my soul, and I want to tell you plainly why. My brother, Peada, and my beloved friend, Oswy, founded a monastery to the glory of Christ and St. Peter, but my brother, as Christ willed it,

[50] On the sources of this and subsequent Peterborough interpolations, see the Introduction.

[51] *E* alone correctly notices Peada's death as having occurred at the Easter following the battle of *Winwidfeld* (see Bede III. 24), but, with *ABC*, incorrectly repeats it under 656 as though it had occurred two years after Penda's death.

[52] Probably Wulfhere's (note "my beloved friend, Oswy" below), but see Earle, *Two of the Saxon Chronicles Parallel,* p. 285.

has gone from this life; and, lo, I pray you, dear friend, have them work rapidly at the building, and I'll find you gold and silver, land and property, and all that is needed for it."

Then the abbot went home and began to work. It went so well, as Christ granted him, that in a few years the monastery was ready. When the king heard this, he was very glad. He ordered sent throughout his whole nation for all his thegns, for the archbishop, and for the bishops, and for his earls, and for all who loved God, that they should come to him; and he set a day on which the monastery was to be consecrated.

When the monastery was consecrated, there were present King Wulfhere and his brother, Æthelred, and his sisters, Cyneburg and Cyneswith. And Archbishop Deusdedit of Canterbury consecrated the monastery, and the bishop of Rochester, Ithamar, and the bishop of London, who was named Wine, and the bishop of Mercia, who was called Jaruman, and Bishop Tuda. And the priest Wilfrith, who later was bishop, was there. And all his thegns who were in his kingdom were there.

When the monastery had been consecrated in the name of St. Peter, St. Paul, and St. Andrew, the king stood up before all his thegns and said in a loud voice: "May the high Almighty God be thanked for this worthy deed that has been done here, and I would this day honor Christ and St. Peter, and I desire you all to confirm my words. I, Wulfhere, today freely give to St. Peter and Abbot Seaxwulf and the monks of the monastery these lands and these waters and meres and fens and weirs and all the lands which adjoin them, which are of my kingdom, so that no one but the abbot and the monks shall have any authority there. This is the gift: from Peterborough to Northborough and so to the place called *Folies,* and then the whole fen straight to Asen Dike, and from Asen Dike to the place called *Feðermuð,* and then ten miles along the straight way to *Cuggedic,* and so to *Raggewilh,* and from *Raggewilh* five miles to the straight stream which goes to Elm and to Wisbeach, and so about three miles to Throckenholt, and from Throckenholt right through the whole fen to *Dereuorð,* which is twenty miles distant, and so to *Grætecros,* and from *Grætecros* through a clear water called *Bradanæ,* and from there six miles to *Paccelad,* and so onward through all the meres and fens which lie toward Huntingdon and these meres and lakes, *Scælfremere* and Whittlesey Mere, and all the others which lie thereabout with the land and with the houses that are on the east half of *Scælfremere,* and from there all the fens to Peterborough and from Peterborough all the way to Wansford, and from Wansford to King's Cliff, and from there to Easton Maudit, and from Easton Maudit to Stamford, and from Stamford, even as the water runs, to the above-mentioned Northborough." These are the lands and the fens which the king gave to St. Peter's monastery.

Then the king said: "This gift is small, but I desire them to hold it so royally and so freely that neither tax nor rent be taken from it except for the monks alone. Thus I desire to free this monastery so that it will be subject only to Rome; and I desire that all of us who cannot go to Rome seek St. Peter here."

In the midst of these words, the abbot requested him to grant him what he asked of him; and the king granted it. "I have here God-fearing monks who would like to spend their lives in an anchoret's cell, if they knew a place. But here is an island called *Ancarig,* and I would make this request—that we may there build a monastery to the glory of St. Mary, so that those may dwell there who want to lead their life in peace and in rest."

Then the king answered and spoke thus: "Lo, beloved Seaxwulf, I thus approve and grant not only what you ask, but everything I know you to desire on our Lord's behalf. And I ask you, brother Æthelred, and my sisters, Cyneburg and Cyneswith, for your souls' salvation, to be witnesses and to write it with your fingers. And I ask all those who come after me, be they my sons, be they my brothers, or kings that come after me, that our gift may stand, even as they wish to be partakers of the eternal life and even as they wish to escape eternal punishment. Whoever shall lessen our gift or the gifts of other good men, may the heavenly gate-keeper lessen him in the kingdom of heaven; and whoever shall increase it, may the heavenly gate-keeper increase him in the kingdom of heaven."

These are the witnesses who were there, and who wrote it with their fingers on the sign of the cross and agreed with their tongues. That was first King Wulfhere who first confirmed it by his word and afterwards wrote it with his fingers with the sign of the cross; and he spoke thus: I, King Wulfhere, with the kings and with the earls and with the army-leaders and with the thegns, the witnesses of my gift, do confirm it before Archbishop Deusdedit with the sign of the cross. And I, Oswy, king of Northumbria, friend of this monastery and of Abbot Seaxwulf, approve it with the sign of the cross. And I, King Sigehere, grant it with the sign of the cross. And I, King Sibbi, write it with the sign of the cross. And I, Æthelred, the king's brother, grant the same with the sign of the cross. And we, the king's sisters, Cyneburg and Cyneswith, we approve it. And I, Deusdedit, archbishop of Canterbury, grant it. After that, all the others who were there agreed to it with the sign of the cross. They were, by name, Ithamar, bishop of Rochester, and Wine, bishop of London, and Jaruman, who was bishop of Mercia, and Bishop Tuda, and the priest Wilfrith, who was later bishop, and the priest Eoppa, whom King Wulfhere sent to preach Christianity in the Isle of Wight,[53] and Abbot Seaxwulf, and Alderman Immine, and Alderman Eadbert, and Alderman Herefrith, and Alderman Wilbert, and Alderman Abba, Æthelbald, Brordan, Wilbert, Ealhmund, Frithogist. These, and many others who were there, thegns

---

[53] This statement is based upon a misunderstanding of Bede's notice (IV. 13) about Eoppa and the conversion of Sussex, not Wight. The same error is made in the Chronicle proper under 661.

of the king, all agreed to it. This charter was written six hundred and sixty-four years after the birth of our Lord, the seventh year of King Wulfhere, the ninth year of Archbishop Deusdedit. Then they laid the curse of God and the curse of all saints and of all Christian people upon him who should undo anything that was done there. So be it, say all —Amen.

When this affair was finished, the king sent to Rome to Vitalian, who was then pope, and asked him to grant with his charter and with his blessing all this matter mentioned above. And the pope then sent his charter, saying thus: I, Pope Vitalian, grant to you, King Wulfhere, and to Archbishop Deusdedit and to Abbot Seaxwulf all the things that you ask, and I forbid any king or any man to have any authority there except the abbot alone, and that he obey no man except the pope of Rome and the archbishop of Canterbury. Whoever violates this in any respect, may St. Peter destroy him with his sword; whoever keeps it, may St. Peter with the keys of heaven open to him the kingdom of heaven. Thus was founded the monastery at *Medeshamsted* which later was called *Burh*.

After that another archbishop came to Canterbury who was called Theodore, a very good and wise man, and he held his synod with his bishops and with the clergy. Then Winefrith, bishop of Mercia, was deposed from his bishopric, and Abbot Seaxwulf was there elected bishop, and Cuthbald, a monk of the same monastery, was elected abbot. This synod was held six hundred and seventy-three years after the birth of our Lord.

658. Here Cenwalh fought against the Welsh at Pen Pits and he chased them as far as the Parrett. This [battle] was fought after he came from East Anglia—he had been there three years in exile. Penda had driven him away and deprived him of his kingdom because he had abandoned his [Penda's] sister.[54]

660. Here Bishop Ægelbert left Cenwalh, and Wine held the bishopric for three years; and Ægelbert received the bishopric of the Parisians on the Seine in Gaul.

661. Here at Easter Cenwalh fought at Pontesbury, and Wulfhere, son of Penda, ravaged as far as [55] Ashdown. And Cuthred, son of Cwichelm, and King Cenbert died in the one year. And Wulfhere, son of Penda, ravaged in Wight and gave the people of Wight to Æthelwald, king of Sussex, because Wulfhere had sponsored him at baptism. And the priest Eoppa, by order of Wilfrith and King Wulfhere, first brought baptism to the people of the Isle of Wight.[56]

[54] Cf. 644.
[55] MS *of;* A *oþ* "as far as"; BC *on* "on."
[56] Cf. the same mistaken assertion in the forged charter under 656.

664. Here the sun was eclipsed on May 3, and in this year a great pestilence came to the island of Britain, and Bishop Tuda died of the pestilence and was buried at *Wagele*. And Eorconbert, king of Kent, died, and his son, Egbert, succeeded to the throne. And Colman, with his companions, went to his country [Ireland].[57] And Ceadda and Wilfrith were consecrated; and in the same year Archbishop Deusdedit died.

667. Here Oswy and Egbert sent the priest Wighard to Rome to be consecrated archbishop, but he died as soon as he arrived there.

668. Here Pope Vitalian consecrated Theodore archbishop and sent him to Britain.

669. Here King Egbert gave Reculver to the priest Bass that he might build a church [there].

670. Here Oswy, king of Northumbria, died on February 15 and Ecgfrith, his son, reigned after him. And Hlothhere, nephew of Bishop Ægelbert, succeeded to the bishopric of Wessex and held it seven years, and Bishop Theodore consecrated him.

671. Here the great mortality of birds occurred.

672. Here Cenwalh died, and Seaxburg, his queen, reigned one year after him.

673. Here Egbert, king of Kent, died; and Archbishop Theodore summoned a synod at Hertford; and St. Æthelthryth founded the minster at Ely.

674. Here Æscwine succeeded to the throne of Wessex.

675. Here Wulfhere, son of Penda, and Æscwine, son of Cenfus, fought at *Bedanheafod;* and the same year Wulfhere died and Æthelred succeeded to the throne.

In his [Æthelred's] time he sent Bishop Wilfrith to Rome to the then pope—he was named Agatho—and showed him by document and by word how his brothers, Peada and Wulfhere, and Abbot Seaxwulf had built a monastery called Peterborough, and that they had freed it of all services to king and to bishop; and he entreated him to agree to it with his charter and with his blessing. And the pope then sent his charter to England, saying thus:

"I, Agatho, pope of Rome, greet well the worshipful Æthelred, king

---

[57] This statement is the only reference in the chronicles to the events of the famous Synod of Whitby at which Colman unsuccessfully defended the Celtic against the Roman practice of fixing the date of Easter and prescribing the form of tonsure. Both *E* and the OE version of Bede, oddly enough, omit any direct mention of the synod (Bede III. 25). *AC,* which here draw upon the Epitome, naturally do not notice it.

of Mercia, and Archbishop Theodore of Canterbury and Seaxwulf, the bishop of Mercia, who was formerly abbot, and all the abbots who are in England, with God's greeting and my blessing. I have heard the wish of King Æthelred and of Archbishop Theodore and of Bishop Seaxwulf and of Abbot Cuthbald, and I would have it in every way as you have said. And I command on behalf of God and of St. Peter and of all saints and of all persons in orders that neither king nor bishop nor earl nor any man have any authority or rent or tax or military service, nor shall anyone exact any kind of service from the abbacy of Peterborough.

"I also command that the bishop of the shire be not so presumptuous as to perform any ordination or consecration in this abbacy unless the abbot ask him, nor have any authority there, neither the bishop's visitation fee nor synod nor anything of the kind. And I will that the abbot be held as legate of Rome over the whole island, and that, whatever abbot shall be elected there by the monks, he be consecrated by the archbishop of Canterbury.

"I will and grant that whatever man shall have vowed a journey to Rome and be unable to perform it either because of sickness or his lord's need of him or because of poverty, or be unable to go there because of any other exigency, be he from England or from whatever other island he may be, let him come to the monastery at Peterborough and have the same forgiveness of Christ and St. Peter and of the abbot and of the monks that he would have if he went to Rome.

"Now I ask you, brother Theodore, to have it ordered throughout all England that a synod be assembled and this charter be read and observed. In like manner I command you, Bishop Seaxwulf, that just as you wished the monastery to be free, so I forbid you and all the bishops that shall come after you, by Christ and all his saints, to have any authority over the monastery except insofar as the abbot wishes.

"Now I will say by word that whoever observes this charter and this decree, may he always dwell with God Almighty in the heavenly kingdom; and whoever breaks it, may he be excommunicated and thrust down in hell with Judas and with all the devils unless he make amends. Amen."

Pope Agatho and one hundred and twenty-five bishops sent this charter to England by Wilfrith, archbishop [58] of York. This was done six hundred and eighty years after the birth of our Lord in the sixth year of King Æthelred.

The king then ordered Archbishop Theodore to arrange an assembly of the whole witan at the place called Hatfield. When they had gathered there, he had the charter read which the pope had sent there, and they all agreed to and fully confirmed it.

Then the king said: "I will that all those things which my brother, Peada, and my brother, Wulfhere, and my sisters, Cyneburg and Cyne-

[58] Properly *bishop* of York; the first archbishop of York was Egbert, who received his pallium in 735.

swith, gave and granted to St. Peter and the abbot, shall stand; and I will in my day enlarge it for [the good of] their souls and for my own.

"Now today I give to St. Peter for his monastery, Peterborough, these lands and all that adjoins them: that is Breedon-on-the-Hill, *Hrepingas, Cedenac,* Swineshead, *Heanbyrig, Lodeshac, Scuffanhalch, Costesford,* Stratford, *Wætteleburne, Lufgeard, Æþelhuniglond,* Bardney. I give these lands to St. Peter just as freely as I myself owned them and so that none of my successors shall take anything from them. If anyone do so, may he have the curse of the pope of Rome and the curse of all bishops and of all those who are here witnesses, and I confirm this with the sign of the cross.

"I, Theodore, archbishop of Canterbury, am witness to this charter of Peterborough, and I confirm it with my signature and I excommunicate all those who break any part of it and I bless all those who hold to it. I, Wilfrith, archbishop of York, I am a witness to this charter and I agree to the same curse. I, Seaxwulf, who was first abbot and now am bishop, I give those who break this my curse and that of all my successors. I, Osthryth, queen of Æthelred, grant it. I, Adrian, legate, agree to it. I, Putta, bishop of Rochester, I subscribe to it. I, Walter, bishop of London, confirm it. I, Abbot Cuthbald, agree to it so that, whoever breaks it, may he have the cursing of all bishops and of all Christian people. Amen."

676. Here Æscwine died, and Hedda succeeded to the bishopric; and Centwine succeeded to the throne of Wessex. And Æthelred, king of Mercia, ravaged Kent.

678. Here the star [called] comet appeared in August and shone like a sunbeam every morning for three months. And Bishop Wilfrith was driven out of his bishopric by King Ecgfrith, and two bishops were consecrated in his place, Bosa to Deira and Eata to Bernicia. And Eadhæth was consecrated bishop of the people of Lindsey; he was the first of the bishops of Lindsey.

679. Here Ælfwine was killed by the Trent where Ecgfrith and Æthelred fought; and here St. Æthelthryth died; and Coldingham was burned by a fire sent from heaven.

680. Here Archbishop Theodore appointed a synod at Hatfield because he wished to set right the faith of Christ. And this year Abbess Hild died in Whitby.

681. Here Trumbert was consecrated bishop of Hexham and Trumwine of the Picts, for at that time they were subject hither.[59]

682. Here in this year Centwine drove the Britons to the sea.

[59] Again (cf. 449) from the point of view of the northern scribe who adapted this annal from Bede (IV. 12), for the Picts were under Northumbrian control. The Canterbury compiler of *F* has substituted *ðider* "thither."

684. Here in this year Ecgfrith sent an army against the Scots, and Briht, his alderman, with it, and they miserably pillaged and burned God's churches.

685. Here King Ecgfrith ordered Cuthbert consecrated bishop, and Archbishop Theodore consecrated him bishop of Hexham on the first day of Easter in York, because Trumbert had been deprived of the bishopric. And the same year King Ecgfrith was killed north of the sea [*i. e.,* the Firth of Forth] and a great army with him on May 20. He had been king fifteen years, and Ealdfrith, his brother, succeeded him to the throne. And here Ceadwalla began to fight for the kingdom; and the same year Hlothhere, king of Kent, died. And John was consecrated bishop [of Hexham] in August, and he stayed there until Wilfrith returned. Later John succeeded to the bishopric of York, for Bishop Bosa had died. Then afterwards Wilfrith [II], his priest, was consecrated bishop of York, and he [John] went to his monastery in Beverley.

686. Here Ceadwalla and Mul, his brother, ravaged Kent and Wight.

This Ceadwalla gave *Hoge* to St. Peter's monastery of Peterborough: it is on an island called *Heabureahg*. The abbot in the monastery at the time was named Ecgbald—he was the third abbot after Seaxwulf. Theodore was then archbishop in Kent.

687. Here Mul was burned in Kent and twelve other men with him. And that year Ceadwalla again ravaged Kent.

688. Here King Ceadwalla went to Rome and received baptism from Pope Sergius, and he gave him the name of Peter, and a week later on April 20 he died in his baptismal garments, and he was buried in St. Peter's church. And Ine succeeded him to the throne of Wessex —he reigned twenty-seven [*for* thirty-seven] [60] years and afterwards went to Rome and remained there until the day of his death.

690. Here Archbishop Theodore died—he had been bishop twenty-two years, and he was buried in Canterbury.

692. Here Beorhtwald was elected archbishop on July 1—he was previously abbot of Reculver. Before this there were Roman bishops, and afterwards there were English. At that time there were two kings in Kent: Wihtred and Webhard.

693. Here Beorhtwald was consecrated archbishop by Godwine,

[60] As in *AC;* see 726.

bishop of Gaul, on July 3. At this time Bishop Gefmund died, and Beorhtwald consecrated Tobias in his place. And Drihthelm [61] was led forth from life.[62]

694. Here the men of Kent made an agreement with Ine and gave him thirty thousand [pence],[63] because they had previously [687] burned Mul. And Wihtred succeeded to the throne of Kent and held it twenty-three [*for* thirty-three] [64] years.

697. Here the Southumbrians killed Osthryth, Æthelred's queen, sister of Ecgfrith.

699. Here the Picts killed Alderman Beorht.

702. Here Cenred succeeded to the throne of the Southumbrians.[65]

703. Here Bishop Hedda died, and he had held the bishopric of Winchester twenty-seven years.

704. Here Æthelred, son of Penda, king of Mercia, became a monk, and he had held the throne twenty-nine years. Then Cenred succeeded [him].

705. Here Ealdfrith, king of Northumbria, died on December 14 at Driffield. Then Osred, his son, succeeded to the throne.

709. Here Bishop Ealdhelm died—he was bishop to the west of the Wood.[66] And in the early days of Daniel, Wessex was divided into two bishoprics, and previously it had been one. Daniel directed one, Bishop Ealdhelm the other—Forthhere succeeded Ealdhelm to it. And Ceolred succeeded to the throne of Mercia; and Cenred went to Rome and Offa with him, and Cenred stayed there until the end of his life. And the same year Bishop Wilfrith died at Oundle, and his body was taken to Ripon. He had been bishop forty-five years—King Ecgfrith had previously driven him away to Rome.[67]

[61] MS *Brihthelm* for *Drihthelm* (*D*) was probably produced by the *Brihtwald* of the preceding sentence.

[62] Temporarily into the other world; see Bede v. 12 for a description of Drihthelm's vision.

[63] *AD* also omit the denomination. *BCF* have *punda* "pounds," but 30,000 *sceattas* or pence, the wergeld of a king of Mercia (Liebermann, *Die Gesetze der Angelsachsen,* I, 462–63), seems much more reasonable.

[64] As in *AD;* cf. 692, 725. Thirty-three years is right if Wihtred's reign is measured from 692.

[65] This annal (also in *DF*) either represents a doublet of 704 (the correct date according to Bede's Epitome) taken from another source, or Cenred may have become joint king with Æthelred in 702.

[66] Apparently the (Hampshire) Weald: F. P. Magoun, Jr., "Aldhelm's Diocese of Sherborne *Bewestan Wuda,*" *The Harvard Theological Review,* XXXII (1939), 103–14.

[67] Cf. 678.

710. Here Acca, Wilfrith's priest, succeeded to the bishopric which he [Wilfrith] had previously held; and the same year Alderman Beorhtfrith fought against the Picts between *Hæfe* and *Cære;* and Ine and Nunna, his kinsman, fought against Geraint, king of the Welsh; and the same year Sigebald [68] was killed.

714. Here Guthlac the saint died.

715. Here Ine and Ceolred fought at *Wodnesbeorh.*

716. Here Osred, king of Northumbria, was killed south of the border; [69] he had [the throne] seven years after Ealdfrith. Then Cenred succeeded to the throne and held it two years, and then Osric, and he held it eleven years. And also in the same year Ceolred, king of Mercia, died, and his body rests at Lichfield and that of Æthelred, son of Penda, at Bardney. And then Æthelbald succeeded to the throne of Mercia and held it forty-one years. And Egbert, the reverend man, [converted] [70] the religious house at Iona to the correct Easter and to St. Peter's tonsure.

718. Here Ingild, brother of Ine, died, and their sisters were Cwenburg and Cuthburg; and this Cuthburg built the monastery at Wimborne, and she was given in marriage to Ealdfrith, king of Northumbria, and they separated while he was yet living.

721. Here Daniel went to Rome; and the same year Cynewulf the atheling was killed. And here died the holy bishop John who had been bishop thirty-three years and eight months and thirteen days, and his body rests at Beverley.

722. Here Queen Æthelburg destroyed Taunton which Ine had previously built; and Ealdbert, the exile, departed to Surrey and Sussex.

725. Here Wihtred, king of Kent, died on April 23; he had reigned thirty-four years. And Ine fought against the South Saxons and there killed Ealdbert the atheling whom he had previously banished.

726. Here Ine went to Rome and Æthelhard, his kinsman, succeeded to the throne of Wessex and held it fourteen years.

727. Here Tobias, bishop of Rochester, died, and in his place Archbishop Beorhtwald consecrated Ealdwulf bishop.

[68] MS *Hygebald;* D *Sigbald;* and Geoffrey Gaimar, *Lestorie des Engles* (ed. C. T. Martin, "Rolls Series," London, 1888), 1. 1633 *Sibald.*
[69] Either the Pictish (at the Firth of Forth) or the Mercian (at the Humber) border may be meant.
[70] From *D.*

729. Here two comets appeared; and the same year Osric died—he had been king eleven years—and the holy Egbert in Iona. Then Ceolwulf succeeded to the throne and held it eight years.

730. Here Atheling Oswald died.

731. Here Archbishop Beorhtwald died on January 13; he had been bishop twenty-seven years and six months and fourteen days. And the same year Tatwine was consecrated archbishop. He had previously been priest at Breedon-on-the-Hill in Mercia. Daniel, bishop of Winchester, and Ingwald, bishop of London, and Ealdwine, bishop of Lichfield, and Ealdwulf, bishop of Rochester, consecrated him on June 10.

733. Here Æthelbald captured Somerton; and the sun was eclipsed; and Acca was driven from his bishopric.

734. Here the moon was as though it were sprinkled with blood; [71] and Archbishop Tatwine died, and also Bede; [72] and Egbert was consecrated bishop.

735. Here Bishop Egbert received the pallium at Rome.

736. Here Archbishop Nothhelm received the pallium from the bishop of the Romans.

737. Here Bishop Forthhere and Queen Frithogyth went to Rome; and King Ceolwulf adopted Peter's tonsure and gave his kingdom to Eadbert, his cousin on his father's side—he reigned twenty-one years. [73] And Bishop Æthelwald and Acca died; and Cynewulf was consecrated bishop. And the same year King Æthelwald [for Æthelbald] [74] ravaged Northumbria.

738. Here Eadbert, son of Eata—Eata, the son of Leodwald—succeeded to the throne of Northumbria and held it twenty-one years; and his brother was Archbishop Egbert, son of Eata; and they both rest in the same chapel in York.

740. Here King Æthelhard died, and Cuthred, his kinsman, succeeded to the throne of Wessex, and held it sixteen years; and he

---

71 The lunar eclipse of January 24; the red coloring referred to is probably produced by the refraction of light through a highly vaporous atmosphere.

72 The conventional date assigned to Bede's death is 735. The various dates in the early sources are listed in Plummer's *Bede*, I, lxxi–ii, n. 3.

73 The notice of Eadbert's accession is repeated in the next annal. His resignation is placed under 757 by *E;* the date given in the northern sources (Plummer, II, 48) is 758, which would make 737 the correct date for his accession.

74 MS *Æðelwold* for *Æðelbald* (*D*), probably from the bishop's name in the preceding sentence.

fought vigorously against Æthelbald, king of Mercia; and Eadbert [*for* Cuthbert] [75] was consecrated archbishop, and Dunn bishop of Rochester.

741. Here York burned.

743. Here Æthelbald, king of Mercia, and Cuthred, king of Wessex, fought against the Welsh.

744. Here Daniel resided [*for* resigned] [76] in Winchester, and Hunfrith succeeded to the bishopric. And there were many shooting stars; and Wilfrith the Younger, who was bishop of York, died on April 29; he had been bishop thirty years.

745. Here Daniel died. At that time forty-six [*for* forty-three] [77] years had passed since he succeeded to the bishopric.

746. Here King Selered was killed.

748. Here Cynric, atheling of the West Saxons, was killed; and Eadbert, king of Kent, died.

750. Here Cuthred, king of Wessex, fought against Æthelhun, the arrogant alderman.

752. Here Cuthred, king of Wessex, in the twenty-second [*for* twelfth] [78] year of his reign fought at *Beorgford* against Æthelbald, king of Mercia, and routed him.

753. Here Cuthred, king of Wessex, fought against the Welsh.

754 [756].[79] Here Cuthred, king of Wessex, died; and Cynehard succeeded Hunfrith to the bishopric of Winchester; and that year Canterbury burned; and Sigebert, his [Cuthred's] kinsman, succeeded to the throne of Wessex and held it one year.

755 [757]. Here Cynewulf and the witan of the West Saxons deprived Sigebert, his kinsman, of his [whole] kingdom except Hampshire, on account of his illegal acts; and he [Sigebert] kept that

[75] As in *AD;* the *E*-form is apparently a careless repetition of the name in 738.
[76] The *gesæt* "resided" of all the chronicles may rest upon a misreading of *resedit* for *recedit* in a Latin source. The word is again mistakenly employed in 779.
[77] As in *ACD.*
[78] As in *ACD.*
[79] With this annal begins the almost century-long (754–845) chronological dislocation running through all the chronicles and presumably produced by the carelessness of the scribe who made the master copy of the Primary Compilation which served as the prototype for the early sections of the existing chronicles. Up to 828 the dating is in most cases two years too early. A chronological discrepancy occurs within many annals of *E* in the case of the Northumbrian entries which the northern redactor correctly inserted under the false dates of the Primary Compilation. The original dates have accordingly been added in brackets only for those annals in which none of this new northern matter appears.

[Hampshire] until he killed the alderman who had stayed with him for a very long time. And then Cynewulf drove him [Sigebert] into the Weald, and he lived there until a herdsman stabbed him at Privett. The herdsman avenged the alderman, Cumbra. And this Cynewulf fought many battles against the Welsh.

And about sixteen [*for* thirty-one] [80] years after he got the throne, he wanted to drive out an atheling named Cynehard. This Cynehard was brother of this Sigebert. And then he [Cynehard] learned that the king with a small retinue [was] at *Merantun* in the company of a woman. And he [Cynehard] surprised him there and surrounded the chamber [of the woman] from the outside before the men who were with the king noticed him. And then the king realized this, and he went to the door [of the chamber] and valiantly defended himself until he set eyes on the atheling [Cynehard]. And then he rushed out at him and severely wounded him; and they [Cynehard's men] all fought against the king until they had killed him. And then from the woman's outcries the king's thegns became aware of the disturbance and ran to the place, whoever was first ready. And the atheling [Cynehard] offered money and life to each of them [Cynewulf's thegns], and none of them would accept it, but they kept on fighting steadily until they [Cynewulf's thegns] were all killed except for a Welsh hostage, and he was seriously wounded.

Then in the morning those of the king's thegns who had been left behind [*i. e.,* not brought to *Merantun*] heard that the king had been killed. Then both his [Cynewulf's] alderman Osric and his thegn Wigfrith and those men who had previously been left behind rode there [to *Merantun*] and came upon the atheling [Cynehard] in the enclosure where the king lay dead; and they [Cynehard's men] had locked the gates [of the enclosure] against them [Osric's men], and they [Osric's men] came right up to them. And then he [Cynehard] offered them [Osric's men] what they wanted of money and land if they [Osric's men] would grant him the throne, and informed them that with him were their [Osric's men's] kinsmen who did not wish to leave him. And then they [Osric's men] said that no kinsman was dearer to them than their lord and that they would never follow his murderer. And then they [Osric's men] offered to let their kinsmen

[80] *ABC xxxi; D xxi.* See below in this annal and 784 [786] where, of course, this story belongs. Actually, according to the chronicles, Cynewulf reigned twenty-nine years (757–86).

go away unharmed, and they [the kinsmen] said that the same offer had been made to their [Osric's men's] companions who had been with the king before. Then they [the kinsmen] said that they considered it [the offer] no more than their [Osric's men's] companions who had been killed with the king. Then they [Osric's men] began fighting about the gates until they got inside [the enclosure] and killed the atheling and all the men who were with him except one who was the alderman's [Osric's] godson, and he escaped with his life, and he was often wounded.

And this Cynewulf reigned thirty-one years, and his body lies at Winchester and the atheling's [Cynehard's] at Axminster. And their direct paternal line goes back to Cerdic.

And the same year [*i. e.,* 757] Æthelbald, king of Mercia, was killed at Seckington, and his body rests at Repton, and he had reigned forty-one years; and then Beornred succeeded to the throne and held it for a short time and unhappily; and the same year Offa drove out Beornred and succeeded to the throne and held it thirty-nine years; and his son, Ecgfrith, held it one hundred and forty-one days. This Offa was the son of Thingfrith.

757. Here Eadbert, king of Northumbria, adopted the tonsure; and his son, Oswulf, succeeded to the throne and reigned one year, and the men of his household killed him on July 24.

758 [760]. Here Archbishop Cuthbert died.

759. Here Bregowine was consecrated archbishop at Michaelmas [Sept. 29]; and Moll Æthelwald succeeded to the throne of Northumbria and reigned six years and then abandoned it.

760. Here Æthelbert, king of Kent, died; and Ceolwulf also died.

761. Here there was the hard winter; and Moll, king of Northumbria, killed Oswine at *Eadwinesclif* on August 6.

762.[81] Here Jænbert was consecrated archbishop on the fortieth day after Christmas; and Bishop Frithowald died at Whithorn on May 7. He had been consecrated at York on August 15 in the sixth year of Ceolwulf's reign, and he had been bishop twenty-nine years. Then Peohtwine was consecrated bishop of Whithorn at Elvet Hall on July 17.

765. Here Ealhred succeeded to the throne of Northumbria and reigned eight years.

[81] *AC* 763, *D* 762. The events in this annal cannot be dated with assurance.

766. Here Archbishop Egbert died in York on November 19—he had been bishop thirty-six years [82]—and Frithobert in Hexham—he had been bishop thirty-four years. And Æthelbert was consecrated to York and Ealhmund to Hexham.

768. Here Eadbert, son of Eata, died on August 19.

769. *Beginning of the reign of King Charles [the Great].*

772 [774]. Here Bishop Mildred died.

774. Here the Northumbrians drove their king, Ealhred, out of York at Easter time and took as their lord Æthelred, son of Moll, and he reigned four years. And men saw a red cross in the sky after sunset.[83] In that year the Mercians and men of Kent fought at Otford. And extraordinary snakes were seen in Sussex.

776. Here Bishop Peohtwine died on September 19—he had been bishop fourteen years.

777. Here Cynewulf and Offa fought at Bensington, and Offa captured the town; and the same year Æthelbert was consecrated bishop of Whithorn at York on June 15.

In the days of King Offa there was an abbot in Peterborough named Beonna. This same Beonna, on the advice of all the monks of the monastery, rented to Alderman Cuthbert ten bondlands at Swineshead with pasture and with meadow and with all that belonged to them; and on such terms that this Cuthbert gave the abbot fifty pounds for it and each year one night's provision or thirty shillings in pennies [*i. e.,* 120 d. at the time], and also that after his day the land should revert to the monastery. The witnesses to this were King Offa and King Ecgfrith and Archbishop Hygebert, and Bishop Ceolwulf, and Bishop Inwona, and Abbot Beonna, and many other bishops and abbots and many other prominent men.

In the days of this same Offa there was an alderman called Brorda. He requested the king, for love of him, to free a monastery of his called Woking because he wished to give it to Peterborough and St. Peter and the then abbot who was named Pusa. This Pusa was the successor of Beonna, and the king loved him very much; and the king then freed the monastery of Woking from king and from bishop and from earl and from all men so that no one should have any authority there except St. Peter and the abbot. This was done in the royal vill called *Freoricburna*.

778. Here on March 22 Æthelbald and Heardbert killed three high reeves: Ealdwulf, son of Bosa, at High Coniscliffe, and Cynewulf and Ecga at *Helaþyrna*. And then Ælfwald succeeded to the

[82] But cf. 734.
[83] The reference is apparently to an aurora borealis.

throne and drove Æthelred out of the country, and he reigned ten years.

Charles [the Great] entered Spain. Charles came to Saxony. Charles destroyed the cities of Pamplona and Saragossa. He joined his army, and after taking hostages and subduing the Saracens, he returned by way of Narbonne in Gascony in the land of the Franks.

779. Here the Old Saxons and the Franks fought; and the high reeves of the Northumbrians burned Alderman Beorn at *Seletun* on December 24. And Archbishop Æthelbert died in York and Eanbald had [previously] [84] been consecrated in his place; and Bishop Cynebald [*for* Cynewulf] [85] resigned in Lindisfarne.

780. Here Ealhmund, bishop of Hexham, died on September 7, and Tilbert was consecrated in his place on October 2; and Hygebald was consecrated bishop of Lindisfarne at Sockburn; and King Ælfwald sent someone [86] to Rome for a pallium and made Eanbald archbishop.

782. Here Wærburg, Ceolred's queen, and Cynewulf, bishop of Lindisfarne, died; and there was a synod at *Aclea*.

784 [786]. Here Cynehard killed King Cynewulf, and he [himself] was killed there and eighty-four men with him [*see* 755]; and then Beorhtric, king of Wessex, succeeded to the throne, and he reigned sixteen years, and his body lies at Wareham; and his direct paternal line goes back to Cerdic.

785. Here Abbot Botwine died in Ripon. And here there was a contentious synod at *Cealchyð,* and Archbishop Jænbert gave up a part of his bishopric, and Hygebert was appointed [bishop] by King Offa; and Ecgfrith was consecrated king; and at this time messengers were sent from Rome by Pope Adrian to England to renew the faith and the peace which St. Gregory had sent us through Bishop Augustine; and they were received with honor.

787 [789]. Here King Beorhtric married Offa's daughter, Eadburg; and in his days [87] for the first time three ships of the Northmen

[84] Supplied from *D*. Æthelbert retired some two years before his death.
[85] As in *D;* cf. 737. The *E*-scribe was probably misled by the preceding *Ean*-bald.
[86] This was the celebrated scholar, Alcuin.
[87] Here again, as in the case of the "Anglo-Saxon" invasion (see 449*n*), the first coming of the Northmen-Danes is dated only approximately—in the reign of Beorhtric, *i. e.*, between 786 and 802. On the general subject of the Vikings and their raids and settlement in England, see A. Mawer, *The Vikings* (Cambridge, 1913); T. D. Kendrick, *History of the Vikings* (London, 1930); W. G. Collingwood,

came from Hardanger [Norway]; and then the reeve rode up and he wanted to drive [them] to the royal vill because he did not know what they were, and he was killed there.[88] Those were the first ships of the Danes to come to England.

788. Here a synod was assembled in Northumbria at *Pincanhealh* on September 2; and Abbot Ealdbert died.

Charles [the Great] went through Alemannic territory to the borders of Bavaria.

789. Here Ælfwald, king of Northumbria, was killed by Sicga on September 23; and a heavenly light was often seen at the spot where he was killed; and he was buried in the church at Hexham. And a synod was assembled at *Aclea*. And Osred, son of Ealhred, succeeded him to the throne—he was his nephew.

790. Here Archbishop Jænbert died; and the same year Abbot Æthelhard was elected archbishop; and Osred, king of Northumbria, was betrayed and driven out of the kingdom, and Æthelred, son of [Moll] Æthelwald, again obtained the throne.

791. Here Bealdwulf was consecrated bishop of Whithorn on July 17 by Archbishop Eanbald and by Bishop Æthelbert.

792. Here Offa, king of Mercia, ordered Æthelbert's head cut off. And Osred—who had been king of Northumbria—after coming home from his exile, was seized and killed on September 14, and his body lies at Tynemouth. And on September 29 King Æthelred married a new wife—she was called Ælfflæd.

793. Here dire portents came over Northumbria and sorely terrified the people; there were great lightnings, and fiery dragons were seen flying in the air. A great famine soon followed these signs, and shortly after that in the same year on January 8 [*for* June 8] [89] an inroad of heathen miserably destroyed God's church in Lindisfarne by plundering and killing. And Sicga died on February 22.

794. Here Pope Adrian and King Offa died; and Æthelred, king of Northumbria, was killed by his own people on April 19; and Bishop Ceolwulf and Bishop Eadbald left the country. And Ecgfrith suc-

Scandinavian Britain (London, 1908); E. Ekwall, "The Scandinavian Settlement," in H. C. Darby, ed., *An Historical Geography of England before A. D. 1800* (Cambridge, 1936), pp. 133–64; Hodgkin, *History*, pp. 473–509, 699 ff.

[88] Ostensibly a king's reeve or high reeve who wanted to collect the king's charges. Ethelwerd (*Monumenta historica Britannica*, p. 509) supplies the name of the reeve, Beaduheard, and of the royal vill, Dorchester.

[89] According to Simeon of Durham (ed. T. Arnold, "Rolls Series" [London, 1882], I, 51)—and a more likely season of the year.

ceeded to the throne of Mercia and died the same year; and Eadbert, who by a second name was called Præn, succeeded to the throne of Kent.[90] And Alderman Æthelhard died on August 1. And the heathen ravaged in Northumbria and looted Ecgfrith's monastery [Jarrow] at the mouth of the Don; and one of their leaders was killed there and in addition some of their ships were broken to pieces by a storm; and many of them were drowned there, and some came to shore alive and were at once killed at the mouth of the river.

795. Here the moon was eclipsed between cockcrow and dawn on March 28.[91] And Eardwulf succeeded to the throne of Northumbria on May 14; and he was afterwards consecrated and raised to his royal seat on May 26 in York by Archbishop Eanbald and [by] Æthelbert and Hygebald and Bealdwulf.

796. Here Offa, [king] of Mercia, died on August 10 [for July 29] [92]—he had reigned forty years—and Archbishop Eanbald on August 10 of the same year, and his body lies in York. And the same year Bishop Ceolwulf died; and a second Eanbald was consecrated in the other's place on August 14. And the same year Ceolwulf [for Cenwulf],[93] king of Mercia, raided the men of Kent and of Romney Marsh, and captured Præn, their king, and led him bound into Mercia.

797. Here the Romans cut out the tongue of Pope Leo and bored out his eyes, and chased him from his see; and soon afterwards, with God's help, he could see and speak, and he was pope again as he formerly had been. And Eanbald received the pallium on September 8; and Bishop Æthelbert died on [October 16, and Heardred was consecrated bishop in his place on] [94] October 30.

798. Here in the spring there was a great fight in Northumbria at Whalley on April 2, and Alric, son of Heardbert, was killed there, and many others with him.

799 [801]. Here Archbishop Æthelred [for Æthelhard] [95] and Cynebert, bishop of Wessex, went to Rome.

800. Here the moon was eclipsed at the second hour of the eve of

[90] The events so far belong to 796 (cf. the second notice of Offa's death under 796), the following northern events to 794.
[91] March 28, 796. Eardwulf's succession is probably also to be placed in that year (Theopold, *Kritische Untersuchungen*, pp. 72–73).
[92] MS *idus* for *kalendas* (D) *Augusti*.
[93] *AD Ceolwulf, BC Cynulf*. The *ADE* form was probably produced through confusion with the next king of Mercia, Ceolwulf. The correct name, Cenwulf, appears in the obit entered under 819.
[94] Supplied from *D*. The *E*-scribe carelessly jumped from one date to the other.
[95] As in *ACD*.

January 16.[96] And King Beorhtric and Alderman Worr died. And Egbert succeeded to the throne of Wessex. And the same day Alderman Æthelmund rode over [the Thames] from the Hwicce at Kempsford. Alderman Weohstan then met him with the men of Wiltshire, and there was a great fight, and both the aldermen were killed there, and the men of Wiltshire won the victory.

King Charles [the Great] was made emperor, and called Augustus by the Romans, and he condemned to death those who had dishonored Pope Leo, but at the entreaties of the pope, tempering death with exile, he banished [them from him]. For Pope Leo himself had consecrated him emperor.

802. Here the moon was eclipsed at dawn on December 20 [*for* May 20] ; [97] and Beornmod was consecrated bishop of Rochester the same year.

803. Here Hygebald, bishop of Lindisfarne, died on June 24, and Egbert was consecrated in his place on June 11; and Archbishop Æthelhard died in Kent, and Wulfred [was] consecrated archbishop.

804 [806]. Here Archbishop Wulfred received the pallium.

805 [807]. Here King Cuthred died in Kent, and Abbess Ceolburg, and Heardbert.

806. Here the moon was eclipsed on September 1. And Eardwulf, king of Northumbria, was driven from his kingdom; and Eanbert, bishop of Hexham, died.

810. *Charles [the Great] made peace with Nicephorus, emperor of Constantinople.*

812 [814]. Here King Charles [the Great] died, and he had reigned forty-five years. And Archbishop Wulfred and Wigbert, bishop of Wessex, went to Rome.

Cireneius sent his messengers with offers of peace to Emperor Charles. Emperor Charles died.[98]

813 [815]. Here Archbishop Wulfred, with the blessing of Pope Leo, returned to his own bishopric; and that year King Egbert ravaged in Cornwall from east to west.

---

[96] The eclipse took place at 8:30 p. m. on January 15, 800.

[97] MS *xiii* *kalendas* *Ianuarii*, with January a mistake for June. A lunar eclipse occurred at 4 a. m. on May 21, 802.

[98] The MS *Cireneius Karolo imperatori legatos suos cum pace mittit. Karolus imperator obiit* is a drastic corruption of the source (*Annales Uticenses*) : *811. Niceforus obiit. Michael imperator, gener eius, qui Karolo imperatori legatos suos cum pace mittit. 814. Karolus imperator obiit.* (Quoted by Theopold, *Kritische Untersuchungen*, p. 87.)

814 [816]. Here Leo, the noble and holy pope, died, and Stephen succeeded him to the papacy.

815 [817].⁹⁹ Here Pope Stephen died, and after him Paschal was consecrated pope; and the same year the English School ¹⁰⁰ burned.

819 [821]. Here Cenwulf, king of Mercia, died, and Ceolwulf succeeded to the throne; and Alderman Eadbert died.

821 [823]. Here Ceolwulf was deprived of his kingdom.

822 [824]. Here two aldermen, Berghelm and Muca, were killed; and [there was] a synod at *Clofesho*.

823 [825]. Here there was a battle between the men of Cornwall and the men of Devon at Galford; and the same year Egbert, king of Wessex, and Beornwulf, king of Mercia, fought at *Ellandun,* and Egbert won the victory, and a great number was killed there. Then he sent his son, Æthelwulf, and Ealhstan, his bishop, and Wulfhard, his alderman, from the fyrd into Kent with a large force, and they drove Bealdred, the king, north over the Thames—and the men of Kent and the men of Surrey and the South Saxons and the East Saxons submitted to him, because they had before been wrongly forced away from his kinsmen.¹⁰¹

And the same year the king and the people of East Anglia sought King Egbert as ally and protector for fear of the Mercians; and the same year the East Angles killed Beornwulf, king of Mercia.

825 [827]. Here Ludica, king of Mercia, was killed, and his five aldermen with him; and Wiglaf succeeded to the throne.

827 [829]. Here the moon was eclipsed on Christmas Eve; and the same year King Egbert conquered the kingdom of Mercia and everything south of the Humber; and he was the eighth king who was Bretwalda.¹⁰² Ælle, king of Sussex, was the first who thus had great [power]; the second was Ceawlin, king of Wessex; the third Æthel-

---

⁹⁹ *ACD* 816. Stephen's death and the burning of the English School both occurred in 817.

¹⁰⁰ The *Schola Saxonum* was the Saxon quarter in Rome, and not a "school" or hospice in any modern sense. W. J. Moore, *The Saxon Pilgrims to Rome and the Schola Saxonum* (Fribourg, Switzerland, 1937); see Stevenson, *Asser's Life,* pp. 243–47; W. E. Lunt, *Financial Relations of the Papacy with England to 1327* (Cambridge, Mass., 1939), pp. 11–15.

¹⁰¹ The historical facts behind this statement cannot be made out with any certainty (see Earle, *Two of the Saxon Chronicles Parallel,* pp. 298 f.; Plummer, II, 71 f.; Oman, *England,* pp. 388 f., 393).

¹⁰² *I. e.,* "ruler or lord of Britain." On the probable significance of the term and the nature of Egbert's *imperium,* see Hodgkin, *History,* pp. 398–402; further, F. M. Stenton, "The Supremacy of the Mercian Kings," *EHR,* XXXIII (1918), 433 ff.

bert, king of Kent; the fourth Redwald, king of East Anglia; the fifth
Edwin, king of Northumbria; the sixth was Oswald, who reigned
after him; the seventh was Oswy, Oswald's brother; the eighth was
Egbert, king of Wessex. And this Egbert led a fyrd to Dore against
the Northumbrians, and there they offered him obedience and peace,
and with that they parted.

828 [830]. Here Wiglaf again [see 825] secured the throne of
Mercia; and Bishop Æthelbald [for Æthelwald] [103] died; and the
same year King Egbert led a fyrd against the Welsh, and he forced
them all into obedient subjection.

829 [832].[104] Here Archbishop Wulfred died.

830 [833]. Here Ceolnoth was elected [arch]bishop and consecrated; and Abbot Feologild died.

831 [834]. Here Archbishop Ceolnoth received the pallium.

832 [835]. Here the heathen ravaged the Isle of Sheppey.

833 [836]. Here King Egbert fought against twenty-five [for
thirty-five] [105] ship crews at Carhampton, and a great number was
killed there, and the Danes retained possession of the battlefield.[106]
And Herefrith and Wigfrith [for Wigthegn],[107] two bishops, died;
and Dudda and Osmod, two aldermen, died.

835 [838]. Here a great Scandinavian fleet came to Cornwall, and
they [Cornishmen and Scandinavians] joined forces and fought [108]
against Egbert, king of Wessex. He then went out to meet them and
fought against them at Hingston Down and there routed both the
Cornishmen and the Danes.

836 [839]. Here King Egbert died; and Offa, king of Mercia,
and Beorhtric, king of Wessex, had formerly exiled him three [for

---

[103] D *Æþelbald*, AC correctly *Æþelwald*.

[104] The chronological dislocation for the next eleven entries appears to increase to
three, and sometimes four, years. Even a few events above—the deaths of Beornwulf
(823) and of Ludica (825)—are most likely also antedated by three years. Only a
few of the following events, however, can be dated with any certainty (Theopold,
Kritische Untersuchungen, p. 51; Plummer, II, 73–77 *passim*). On the annals for
840 and 845, see Theopold, pp. 62 f.

[105] *AC xxxv, D xxv.*

[106] This recurring and obscure phrase, employed even where the Scandinavians are
defeated, as well as when they gain the victory, probably means that, whatever the
outcome of the battle, the Danes neither gained nor lost ground, but preserved their
original position—in a fort or behind a series of earthworks.

[107] *AC Wigþen, D Wigferð*. The *DE* form is probably due to the preceding *Here-
ferð*.

[108] *DE wuniende wæron* "dwelt" for *AC winnende wæron* "fought" or "continued
fighting."

thirteen] [109] years from England to the land of the Franks before he was king; and this Egbert had reigned thirty-seven years and seven months; and Æthelwulf, his son, succeeded to the throne of Wessex, and Æthelstan, his other son, succeeded to the throne of Kent [and of Essex] [110] and to Surrey and to the throne of Sussex.

837 [840]. Here Alderman Wulfhard fought against thirty-three ship crews at Southampton and there killed a great number and won the victory. And that year Wulfhard died. And Alderman Æthelhelm fought with the men of Dorset against the Danes at Portland, and the alderman was killed, and the Danes retained possession of the battlefield.

839 [842]. Here there was a great slaughter at London and at Quentavic and at Rochester.

840 [844]. Here King Æthelwulf fought at Carhampton against thirty-five ship crews, and the Danes retained possession of the battlefield.

845 [850]. Here Alderman Earnwulf [*for* Eanwulf],[111] with the men of Somerset and Bishop Ealhstan and Alderman Osric with the men of Dorset fought at the mouth of the Parrett against the Danish army and there killed a great number and won the victory.

851.[112] Here Alderman Ceorl with the men of Devon fought against the heathen at Wigborough and there killed a great number and won the victory; and the heathen settled on the Isle of Thanet over the winter. And the same year three hundred and fifty ships came to the mouth of the Thames, and [the Scandinavians] stormed Canterbury and routed Beorhtwulf, king of Mercia, with his fyrd, and then went south over the Thames into Surrey; and King Æthelwulf and his son, Æthelbald, with the West Saxon fyrd fought against them at *Aclea* and there killed the greatest number among the heathen army that we ever heard tell of and there won the victory. And the same year King Æthelstan and Alderman Ealhhere fought in ships and killed a large force at Sandwich and captured nine ships and routed the others.

[109] This correction of a reading common to all the Old English Chronicles and later Latin authorities was first made by J. M. Lappenberg, *Geschichte von England* (Hamburg, 1834–37), I, 270 n. 1, and is generally subscribed to (see Plummer, II, 75). Oman (*England,* p. 389 n. 1), however, accepts the original duration of three years as correct.

[110] From *AC;* also omitted in *D.*

[111] *D Earnulf, AC* correctly *Eanulf.*

[112] The blank annals 846–50 lead here to the restoration of the original chronology of the Primary Compilation.

852. Here at this time Abbot Ceolred of Peterborough and the monks rented the land of Sempringham to Wulfred, on the agreement that after his day the land should revert to the monastery and that Wulfred should give the land of *Sleaford* to Peterborough, and [that] each year he should give to the monastery sixty loads of wood and twelve loads of brushwood and six loads of faggots and two butts full of clear ale and two cattle for slaughter and six hundred loaves and ten measures of Welsh ale, and each year a horse and thirty shillings and one night's provision. Here were present King Burgred, and Archbishop Ceolred [*for* Ceolnoth], and Bishop Tunbert, and Bishop Cenred [*for* Ceolred], and Bishop Ealhhun, and Bishop Beorhtred, and Abbot Wihtred, and Abbot Weorhthard, and Alderman Æthelhard, Alderman Hunbert, and many others.

852*b* [853]. Here Burgred, king of Mercia, subdued the Welsh with the aid of King Æthelwulf. And the same year Ealhhere with the men of Kent and Hudda with the men of Surrey fought on the Isle of Thanet against the heathen army, and many on either side were killed and drowned there, and the aldermen [were] both dead. And Burgred, king of Mercia, married the daughter of Æthelwulf, king of Wessex.

855. Here the heathen first settled on the Isle of Sheppey over the winter; and the same year King Æthelwulf by charter gave the tenth part of his own land in all his kingdom for the glory of God and his own eternal salvation.[113] And the same year he went to Rome with great pomp and remained there a year. And while he was on his homeward journey, he married the daughter of Charles [the Bald], king of the Franks, and came home safe. And then in about two years he died [Jan. 13, 858], and his body lies in Winchester, and he had reigned nine years. He was the son of Egbert.[114] And then his two sons succeeded to the throne—Æthelbald to the throne of Wessex and of Surrey,[115] and he [Æthelbald] reigned five years.

860. Here King Æthelbald died, and his body lies at Sherborne, and Æthelbert succeeded to the entire kingdom of his brother; and in his day a great fleet landed and stormed Winchester; and Alderman Osric with the men of Hampshire and Alderman Æthelwulf with the

[113] Apparently Æthelwulf made his famous "donation" by granting land to his thegns with a reversion to a religious foundation (see Stevenson, *Asser's Life,* pp. 186–91).
[114] E alone omits the long genealogy which appeared here in the Primary Compilation and is generally held to mark the end of the earlier Æthelwulfian Chronicle.
[115] A correctly records Æthelbald's succession to Wessex and Æthelbert's to Kent, Essex, Surrey, and Sussex; D, probably following two sources, first has Æthelbald succeeding to Surrey and Wessex, as in E, then a second version as in A. E has simply adopted the wrong account.

men of Berkshire fought against the Scandinavians and routed the army and retained possession of the battlefield. And this Æthelbert reigned five years, and his body lies at Sherborne.

865. Here the heathen army settled on the Isle of Thanet and made peace with the men of Kent, and the men of Kent promised them money in return for the peace; and [during the peace and] [116] the promise of money the Scandinavians stole inland by night and ravaged all of eastern Kent.

866. Here Æthelred, brother of Æthelbert, succeeded to the throne of Wessex. And the same year a great heathen army came to England and set up winter quarters in East Anglia, and they were there provided with horses, and they [the East Angles] made peace with them.

867. Here the Scandinavian army went from East Anglia over the mouth of the Humber to York in Northumbria. And there was great discord there among the people, and they had thrown out their king, Osbert, and had received as king Ælle, [who was] not of royal blood. And late in the year they determined to fight against the Scandinavians and, moreover, gathered a great fyrd and sought out the army at York and stormed the town, and some of them got inside; and a great number of the Northumbrians were killed there, some inside, some outside, and both the kings were killed, and the remainder made peace with the Scandinavians. And the same year Bishop Ealhstan died, and he had had the bishopric at Sherborne fifty years, and his body lies there in the cemetery. [117]

868. Here the same army went into Mercia to Nottingham and there set up winter quarters; and Burgred, king of Mercia, and his witan asked Æthelred, king of Wessex, and Alfred, his brother, to help him fight against the Scandinavians. And then they went with the West Saxon fyrd into Mercia as far as Nottingham and there found the army inside the fortress and besieged it there; and no serious fighting took place there, and the Mercians made peace with the Scandinavians.

869. Here the Scandinavian army again went to York and stayed there one year.

870. Here the Scandinavian army went across Mercia into East

[116] From *A;* omitted from *DE* through repetition of the word "peace."
[117] "In the cemetery" for the MS *on tune* (generally translated "in the town") follows F. M. Stenton, "The Southwestern Element in the Old English Chronicle," *Essays in Medieval History Presented to T. F. Tout* (Manchester, 1925), p. 18.

Anglia and set up winter quarters at Thetford; and in the same year St. Edmund, king [of East Anglia], fought against them, and the Danes won the victory and killed the king and conquered the whole country.

And [they] destroyed all the monasteries to which they came. At that time they came to Peterborough and burned and destroyed it, killing the abbot and the monks and all whom they found there. They brought it about that, where it had previously been very rich, it was reduced to nothing.

And that year Archbishop Ceolnoth died.

871. Here the Scandinavian army rode to Reading in Wessex; and three days later two jarls rode up-country. Then Alderman Æthelwulf met them at Englefield and fought against them there and won the victory, and one of them [the jarls], named Sidrac, was killed there. Then four days later King Æthelred and Alfred, his brother, led a great fyrd there to Reading and fought against the Scandinavian army, and a great number was killed there on both sides, and Alderman Æthelwulf was killed, and the Danes retained possession of the battle-field. And four days later King Æthelred and Alfred, his brother, fought against the entire army at Ashdown; and they [the Scandinavians] were in two divisions. In one were Bachsecg and Halvdan, the heathen kings, and in the other were the jarls. And then King Æthelred fought against the troops of the kings—and King Bachsecg was killed there—and Alfred, his brother, against the troops of the jarls, and Jarl Sidrac the Elder was killed there, and Jarl Sidrac the Younger, and Jarl Asbjǫrn, and Jarl Fræna, and Jarl Harald. And both the armies were routed and many thousands killed, and they kept on fighting until night. And a fortnight later King Æthelred and Alfred, his brother, fought against the Scandinavian army at Basing, and there the Danes won the victory. And two months later Æthelred and Alfred, his brother, fought against the army at *Mæredun;* and they were in two divisions; and they routed both, and late in the day were victorious; and there was great slaughter on either side, and the Danes retained possession of the battlefield; and Bishop Heahmund and many good men [were] killed there. And after this fight a great summer army [118] came to Reading. And then after Easter King Æthel-

[118] This term designates a band of raiders who returned to their continental base (often Flanders) for the winter.

red died; and he had reigned five years, and his body lies at Wimborne church.

Then his brother, Alfred, son of Æthelwulf, succeeded to the throne of Wessex. And then one month later King Alfred with a small band fought against the entire army at Wilton and late in the day routed them, and the Danes retained possession of the battlefield. And this year nine pitched battles were fought against the Scandinavian army in the kingdom south of the Thames, besides those raids which Alfred, the king's brother, and the aldermen and king's thegns often made upon them, which no one has kept count of. And that year nine jarls and one king were killed; and that year the West Saxons made peace with the Scandinavians.[119]

872. Here the Scandinavian army went from Reading to London and there set up winter quarters; and then the Mercians made peace with the Scandinavians.

873. Here the Scandinavian army set up winter quarters at Torksey.

874. Here the Scandinavian army went from Lindsey to Repton and there set up winter quarters and drove King Burgred overseas about twenty-two years after he had succeeded to the throne, and conquered the whole country [Mercia]; and he went to Rome and stayed there, and his body lies in St. Mary's church at the English School. And that same year they gave the kingdom of Mercia into the keeping of Ceolwulf, an unwise thegn of the king, and he swore oaths to them and gave hostages that it [Mercia] would be ready for them on whatever day they wanted to have it, and he would be ready himself and with all those who wanted to follow him, as the Scandinavians might require.

875. Here the Scandinavian army left Repton, and Halvdan went with part of the army into Northumbria and set up winter quarters on the Tyne; and the Scandinavians conquered the country and ravaged frequently among the Picts and the Strathclyde Welsh. And Guthrum and Ascytel and Anwend, the three kings, went with a large army from Repton to Cambridge and stayed there one year. And that sum-

---

[119] On the dates of the battles enumerated in this annal, see M. L. R. Beaven, "The Beginning of the Year in the Alfredian Chronicle (866–87)," *EHR*, XXXIII (1918), 328–42. For the chronology of the Danish movements in this and the following annals and the identification of the continental battles, see most conveniently Smith, *The Parker Chronicle*, pp. 26–41.

mer King Alfred went to sea with a fleet and fought against seven ship crews and captured one of them and routed the rest.

876. Here the Scandinavian army stole away from the West Saxon fyrd to Wareham, and afterwards the king made peace with the Scandinavians, and they gave to the king as hostages those who were most honored in the Scandinavian army, and they swore oaths to him on the holy ring—which they previously had not been willing to do to any people—that they would at once leave his kingdom. And then, meanwhile, they—the mounted division of the army—stole away from the fyrd by night to Exeter. And that year Halvdan divided up Northumbria, and they [the Scandinavians] ploughed and provided for themselves.

Rollo and his men entered Normandy, and he reigned fifty-three years.

877. Here the Scandinavian army came to Exeter from Wareham, and the Scandinavian fleet sailed out around west; and then a great storm overtook them at sea, and on that occasion a hundred and twenty ships were destroyed at Swanage. And King Alfred with the fyrd rode after the mounted division up to Exeter, and they were unable to overtake them from behind before they [the Scandinavians] were in the fortress where no one could get at them; and they [the Scandinavians] there gave him chief hostages, as many as he wanted to have, and swore great oaths, and then they kept a good peace. And then in the autumn the Scandinavian army went into Mercia and divided up a part of it and gave a part to Ceolwulf.

878. Here at Christmas time after Twelfth-night [Jan. 5] the Scandinavian army stole away to Chippenham and overran Wessex and occupied it and drove many of the people overseas, and conquered the greater part of the rest except King Alfred [who] with a little band under difficulties skirted the woods and [sought refuge] in swamp forts. And that same winter the brother of Ingwar and of Halvdan [Ubba], was in Devon in Wessex,[120] and he was killed there and eight hundred men with him and forty [chief] [121] men of his

---

[120] At this time Devon was a part of Wessex.

[121] The emendation of the *manna* of the MS to [*heafod*]*manna* "chief men" (Hoffmann-Hirtz, *Une Chronique anglo-saxonne*, p. 80, n. 4) appears to be the simplest and most reasonable way of injecting some sort of sense into what stands in the text as an utterly meaningless distinction. See also the alternative emendation (*hiredes* "retinue" for *heres* "army") suggested in Smith, *The Parker Chronicle*, p. 31.

army; and the war banner which they called "Raven" was captured there. And then at Easter King Alfred with a little band built a fort at Athelney, and from this fort he and the men of Somerset who were nearest to it fought against the Scandinavians. Then in the seventh week after Easter he rode to *Ecgbrihtesstan,* east of Selwood Forest, and all the men of Somerset, and the men of Wiltshire and those of the men of Hampshire who were on this side of the sea,[122] came to meet him; and they rejoiced in him. And one day later he went from that camp to *Iglea* and the following day to *Eðandun,* and there fought against the entire army and routed them and rode after them up to the fort [at Chippenham] and stayed there a fortnight. And then the Scandinavians gave him hostages and [swore] many oaths that they would leave his kingdom, and they also promised him that their king would receive baptism, and they carried that out. And three weeks later King Guthrum with twenty-nine men of those who were most honored in the army came to Aller—and that is opposite Athelney—and the king received him there at baptism, and his chrism-loosing [123] was at Wedmore; and he remained twelve days with the king, and he [Alfred] greatly honored him and his companions with money.

879.[124] Here the Scandinavian army went from Chippenham to Cirencester and stayed there one year. That year a band of vikings gathered and settled at Fulham on the Thames. And the same year the sun was eclipsed for one hour of the day.[125]

880. Here the Scandinavian army went from Cirencester into East

---

[122] Possibly the Solent. Smith, *op. cit.,* p. 32, follows Asser in suggesting that the men of Hampshire stipulated are simply those whom the Danes had not yet forced overseas. As the text stands, the clause encloses a double ambiguity: of "this" and "sea."

[123] The ceremonial removal, after a stated time, of the linen band preserving the unction placed on the head during the baptismal rite.

[124] The description of the Scandinavian movements in some of the annals of *E* from 879 to 892 is a year ahead of the Continental sources when the year is reckoned from Christmas (see Plummer, II, 95). M. L. R. Beaven, "The Beginning of the Year in the Alfredian Chronicle (866–87)," *EHR,* XXXIII (1918), 328–42, and R. H. Hodgkin, "The Beginning of the Year in the English Chronicle," *EHR,* XXXIX (1924), 497–510, have shown clearly that the annals up to 890 begin their year in the fall, probably on September 24 according to the Caesarean indiction, and that the chronological discrepancies between these entries and other sources are thereby removed.

[125] This solar eclipse is that of October 29, 878, which, according to the indictional reckoning, would be entered under 879; on this eclipse, see Stevenson, *Asser's Life,* pp. 280–86.

Anglia and occupied the land and divided it up; and the same year the Scandinavian army which had settled at Fulham went overseas to Ghent in the land of the Franks and stayed there one year.

881. Here the Scandinavian army went farther inland into Frankish territory, and the Franks fought against them, and then the Scandinavian army was there provided with horses after the battle.

882. Here the Scandinavian army went up along the banks of the Meuse farther into Frankish territory and stayed there one year. And the same year King Alfred went out to sea with his ships and fought against four ship crews of Danes and captured two of the ships and killed the men, and two [ship crews] surrendered to him, and many men were killed and wounded before they surrendered.

883. Here the Scandinavian army went up the Escaut to Condé-sur-l'Escaut and stayed there one year. And Pope Marinus sent the *lignum Domini* to King Alfred. And the same year Sigehelm and Æthelstan carried to Rome and also to India, to St. Thomas and St. Bartholomew, the alms which King Alfred had promised [to send] there when they were encamped opposite the Scandinavian army at London; [126] and by the grace of God they were very successful there in their prayers according to the vows.

884. Here the Scandinavians went up the Somme to Amiens and stayed there one year.

885. Here the Scandinavian army mentioned above separated into two parts, the one [going] east, the other part to Rochester, and besieged the city and built another fortification around themselves. And they [the citizens of Rochester] nevertheless defended the city until King Alfred arrived from outside with a fyrd. Then the Scandinavians went to their ships and abandoned the fortification; and they were there deprived of their horses, and at once that same summer again departed overseas.

The same year King Alfred sent a fleet from Kent to East Anglia. As soon as they came to the mouth of the Stour they met sixteen ships of vikings and fought against them and captured all the ships and killed the men. While they were on their way home with the

---

[126] This action may have occurred in 872 or 879, *q.v.*, though Beaven, "King Edmund I," *EHR*, XXXIII (1918), 341 f., refers the event to 885, considering this part of the present entry—which does not appear in *A*—an interpolation originally dated 886.

spoils, they met a large fleet of vikings and fought against them the same day, and the Danes won the victory.

And the same year before Christmas Carloman, king of the Franks, died—a wild boar killed him. And one year earlier his brother [Louis] had died—he had also had the west kingdom [Neustria]; [they were both the sons of Louis (the Stammerer) who also had had the west kingdom].[127] He [Louis] died in the year when the sun was eclipsed;[128] he was the son of Charles [the Bald], whose daughter [Judith] Æthelwulf, king of Wessex, had for his queen.

[The same year a great fleet gathered against the Old Saxons, and there was a great fight twice in the year, and the Saxons won the victory; and Frisians were there with them. The same year Charles (the Fat) succeeded to the west kingdom and to the entire kingdom on this side of the Mediterranean and beyond this sea,[129] just as his great-grandfather (Charlemagne) had had it, except for Brittany. This Charles was the son of Louis (the German); this Louis was the brother of Charles (the Bald), who was the father of Judith whom King Æthelwulf had married—and they were the sons of Louis (the Pious). This Louis was the son of the old Charles (Charlemagne); this Charles was the son of Pippin.][130]

The same year the good Pope Marinus died; he had freed[131] the English School at the prayer of Alfred, king of Wessex, and he [Marinus] had sent him great gifts and a part of the cross on which Christ suffered;[132] and the same year the Scandinavian army went into East Anglia and broke the peace with King Alfred.

886. Here the Scandinavian army, which had previously gone east, again went west and then up the Seine and there set up winter quarters at the city of Paris. The same year King Alfred occupied London, and all the English who were outside the control of the Danes submitted to him, and he then placed the town in the keeping of Alderman Æthelred.

887. Here the Scandinavian army went inland over the bridge at

---

[127] From *D*.
[128] See 879 and n. Louis died on April 10, 879.
[129] "This sea" most likely refers to the English Channel.
[130] From *D* (also in *AC*). The omission of this long passage is apparently due to the recurrence of the phrase, "the same year."
[131] *Ab omni tributo et telonio*, adds Asser (Stevenson, *Asser's Life*, p. 53).
[132] See 883.

Paris, and then up along the Seine as far as the Marne, and then up on the Marne as far as Chézy-sur-Marne, and then stayed there [and] [133] within [the junction of the Seine and] the Yonne—two winters in the two places.

And the same year Charles [the Fat], king of the Franks, died, and six weeks before he died, Arnulf, his brother's [Carloman's] [natural] son, deprived him of the kingdom; and the kingdom was then divided into five [parts], and five kings were consecrated to them. This was [done], however, with Arnulf's consent. And they said that they would hold it of [in fealty to] him because no one of them was born [descended from Charles] on the paternal side except him alone. Arnulf occupied the country east of the Rhine, and Rudolph succeeded to the middle kingdom [Upper Burgundy], and Odo to the west part [Neustria], and Berengarius and Guido to Lombardy and to the lands on the far side of the Alps. And they [Berengarius and Guido] held that with great strife and fought two pitched battles and frequently ravaged that country [Italy] and each repeatedly drove out the other.

And the same year that the Scandinavian army went inland over the bridge at Paris, Alderman Æthelhelm carried the alms of the West Saxons and of King Alfred to Rome.[134]

888. Here Alderman Beocca and Queen Æthelswith, who was King Alfred's sister, carried the alms of the West Saxons and of King Alfred to Rome; and she died, and her body lies at Pavia. And in this year Archbishop Æthelred and Alderman Æthelwald died in the same month.

889. In this year there was no journey to Rome except that King Alfred sent two couriers with letters.

890. Here Abbot Beornhelm carried the alms of the West Saxons and of King Alfred to Rome. And Guthrum, the northern king, whose baptismal name was Æthelstan, died. He was the godson of King Alfred, and he lived in East Anglia and first settled that country. And the same year the Scandinavian army went from the Seine to St. Lô,

---

[133] From *AC*.

[134] These "alms" of the West Saxons and King Alfred are probably identical with the later payments made to Rome under the name of Peter's Pence. They are mentioned again in 888 and 890 and their non-payment noted in 889. On the origin and pre-Conquest history of these payments, see William E. Lunt, *Financial Relations of the Papacy with England to 1327* (Cambridge, Mass., 1939), pp. 3–30.

which is between the Bretons and the Franks; and the Bretons fought against them and won the victory, and they drove them out into a river and drowned many.

Here Archbishop Plegmund was elected by God and all the people.

892.[135] Here the great Scandinavian army, about which we spoke some time ago, again went out of the eastern kingdom [Austrasia] west to Boulogne-sur-Mer and there were shipped so that they crossed at one time with horses [and] with everything. And they landed at the mouth of the Lympne with two hundred and fifty ships—the mouth is in the east of Kent at the east end of the great forest which we call the Weald; the forest is one hundred and twenty miles long or longer from east to west, and thirty miles broad. The river of which we spoke before flows out of the forest. In this river they pulled up their ships as far as the forest, four miles from the outside of the mouth, and there stormed a fort in the fen.[136] In it sat a few churls, and it was only half finished. Then a short time later Hæsten came up with eighty ships into the mouth of the Thames and built himself a fort at Milton Royal and the other army [built a fort] at Appledore.

Here Wulfhere, archbishop of Northumbria, died.

901. Here King Alfred died on October 26,[137] and he had held the throne twenty-eight and a half years; and then Edward, his son, succeeded [to] the throne.

906. Here King Edward was forced to make peace both with the army of the East Angles and with the Northumbrians.

910. Here the English and Danish armies fought at Tettenhall; and Æthelred, leader of the Mercians, died; and King Edward got possession of London and of Oxford and of all the lands which belonged to them. And a great Scandinavian fleet came here from the

---

[135] *ACD* 893 (*A* originally 892). The annal with the story of the three Irish exiles (*A* 891, *CD* 892) is, oddly enough, omitted from *E*.

[136] MS *fænne, A fenne* "fen"; *CD fæsten(n)e* "fort." Plummer (I, 85), on the basis of the context (?) and from the evidence of the Latin historians, restores the *CD* reading in *E*; however, the passage can be more correctly construed by retaining *fænne* and simply changing the usual punctuation (Smith, *The Parker Chronicle,* p. 42).

[137] The date of Alfred's death has provoked considerable discussion: see B. A. Lees, *Alfred the Great* (New York, 1915), pp. 427-32, where the evidence is reviewed. The conventional date (900) has been challenged in favor of 899 by M. L. R. Beaven, "The Regnal Dates of Alfred, Edward the Elder, and Athelstan," *EHR*, XXXII (1917), 517-31, where W. H. Stevenson's original suggestion, "The Date of King Alfred's Death," *EHR*, XIII (1898), 71-77, is supported with a convincing array of evidence.

south from Brittany and ravaged a great deal along the Severn, but later they were almost all destroyed there.

918. Here Æthelflæd, lady of Mercia, died.

921. Here King Sihtric killed Niall, his brother.[138]

923. Here King Ragnall won York.

924. Here King Edward died, and Æthelstan, his son, succeeded to the throne.[139]

925. Here [Arch]bishop Wulfhelm was consecrated; [140] and the same year King Edward died.

927. Here King Æthelstan drove out King Guthfrith; and here Archbishop Wulfhelm went to Rome.

928. *William succeeded to the throne [of Normandy] and reigned fifteen years.*

933. Here Atheling Edwin drowned in the sea.[141]

934. Here King Æthelstan went to Scotland, both with a land force and with a fleet, and he ravaged a large part of it.

937. Here King Æthelstan led a fyrd to *Brunanburh*.[142]

940. Here King Æthelstan died, and Edmund, his brother, succeeded to the throne.[143]

942. Here King Olaf [Godfreyson] died.

And Richard the Elder succeeded to the throne [of Normandy] and reigned fifty-two years.

944. Here King Edmund conquered the whole of Northumbria, and banished two men of royal blood, Olaf [Sitricson] and Ragnall.

945. Here King Edmund ravaged the whole of Cumberland.

[138] This statement is based upon a confusion of two separate events: in 888 Sihtric killed his brother, Sicfrith; in 919 he killed Niall Glundubh, king of Ireland: *Annals of Ulster,* ed. W. H. Hennessey (Dublin, 1887–1901), I, 407, 439.

[139] This annal is crossed out in the MS by a later hand—see 925. *CD* enter Edward's death under 924, *A* under 925; the correct date is uncertain: see Beaven, *op. cit.;* J. A. Robinson, *The Times of St. Dunstan* (Oxford, 1923), pp. 27–36.

[140] More correctly, "translated," for he had previously been consecrated to Wells. The same mistaken use of "consecrate" is made in 989 (Sigeric), 996 (Ælfric).

[141] This entry is peculiar to *E.* The drowning of the atheling gave rise to several later legendary treatments (see Plummer, II, 137 f.), but he apparently was simply drowned in a shipwreck.

[142] The spirited poem on the battle of Brunanburh, edited by A. Campbell, *The Battle of Brunanburh* (London, 1938), inserted here by *ACD,* is omitted in *EF.*

[143] According to Beaven, *op. cit.,* Æthelstan died on October 26–27, 939, forty years (see *BCD* 941) after Alfred's death in 899, and fourteen years (*ibid.*) since the death of Edward the Elder in 925. A corrected chronology of Edmund's reign, taking 939 as the date of Æthelstan's death, has been sketched by the same writer in "King Edmund I and the Danes at York," *EHR,* XXXIII (1918), 1–9.

948.[144] Here King Edmund was stabbed, and Eadred, his brother, succeeded to the throne; and he at once brought the whole of Northumbria into his power; and the Scots swore him oaths that they would [do] everything he wished.

949. Here Olaf Cuaran [Sitricson] came to Northumbria.

952. Here the Northumbrians drove out King Olaf and received Eric, Harald's son.

954. Here the Northumbrians drove out Eric, and Eadred succeeded to the throne of Northumbria.

955. Here King Eadred died, and Eadwig, son of Edmund, succeeded to the throne.

956. Here Archbishop Wulfstan died.

959. Here King Eadwig died, and Edgar, his brother, succeeded to the throne.

In his days things went very well;
And God granted him to dwell in peace while he lived.
And he did what was required of him, eagerly earned it.

　　Far and wide he disseminated the glory of God;
And loved God's law and improved the peace of the people,
Most of all the kings who preceded him in the memory of men.
And God also helped him so that kings and nobles gladly submitted
　　　　to him
And were subject to what he wished;
And without strife he governed everything that he really wanted to.

　　He was greatly honored
Far and wide in all countries,
Because he zealously honored God's name
And often and repeatedly meditated on God's law,
And spread God's glory far and wide,
And counselled wisely, often and on all occasions,
All his people, before God and before the world.

　　Yet one fault he had [namely],
That he loved bad foreign habits too much
And brought too quickly
Heathen customs into this country,

---

[144] *AD* 946, the true date of Edmund's death.

And invited foreigners here
And attracted vicious people to this land.

   But God grant him that his good deeds
Be stronger than [his] misdeeds
As a protection for his soul on the long journey.[145]

   963. Here St. Æthelwald was appointed by King Edgar to the bishopric of Winchester, and the archbishop of Canterbury, St. Dunstan, consecrated him bishop on the first Sunday in Advent, which was on November 29.

   In the year after he was consecrated, he established many monasteries and drove the [secular] clerics out of the bishop's seat because they would not observe any rule, and set monks there. He there set up two abbacies: one of monks [New Minster], one of nuns [Nuns' Minster]—that was all in Winchester. Afterwards he came to King Edgar and asked him to give him all the monasteries which the heathen had formerly destroyed because he wished to restore them, and the king granted it gladly. And the bishop then went first to Ely, where St. Æthelthryth lies, and had the monastery built. Then he gave it to one of his monks, who was named Brihtnoth, consecrated him abbot, and appointed monks there, where formerly there had been nuns, to serve God. Then he bought many villages from the king and richly endowed it [the monastery].

   Later Bishop Æthelwald came to the monastery which was called Peterborough, which had formerly been destroyed by the heathen; he found there nothing but old walls and wild woods. There he found, hidden in the old wall, documents which Abbot Headda had formerly written—how King Wulfhere and Æthelred, his brother, had built it, and how they had made it free of king and of bishop and of all secular service, and how Pope Agatho had confirmed this with his charter [see 675], and Archbishop Deusdedit [see 656]. Then he had the monastery built, and appointed an abbot there named Ealdwulf, and placed monks where before there had been nothing. Then he came to the king and had him look at the documents which had previously been found, and the king then answered and said: "I, Edgar, grant and give today, before God and before Archbishop Dunstan, freedom from king and from bishop to the monastery of St. Peter, Peterborough, and all the villages which belong to it: namely, Eastfield and Dogsthorpe and Eye and Paston. And I free it in such fashion that no bishop shall have any authority there except the abbot of the monastery.

   "And I give the town which is called Oundle with all that belongs to it

[145] On the form of this and the following "poems," see W. J. Sedgefield, *The Battle of Maldon and Short Poems from the Saxon Chronicle* (Boston and London, 1904), ix–x, xx–xxi.

—that is, what is called *Eahte hundred,* and market and toll—so freely that neither king nor bishop nor earl nor sheriff shall have any authority there, nor any man except the abbot alone and him whom he shall appoint to it.

"And I give to Christ and St. Peter, and through the prayer of Bishop Æthelwald, these lands: namely, Barrow, Warmington, Ashton, Kettering, Castor, Ailsworth, Walton, Werrington, Eye, *Thorp;* and one moneyer in Stamford. These lands, and all the others which belong to the monastery, I declare free; namely, [of] sac and soc, toll and team, and infangthief.[146] These rights and all others I declare free to Christ and St. Peter.

"And I give the two parts of Whittlesey Mere with the waters and with the weirs and fens, and so on through *Merelad* to the river called the Nene, and so eastward to King's Delph. And I will that there be a market in the same town and that there be no other between Stamford and Huntingdon.

"And I will that the toll be thus given: first, from Whittlesey Mere all the way to the king's toll of Normancross Hundred, and then back again from Whittlesey Mere through *Merelad* straight to the Nene, and so, as the river runs, to Crowland, and from Crowland to the *Must,* and from the *Must* to King's Delph and to Whittlesey Mere.

"And I will that all the freedoms and all the indulgences that my predecessors have given shall stand; and I write and confirm it with the sign of the cross."

Then Archbishop Dunstan of Canterbury answered and said: "I grant that all the things which here are given and mentioned, and all the things which your predecessors and mine have granted—I will that these stand; and whoever breaks it, I give him the curse of God and of all saints and of all persons in orders and of myself, unless he make amends. And I give in acknowledgement to St. Peter my mass vestment and my stole and my robe for the service of Christ.

"I, Oswald, archbishop of York, agree to all these words by the holy cross on which Christ suffered. I, Bishop Æthelwald, bless all who shall hold to this, and I excommunicate all who shall break this, unless he make amends."

Here were present Bishop Ælfstan, Bishop Æthelwulf, and Abbot Æscwig, and Abbot Osgar, and Abbot Æthelgar, and Alderman Ælfhere, Alderman Æthelwine, Brihtnoth, Alderman Oslac, and many other prominent men; and all agreed to it and all signed it with the sign of the cross. This was done nine hundred and seventy-two years after the birth of our Lord, the sixteenth year of the king.

Then Abbot Ealdwulf bought many lands and in addition richly endowed the monastery. And then he stayed there until Archbishop Oswald

---

[146] The OE terms *sac, soc, team,* and *infangenþef* denote certain jurisdictional rights generally given to the grantee in the grant of lands from the king; see *New English Dictionary, svv.* and Jolliffe, *The Constitutional History of Medieval England,* p. 70.

of York died, and then he was elected archbishop. And then another abbot named Cenwulf was at once elected from the same monastery; he was later bishop of Winchester. And he first built the rampart around the monastery. He then named it *Burh* which had previously been called *Medeshamsted*. He stayed there until he was elected bishop of Winchester. Then another abbot named Ælfsige was elected from the same monastery. This Ælfsige was the abbot from then on for fifty years. He exhumed St. Cyneburg and St. Cyneswith, who were buried at Castor, and St. Tibba, who was buried at Ryhall, and translated them to Peterborough and offered them all to St. Peter in one day, and then kept [the relics] while he was there.

964. *Here the monks were expelled from the Old Minster* [*at Winchester*].

966. Here Thored, son of Gunner, ravaged Westmorland; and the same year Oslac became an alderman.

969. Here in this year King Edgar ordered all of the Isle of Thanet to be ravaged.

970.[147] Here Atheling Edmund died.

972.[148] Here Atheling Edgar was consecrated king at Bath on the feast of Pentecost on May 11 in the thirteenth year after he succeeded to the throne, and he was then twenty-nine years old. And soon after that the king led his whole fleet to Chester, and six kings came there to meet him, and all pledged themselves to cooperate with him on sea and on land.

975.

Here Edgar died,
Ruler of the English,
Friendly lord of the West Saxons,
And protector of the Mercians.

It was widely known
Throughout many nations
That kings honored him,
Son of Edmund,
Far and wide
Over the gannet's bath,
Bowed to the king
As it befitted them.

[147] *A* 971, *C* 972, *D* 970; the correct date is uncertain.
[148] *A* 973, *C* 974, *D* 972. Pentecost fell on May 11 in 973.

> No fleet was so proud,
> No army so strong,
> That it took booty
> From him in England
> While the noble king
> Ruled his throne.[149]

And here Edward, son of Edgar, succeeded to the throne; and then at once in the autumn of the same year the star [called] comet appeared; and then in the following year a very great famine and very frequent disturbances occurred throughout England. And Alderman Ælfhere ordered the many monasteries destroyed which King Edgar had formerly commanded the holy Bishop Æthelwald to found. And also at that time Oslac, the famous earl, was driven out of England.

978. Here in this year all the chief witan of England fell from an upper story at Calne, with the sole exception of the holy Archbishop Dunstan, who was standing upon a beam. And some were severely injured there and some did not come through it with their lives.

979.[150] Here King Edward was killed in the evening at Corfe Castle on March 18 and was buried at Wareham without any royal honors.

> No worse deed was done in England than this was,
> Since they [the English] first came to Britain.
>> Men murdered him,
>> But God honored him.
> In life he was an earthly king—
> Now, after death, he is a heavenly saint.
>> His earthly kinsmen
>> Would not avenge him,
>> But his heavenly father
>> Has greatly avenged him.
> The earthly murderers wanted to blot out
>> His memory on earth;
> But the Avenger on high has spread abroad
> His memory in heaven and on earth.

---

[149] These verses represent a short version (also in *D*) of the poem in *AC*. Max Förster, "König Eadgars Tod (†975)," *Englische Studien,* LXXII (1937), 10–13, furnishes the circumstances of Edgar's death from a Welsh source.
[150] *AC* 978, *D* 979; Edward probably died in 978.

Those who before would not
Bow down to his living body,
    They now humbly
Bend on their knees to his dead bones.

Now we are able to understand
    That men's wisdom,
    And intrigues,
    And their counsels,
    Are as nothing
    Against God's will.

And here Æthelred succeeded to the throne, and very soon after that he was consecrated king at Kingston-upon-Thames to the great joy of the witan of England.

980. Here in this year Alderman Ælfhere fetched the body of the holy king [Edward] from Wareham and conveyed it with great honor to Shaftesbury.

981. Here the seven ships first came and pillaged Southampton.

983. Here Alderman Ælfhere died, and Ælfric succeeded to the aldermanship.

984. Here the holy Bishop Æthelwald, father of monks, died; and here Edwin was consecrated abbot at Abingdon.

985. Here Alderman Ælfric was driven out.

986. Here the king did away with the bishopric of Rochester. And here the great cattle plague first came to England.

987. Here Watchet was ravaged.

988. Here Goda, thegn of Devon, was killed, and many slaughtered with him; and here Dunstan, the holy archbishop, departed from this life and journeyed to the heavenly [life]; and Bishop Æthelgar succeeded him to the archiepiscopal see, and he lived only a short time after that—just a year and three months.

989. Here Abbot Edwin died, and Wulfgar succeeded him; and here Sigeric was consecrated archbishop.

991. Here Ipswich was pillaged, and very soon after that Alderman Brihtnoth was killed at Maldon. And in that year it was decided that tribute should for the first time be given to the Danes because of the great terror which they caused along the seacoasts—that was first ten thousand pounds. Archbishop Sigeric advised that [course].

992. Here Oswald, the holy archbishop, departed this life and attained the heavenly [life]. And Alderman Æthelwine died in the same year. Then the king and all his witan decided that the ships which were any good should be assembled at London; and the king then entrusted the fyrd to the leadership of Alderman Ælfric and Earl Thored and Bishop Ælfstan [for Ælfric] [151] and Bishop Æscwig, and they were supposed to try to trap and surround the Scandinavians anywhere. Then Alderman Ælfric sent and warned the Scandinavians; and then on the night before the day on which they were supposed to come together, he, to his great shame, fled from the fyrd, and the Scandinavians then escaped except for one ship [crew] that was killed there. And the Scandinavians then met the ships from East Anglia and from London, and they killed a great number there and captured the ship, fully armed and equipped, in which the alderman [Ælfric] had been. And then after the death of Archbishop Oswald, Abbot Ealdwulf of Peterborough succeeded to the bishopric of York and of Worcester, and Cenwulf to the abbacy of Peterborough.

993. Here in this year Bamborough was stormed and much booty taken there; and after that the Scandinavian army came to the mouth of the Humber and there did much damage, both in Lindsey and in Northumbria. Then a very large fyrd was assembled, and when they were supposed to come together, the leaders were the first to run away —that was Fræna and Godwine and Frithogist. In this same year the king ordered Ælfgar, son of Alderman Ælfric, to be blinded.

994. Here in this year Olaf and Svein came to London on the Nativity of the Virgin [Sept. 8] with ninety-four ships, and they resolutely attacked the town and also tried to set it on fire; but they suffered more injury and harm there than they ever supposed any townsmen could inflict on them. For the holy Mother of God on that day showed her mercy to the townsmen and rescued them from their enemies. And they went from there and did the most damage that any army might ever do in burning and ravaging and in killing both along the seacoast in Essex and in Kent and in Sussex and in Hampshire; and finally they got horses and rode as far as they wished and did inexpressible harm.

The King and his witan then determined to send to them and prom-

[151] An error common to all the chronicles. The obit of Bishop Ælfstan is entered under C 981.

ise tribute and provisions on condition that they cease their ravaging; and they accepted that. And the whole army then came to Southampton and there set up winter quarters, and they were fed there from the whole kingdom of Wessex, and they were paid sixteen thousand pounds. Then the king sent Bishop Ælfheah and Alderman Æthelward for King Olaf, and hostages were meanwhile delivered to the ships; and they then conducted Olaf with great honor to the king at Andover, and King Æthelred received him at the hands of the bishop [152] and royally presented him with gifts. And Olaf then promised him, as he also carried it out, that he would never again come with hostile intent to England.

Here Richard the Elder died and Richard, his son, succeeded to the throne [of Normandy] and reigned thirty-one years.

995. Here in this year the star [called] comet appeared; and Archbishop Sigeric died.

996. Here in this year Ælfric was consecrated archbishop to Christ Church [Canterbury].

997. Here in this year the Scandinavians went around Devon into the mouth of the Severn [Montgomeryshire, Wales] and ravaged there, both in Cornwall and in Wales and in Devon, and then landed at Watchet and there did much damage by burning and by killing. And after that they returned around Land's End on the south side and then turned into the Hamoaze and then went inland until they came to Lydford and burned and destroyed everything they came upon; and they burned Ordwulf's monastery at Tavistock and brought countless booty with them to their ships.

998. Here the Scandinavian army turned eastward again into the mouth of the Frome and there went inland everywhere as far as they wished into Dorset. And the fyrd was often assembled against them, but every time they were supposed to meet, they [the English] for some reason always determined on flight, and in the end they [the Scandinavians] always won the victory. And another time they were on the Isle of Wight and provisioned themselves for the time being from Hampshire and from Sussex.

999. Here the Scandinavians again came around into the Thames and then went up along the Medway to Rochester; and then the Kentish fyrd came against them and they met resolutely there, but alas!

[152] *I. e.,* sponsored him at his confirmation; he had already been baptized.

that they gave way too quickly and fled, because they did not have the help that they should have had; and the Danes retained possession of the battlefield. And then they [the Danes] got horses and rode as far as they wished, and destroyed and ravaged almost all of West Kent. Then the king and his witan determined to attack them with a fleet and also with a land force, but when the ships were ready, they delayed from day to day and distressed the poor people who were in the ships. And every time things should have been farther advanced, there was a delay from one time to another; and they [the English] always let their enemy's force increase, and they always withdrew from the sea, and they [the Scandinavians] kept after them. And then in the end the naval expedition effected nothing except the people's distress and a waste of money and the encouragement of their enemies.

1000. Here in this year the king went into Cumberland and ravaged very nearly all of it; and his ships went out around Chester and were supposed to come to meet him, but they could not. Then they ravaged the Isle of Man. And the enemy fleet went this summer to Richard's kingdom [Normandy].

1001. Here the Scandinavians came to the mouth of the Exe and then went up to the town [Exeter] and fought resolutely there, but they were very resolutely and sturdily opposed. Then they went about the country and did exactly as they were accustomed to—killed and burned. Then a great fyrd of the people of Devon and Somerset was assembled there, and they then met at Pinhoe; and as soon as they came to grips with each other, the English fyrd gave way; and they [the Scandinavians] killed a great number there and then overran the country, and their latest raid was always worse than the preceding one. And they brought much booty with them to the ships; and from there they went to the Isle of Wight, and there they went about as they pleased and met with no resistance; nor did any fleet dare meet them at sea, nor any land force, no matter how far inland they came. It was a grievous time then in every way because they never ceased their evil-doing.

1002. Here in this year the king and his witan determined that tribute should be paid to the Scandinavian fleet and peace made with them on condition that they cease their evil-doing. Then the king sent Alderman Leofsige to the fleet, and he then arranged a truce with them on the word of the king and of his witan, and [arranged] that they should receive provisions and tribute; and they then accepted that, and they were then paid twenty-four thousand pounds. Then in the meantime Alderman Leofsige killed Æfic, the king's high reeve, and the king then banished him from the country. And then in the same spring the Lady [Ælfgifu], Richard's daughter, came here to England. In the same summer Archbishop Ealdwulf died. And in that year the king ordered all the Danes who were in England to be killed on St. Brice's Day [Nov. 13], because the king had been informed that they planned to trick him of his life and afterwards all his witan, and after that to have his throne.

1003. Here, through the French churl, Hugh, whom the Lady [Ælfgifu] had appointed as her reeve, Exeter was stormed, and the Scandinavians completely destroyed the town and seized a great deal of booty there. Then a very large fyrd was assembled from Wiltshire and from Hampshire, and with great determination they made for the Scandinavian army. Then Alderman Ælfric was supposed to lead the fyrd, but he took to his old tricks; as soon as they were so close that either of them might look at the other, he feigned himself sick and began retching in order to vomit, and said that he had fallen ill, and so deceived the people whom he should have led—as it is said: When the leader is weak, the whole army is greatly handicapped. When Svein saw that they were not of one mind and that they were all confused, he led his army to Wilton and they ransacked the town and burned it; and then he went to Old Sarum, and from there went again to the sea where he knew his sea horses were.

1004. Here Svein came with his fleet to Norwich and completely sacked and burned the town. Then Ulfcytel, with the witan of East Anglia, decided that it would be better for them to buy peace from the Scandinavians before they did too much harm in the country; for they had come unawares, and he did not have time to assemble his fyrd. Then under the truce which was supposed to be existing between them, the Scandinavians stole up from the ships and made their way to Thetford. When Ulfcytel realized that, he sent to have the ships cut to pieces, but those whom he appointed to do it failed him, and he then assembled his fyrd as secretly as he could. And the Scandinavian army then came to Thetford within three weeks after they had ravaged Norwich, and they were inside the town one night and sacked and burned it. Then on the next day, as they planned to go to their ships, Ulfcytel came with his force, and they stoutly came to grips there, and a great number was killed there on either side. The chief men of the people of East Anglia were killed there; but if the full force had been present, they [the Scandinavians] would never have returned to their ships, as they themselves admitted.

1005. Here in this year there was the great famine in England, more severe than any man ever remembered before. And the Scandinavian fleet in this year went from this country to Denmark and returned in a short time.

1006. Here Archbishop Ælfric died, and after him Bishop Ælfheah succeeded to the archbishopric; and Bishop Brihtwald succeeded to the [bishop]ric of Wiltshire. And Wulfgeat was deprived of all his property, and Wulfheah and Ufegeat were blinded, and Alderman Ælfhelm was killed, and Bishop Cenwulf died. And then after midsummer [June 24] the Danish fleet came to Sandwich and did exactly as they had previously been accustomed to—pillaged and burned and killed wherever they went. Then the king ordered all the people of Wessex and Mercia called out, and they were out then all that autumn on an expedition against the Scandinavians; but this was of no more use than it had often been before. But for all this, the Scandinavian army went about as it wished, and the [English] expedition imposed all sorts of hardships on the people, so that neither profited them [the English people]—neither the native army nor the foreign army.

When winter approached, the fyrd went home; and the Scandinavian army then came after Martinmas [Nov. 11] to their place of refuge on the Isle of Wight and there procured what they needed from all over. And then at Christmas they went out through Hampshire into Berkshire to their well-stocked food depot at Reading, and they did as their custom was—lighted their beacons as they went. And then they went to Wallingford and burned it all up, and then went along Ashdown [to Cuckhamsley Barrow and stayed there out of bravado; for it has often been said that if they] [153] reached Cuckhamsley Barrow, they would never get to the sea again. Then they went home by another route. Then a fyrd was assembled there at East Kennet, and they came together there, and they [the Scandinavians] soon routed that force and afterwards carried their booty to the sea. There the

153 Supplied from *CD;* omitted because of the repetition of the place name.

people of Winchester could see a proud and fearless army going by their gates to the sea and fetching food and treasures for themselves more than fifty miles from the sea.

Then the king went across the Thames into Shropshire and set up his quarters there at Christmas time. Then the fear of the Scandinavians became so great that no man could think or devise how they might be driven from the country, or this country held against them, for they had sorely marked every shire in Wessex with burning and with ravaging. The king began earnestly to consider with his witan what seemed most advisable to them all that this country might be saved before it was completely destroyed. Then the king and his witan determined, for the need of the whole nation, though it was hateful to them all, that they must pay tribute to the [Scandinavians].[154] Then the king sent to the Scandinavian army and let them know that he wished there to be a truce between them, and that tribute and provisions would be given them; and they then accepted all that; and they were provisioned from throughout England.

1007. Here in this year the tribute was delivered to the enemy army —that was thirty thousand [155] pounds. And also in this year Eadric was appointed alderman in the kingdom of Mercia.

1008. Here the king commanded ships diligently to be built in all England: that is, from three hundred hides and from ten hides one small vessel,[156] and from eight hides a helmet and a coat of mail.

1009. Here in this year the ships about which we spoke before [1008] were ready, and there were more of them—from what books tell us—than had ever before been in England in the day of any king. And they were all assembled at Sandwich and they were all to remain there and protect this country against any foreign army. But still we had neither the good luck nor the honor that this fleet should be of use to this country, any more than it had been on previous occasions.

Then it happened at this same time or a little earlier that Brihtric, brother of Alderman Eadric, accused Child Wulfnoth, the South Saxon, before the king, and he [Wulfnoth] then went out and enticed [English] ships to him until he had twenty, and then he pillaged

---

154 From *D;* inadvertently omitted by *E.*
155 *EF xxx; CD xxxvi.*
156 This (apparently corrupted) clause ought perhaps to be emended to read: "from three hundred hides one (full-sized) ship and from ten hides one *sceg∂* (a considerably smaller vessel)," as in *D,* but see Plummer, II, 185, and Margaret Ashdown, *English and Norse Documents* (Cambridge, 1930), pp. 98 f.

everywhere along the south coast and did all sorts of damage. Then the [English] fleet was informed that they might easily overtake them [Wulfnoth's ships] if they would try to. Then Brihtric took eighty ships and imagined that he would win great fame for himself if he should catch Wulfnoth dead or alive. But while they were on their way there, such a wind came against them as no man before remembered, and it completely dashed and beat the ships to pieces and cast them ashore, and Wulfnoth came at once and burned the ships. When the fate of the others [Brihtric *et al.*] became known to the other ships with which the king was, nobody knew what to do, and the king and the aldermen and the chief counsellors went home and so without further ado abandoned the ships. And then the people who were in the ships brought the ships again to London; and they let the work of all the people thus casually go to waste—and no better was the victory [157] which all the English people had hoped for.

When this naval expedition had thus ended, the immense army of the enemy came to Sandwich soon after Lammas [Aug. 1], and they at once made their way to Canterbury and would quickly have captured the town if they [the townsmen] had not [even] more quickly begged them for peace; and all the men of East Kent made peace with the Scandinavians and gave them three thousand pounds. And then soon after that the Scandinavians went about till they came to the Isle of Wight, and everywhere in Sussex and in Hampshire and also in Berkshire they ravaged and burned as they were accustomed to. Then the king commanded the whole people to be called out, that they [the Scandinavians] should be resisted on every side; but lo! in spite of that, they went about as they pleased. Then, on one occasion, as they wanted to go to their ships, the king had intercepted them with the whole fyrd, and all the people were ready to attack them, but then, as it always was, it [the attack] was prevented by Alderman Eadric. Then after Martinmas [Nov. 11] they [the Scandinavians] returned to Kent and set up their winter quarters on the Thames, and lived [on supplies] from Essex and from the shires which adjoined it on both sides of the Thames; and they often fought against the city of London, but praise be to God that it still [158] stands safe and sound. And they [the Scandinavians] always got on badly there. Then after Christ-

[157] MS *ege* "fear" for *CD sige* "victory."
[158] This statement must have been written before the capitulation of London to Svein in 1013.

mas they followed an inland route through the Chiltern Hills, and so to Oxford and there burned the town; and they then took it [the booty] on both sides of the Thames to the ships. They were then warned that there was a fyrd at London [assembled] against them. They then crossed over [the Thames] at Staines; and so they carried on all that winter, and that spring they were in Kent and repaired their ships.

1010. Here in this year the above-mentioned army came to [East] Anglia after Easter and landed at Ipswich and at once went to where they learned Ulfcytel [was] with his fyrd—this was on May 18. And the East Angles soon fled. Cambridgeshire stood firmly against them. Æthelstan, the king's son-in-law [or brother-in-law][159] was killed there, and Oswy, his son, and Wulfric, Leofwine's son, and Eadwig, Æfic's brother, and many other good thegns and countless people. Thurcytel Myranheafod first began the flight; and the Danes retained possession of the battlefield. And they were there horsed and afterwards got control of East Anglia, and ravaged and burned the land for three months. They even went into the wild fens, and they killed men and cattle and burned throughout the fens. And they burned Thetford and Cambridge; and afterwards they again turned south to the Thames, and the mounted men rode towards the ships; and afterwards they quickly turned west into Oxfordshire and from there into Buckinghamshire and so along the Ouse until they came to Bedford, and so on to Tempsford; and they always burned as they went. Then they again went to their ships with their booty. And when they had scattered to their ships, the fyrd should have gone out again to keep them from landing; but it went home. And when they were in the east, the fyrd was kept to the west; and when they were in the south, our fyrd was in the north. Then all the witan was summoned to the king, and they were then to take counsel how this country might be defended; but, although they came to some decision, it did not hold even one month. At last there was no chief who would assemble a fyrd, but each fled as best he could; nor at the last would one shire even help another.

Then before St. Andrew's Day [Nov. 30] the Scandinavians came to Northampton and at once burned the town and seized everything in the vicinity that they wanted, and from there went across the Thames

159 MS *aðum* may signify either.

into Wessex and so towards *Caninganmersc,* and they burned it all. When they had gone as far as they then wished, they came at Christmas to the ships.

1011. Here in this year the king and his witan sent to the Scandinavian army and asked for peace and promised them tribute and provisions on condition that they cease their raids.

They had then overrun: (1) East Anglia, and (2) Essex, and (3) Middlesex, and (4) Oxfordshire, and (5) Cambridgeshire, and (6) Hertfordshire, and (7) Buckinghamshire, and (8) Bedfordshire, and (10) [*for* 9] [160] half of Huntingdonshire, and to the south of the Thames all Kent and Sussex and [the district of] Hastings and Surrey and Berkshire and Hampshire and a large part of Wiltshire.

All these misfortunes happened to us through bad counsel; tribute was not offered them in time [nor were they fought against] ; [161] but when they had done the most harm, then truce and peace were made with them. And yet in spite of all this truce and peace and tribute, they went everywhere in bands and pillaged and captured and killed our miserable people.

And in this year, between the Nativity of the Virgin [Sept. 8] and Michaelmas [Sept. 29], they invested Canterbury and got into it by treachery because Ælfmær, whose life Archbishop Ælfheah had once saved, betrayed Canterbury to them; and there they seized Archbishop Ælfheah and Ælfward, the King's reeve, and Abbess Leofwine [*for* Leofrun] [162] and Bishop Godwine; and they let Abbot Ælfmær go free. And they seized everyone in orders in the town, both men and women—it was impossible to tell anyone how many people there were; and afterwards they stayed on in the town as long as they wanted to; and when they had looked the town all over, they went to their ships and took the archbishop with them.

> He was then captive, who before had been
> Head of the English people and of Christendom.
> Then misery could there be seen
> Where before joy had been seen
> In that wretched city [Canterbury] whence first came to us
> Christendom and joy for God and for the world.

[160] *CD* have *Hamtunscire, i. e.,* Northamptonshire, as the tenth county.
[161] From *C.*
[162] MS *Leofwine* for *Leofrune* (*CD*), probably on account of the following *Godwine.*

And they kept the archbishop with them up to the time that they martyred him.

1012. Here in this year Alderman Eadric and all the chief witan of England, ordained and lay, came to London before Easter—that year Easter Day was on April 13—and they stayed on there after Easter until the tribute was all paid: that was eight [*for* forty-eight] [163] thousand pounds.

Then on the Saturday [April 19] the Scandinavians were greatly stirred up against the [arch]bishop because he would not promise them any money, in fact forbade that anything should be given to ransom him. They were also very drunk because wine had been brought there from the south. They then took the [arch]bishop, led him to their council on the Saturday [April 19] of the Octave of Easter, and there pelted him with bones and skulls of cattle.[164] And then one of them hit him on the head with the pointed back of an axe so that he collapsed under the blow, and his holy blood fell on the earth, and he sent his holy soul to God's kingdom. And on the next day Bishops Eadnoth and Ælfhun and the townsmen received the holy body and carried it to London with all honor and buried it in St. Paul's church; and there God now [165] reveals the miraculous powers of the holy martyr.

When the tribute was paid and the oaths of peace were sworn, the Scandinavian army scattered as widely as it had previously been concentrated. Then forty-five ships of the Scandinavians submitted to the king and promised him to defend this country; and he was to feed and clothe them.

1013. In the year after that in which the archbishop was martyred, the king appointed Bishop Lifing to the archbishopric of Canterbury; and in this same year, before the month of August, King Svein came with his fleet to Sandwich and then went very rapidly round East Anglia into the mouth of the Humber and so up along the Trent, until he came to Gainsborough. And then Earl Uhtred and all the Northumbrians at once submitted to him, and all the people of Lindsey, and afterwards the people of the Five Boroughs, and shortly after that all

[163] As in *CD*.
[164] For a Scandinavian parallel to this episode, see R. W. Chambers, *Beowulf: An Introduction*, 2d ed. (Cambridge, 1932), p. 143.
[165] An approximately contemporary reference; see 1023, where the translation of the relics to Canterbury is recorded.

the Scandinavians north of Watling Street; and hostages were given him from every shire. After he saw that all the people had submitted to him, he ordered his army to be provisioned and horsed, and then later he went south with the whole fyrd and entrusted his ships and the hostages to his son, Canute. And after he had crossed Watling Street, they did the greatest damage that any army could do. Then he went to Oxford, and the townsmen at once submitted and gave hostages, and from there to Winchester and they [the townsmen] did the same. From there they went east to London, and many of his [Svein's] people were drowned in the Thames because they did not [trouble to] look for any bridge. When he came to the town [London], the townsmen refused to submit, but resisted him with all their might, for King Æthelred was inside there, and Thurcytel with him. Then King Svein went from there to Wallingford, and so over the Thames west to Bath, and there took up his position with his fyrd. And Alderman Æthelmær came there, and the western thegns with him, and they all submitted to Svein and gave hostages. When he had thus accomplished everything, he went north to his ships, and all the people held him for absolute king. And after that the townsmen in London submitted and gave hostages, because they feared that he would destroy them. Svein then gave orders for the payment of the full Danegeld and for provisions for his army that winter, and Thurcytel gave similar orders for the Scandinavians who were at Greenwich [the 45 ships of 1012]; and in spite of that they raided as often as they pleased.

In that time nothing helped this people [the English] either from the south or from the north. Then for a time the king stayed with the fleet that was in the Thames, and the Lady [Ælfgifu] then went overseas to her brother, Richard [of Normandy], and Ælfsige, abbot of Peterborough, [went] with her. The king also sent Bishop Ælfhun overseas, with the athelings Edward and Alfred, to take care of them. And then at Christmas the king left the fleet and went to Wight and was there during that season; and after that season he went overseas to Richard and stayed there with him until the fortunate occasion of Svein's death.

And while the Lady [Ælfgifu] was with her brother overseas, Ælfsige, abbot of Peterborough, who was there with her, went to the monastery called Bonneval, where St. Florentine's body lay. There he found a poor place, a poor abbot, and poor monks, for they had been plundered. Then he bought St. Florentine's body from the abbot and from the monks there, all except the head, for five hundred pounds; and when he returned, he made an offering of it to Christ and St. Peter [*i. e.*, to Peterborough].

1014. Here in this year King Svein ended his days about Candlemas on February 3, and the whole fleet elected Canute king. Then all the witan, ordained and lay, determined to send for King Æthelred, and they said that no lord was dearer to them than their native lord, if he would govern them more justly than he had before. Then the king sent his son, Edward, here with his messengers, and bade them greet all his people, and said that he would be a kind lord to them and amend all those things which they all hated; also that all of those things which they had done or said against him would be forgiven on condition that they all would unanimously return to him without treachery. And then complete friendship was established on both sides by word and pledge, and they pronounced every Danish king outlawed from England. Then in Lent King Æthelred came home to his own people, and he was gladly received by them all. And after Svein was dead, Canute remained with his army at Gainsborough until Easter; and it was agreed between him and the people of Lindsey that they would supply him with horses and that afterwards they would all go off together and raid. Then King Æthelred came there to Lindsey with the whole fyrd before they [the Scandinavians] were ready, and then they ravaged and burned and killed all the people [renegade English] whom they could get at. Canute went out to sea with his fleet, and the wretched people were thus deceived by him, and then he went south until he came to Sandwich and there let ashore the hostages who had been given to his father and cut off their hands and their noses; and in addition to all these evils the king ordered the Scandinavians who were at Greenwich to be paid twenty-one thousand pounds.

And in this year on Michaelmas eve [Sept. 28] the high tide came far in over this country and ran farther inland than it had ever done before and inundated many villages and drowned a countless number of people.

1015. In this year there was the great assembly at Oxford, and there Alderman Eadric betrayed Sigefrith and Morcar, the chief thegns in the Seven Boroughs—he enticed them into his chamber, and they were treacherously killed there. And the king then took all their property and ordered Sigefrith's widow to be seized and brought to Malmesbury. Then after a short time Atheling Edmund went there and took the woman against the king's will and married her. Then before the Nativity of the Virgin [Sept. 8] the Atheling went from the west north to the Five Boroughs and at once took possession of all Sigefrith's and Morcar's property, and the people all submitted to him. And then at the same time King Canute came to Sandwich and at once went round Kent into Wessex until he came to the mouth of the Frome, and then he ravaged in Dorset and in Wiltshire and in Somerset. The king was then lying sick at Cosham. Then Alderman Eadric assembled a fyrd, and Atheling Edmund in the north [did the same]. When they met, the alderman wanted to betray the atheling, and for that reason they then separated without a fight [against the Danes] and retired before their enemies. And then Alderman Eadric lured forty ships away from the king and then submitted to Canute; and the West Saxons submitted and gave hostages and supplied the Scandinavian army with horses; and it stayed there until Christmas.

1016. Here in this year Canute with his army of one hundred and sixty ships [crews],[166] and Alderman Eadric with him, crossed the Thames at Cricklade into Mercia, and then went to Warwickshire at Christmas time and ravaged and burned and killed everything they came upon. Then Atheling Edmund began to assemble a fyrd. When the fyrd was assembled, they would not be satisfied unless the king was there, and [unless] they had the help of the townsmen of London. Then they gave up the expedition and each man went home. Then after that time the fyrd was again ordered out on pain of the full penalty [of the law],[167] that each man who was fit for service should go out; and they sent to the king at London and prayed him to come to meet the fyrd with such help as he could gather. When they had all come together, it did no more good than it had often done before. The king was then informed that those who should have helped him planned to betray him. Then he left the fyrd and returned to London.

---

[166] The phrase, "one hundred and sixty ships," appears only in *EF* and may be due, as Plummer (II, 195) suggests, to the mistaken notion of a scribe that *here* "army" implies ships. The emendation at least makes sense out of the passage.

[167] Penalties for evading service are mentioned several times in Æthelred's law code (see Liebermann, *Die Gesetze der Angelsachsen*, I, 244, 256).

Then Atheling Edmund rode into Northumbria to Earl Uhtred, and everyone imagined that they would assemble a fyrd against King Canute. They then went into Staffordshire and into Shropshire and to Chester, and they ravaged on their part and Canute on his. And he [Canute] went out through Buckinghamshire into Bedfordshire and from there to Huntingdonshire and along the fens to Stamford and then into Lincolnshire, from there to Nottinghamshire and so to Northumbria towards York. When Uhtred learned this, he abandoned his raiding and hurried north, and then of necessity submitted, and all the Northumbrians with him, and he gave hostages; and nevertheless they killed him, and with him Thurcytel, son of Nafen. And then after that King Canute appointed Eric earl of Northumbria just as Uhtred had been. And afterwards they went south by another route, quite [far] to the west, and then before Easter the whole Scandinavian army took to their ships. And Atheling Edmund went to London to his father; and then after Easter King Canute went with all his ships toward London.

Then it happened that King Æthelred died before the ships came —he ended his days on St. George's Day [April 23] after the great labor and hardships of his life. And then after his death all the witan who were in London and the townsmen elected Edmund king, and while he lived, he sturdily defended his kingdom.

Then the ships came to Greenwich at the Rogation days [the three days before Ascension] and within a short time went to London, and there they dug a big ditch on the south side and brought their ships to the west side of the bridge, and afterwards they built a dike around the town on the outside so that no man could go in or out; and they constantly attacked the town, but they [the townsmen] sturdily resisted them. King Edmund had left [London] before that, and he overran Wessex, and all the people submitted to him; and shortly after that he fought against the Scandinavian army at Pen Pits near Gillingham. And he fought a second battle after midsummer [June 24] at Sherston, and a great number was killed there on both sides, and the armies voluntarily abandoned the fight, and Alderman Eadric and Ælfmær Darling were helping the Scandinavians against King Edmund. And then for the third time he [Edmund] assembled a fyrd and went to London and delivered the townsmen and chased the Scandinavian army to the ships. And then two days later the king crossed [the Thames] at Brentford and then fought against the Scandinavian army and routed them, and many of the English people—those who went in front of the fyrd and wanted to get booty—were drowned there through their own carelessness. And after that the king went into Wessex and assembled his fyrd. Then the Scandinavian army at once went to London and besieged the town from the outside and fought strongly against it both by water and by land, but Almighty God delivered it.

After that the Scandinavians then went from London with their ships into the *Arwe* and went up it and proceeded into Mercia and killed and burned whatever they came upon, as their custom was; and they provided themselves with food and brought both their ships and their cattle into the Medway. Then for the fourth time King Edmund assembled the whole English nation and crossed the Thames at Brentford and went into Kent, and the Scandinavians fled in front of him with their horses to the Isle of Sheppey, and the king killed as many of them as he could overtake. And Alderman Eadric went there to [submit to] the king at Aylesford—no worse advice than that was ever given.[168]

The Scandinavian army again turned inland into Essex and went into Mercia and destroyed everything it came upon. When the king learned that the Scandinavian army was inland, he for the fifth time assembled the whole English nation and followed them and overtook them in Essex at the hill called Assa's hill [now Ashingdon], and there they resolutely engaged. Then Alderman Eadric did as he had often done before. He, with the people of the Maund district, first began the retreat and so betrayed his royal lord and the entire nation. There Canute won the victory and conquered all England for himself. [Bishop] [169] Eadnoth was killed there, and Abbot Wulfsige and Alderman Ælfric and Alderman Godwine and Ulfcytel of East Anglia and Æthelward, son of Alderman Æthelsige [*for* Æthelwine],[170] and all the best men of the English people.

After this battle King Canute then went inland with his army into Gloucestershire, where he had heard that King Edmund was. Then Alderman Eadric and the witan who were there advised the kings to

---

[168] Expressing the chronicler's contempt for Edmund's acceptance of Eadric's submission.
[169] From *CD*.
[170] According to *C*; *D Ælfwine* (see Plummer, II, 198).

make peace between themselves; and they gave hostages to each other, and then the kings met at *Olanig* and there confirmed their friendship with both pledge and oath and arranged the tribute for the Scandinavian army; and then on this agreement they separated, and King Edmund took possession of Wessex and Canute of Mercia.

Then the Scandinavians went to the ships with the things they had seized, and the men of London made a truce with the Scandinavian army and bought themselves peace; and the Scandinavians brought their ships into London and set up their winter quarters there.

Then on St. Andrew's Day [Nov. 30] King Edmund died, and he is buried with his grandfather, Edgar, in Glastonbury; and in the same year Wulfgar, abbot of Abingdon, died and Æthelsige [*for* Æthelwine] [171] succeeded him.

1017. Here in this year King Canute succeeded to the entire kingdom of England and divided it into four parts: Wessex to himself, East Anglia to Thurcytel, Mercia to Eadric, and Northumbria to Eric. And in this year Alderman Eadric was killed, and [also] Northman, son of Alderman Leofwine, and Æthelward, son of Æthelmær the Stout, and Brihtric, son of Ælfgeat [*for* Ælfheah] [172] in Devon; and King Canute banished Atheling Eadwig and Eadwig, king of churls. [173] And then before August 1 the king commanded that Richard's daughter [Ælfgifu], widow of the other king, Æthelred, he brought over to be his queen.

1018. In this year the Danegeld was paid throughout all England; that was altogether seventy-two thousand pounds in addition to what the townsmen in London paid—eleven thousand [*for* 10,500] [174] pounds. And then a part of the Scandinavian army went to Denmark, and forty ships remained with King Canute. And the Danes and the English came to an agreement at Oxford. And here Abbot Æthelsige died at Abingdon, and Æthelwine succeeded him. [175]

171 See 1018 and n.
172 As in *D*.
173 The significance of the title *ceorla cyng* has never been fixed; see Oman, *England*, p. 584.
174 MS *xi þusend,* apparently a misreading of *endlifte healf þusend* (*CD*) = 10,500.
175 This sentence, absent from *C,* the Abingdon Chronicle, was apparently produced by the chronicler's attempt to clear up the confusion that resulted from his mistakenly writing Æthelsige for Æthelwine at the end of the annal for 1016; having thus manufactured two abbots out of one, he was compelled to remove the fictitious Æthelsige in order to make room for the actual Æthelwine (see Plummer, II, 200, 202).

1019. Here King Canute went to Denmark and stayed there all winter.

1020. Here King Canute came to England; and then at Easter there was a great council in Cirencester—Alderman Æthelward was outlawed on that occasion. And in this year the king went to Ashingdon; and Archbishop Lifing died, and the same year Æthelnoth, monk and dean at Christ Church [Canterbury], was consecrated [arch]bishop of it [Canterbury].

1021. Here in this year King Canute outlawed Earl Thurcytel at Martinmas [Nov. 11].

1022. Here King Canute went out to the Isle of Wight with his ships. And [Arch]bishop Æthelnoth went to Rome and was received there by Pope Benedict with great honor; and with his own hands he set the pallium on him and with honor consecrated him archbishop; and afterwards he celebrated mass there with the pallium as the pope instructed him, and after that he dined with the pope and then went home with a full blessing. And Abbot Leofwine, who had been unjustly expelled from Ely, was his companion and cleared himself of everything that had been said against him, as the pope directed him, by testimony of the archbishop and of all the company that was with him.

1023. Here Archbishop Wulfstan died and Ælfric succeeded him; and the same year Archbishop Æthelnoth carried the remains of Archbishop St. Ælfheah from London to Canterbury.

1024. *Here Richard II [of Normandy] died. Richard, his son, reigned about one year, and after him Robert, his brother, reigned eight years.*

1025. Here King Canute went with ships to Denmark to the island in the Helge å,[176] and Ulf and Ecglaf and a very great army, both a land force and a fleet, came against him there from Sweden; and very many men perished there on King Canute's side, both of Danes and of English; and the Swedes retained possession of the battlefield.

1028. Here King Canute went with fifty ships from England to Norway and drove King Olaf out of the country and made good his claim to that country.

1029. Here King Canute came home again to England.

[176] Presumably rather in Helge Sjö (Småland), an expansion of the Helge å about ten miles from the Baltic.

1030. Here King Olaf came again to Norway, and the people gathered against him and fought against him, and he was killed there.

1031. Here King Canute went to Rome; and the same year he went to Scotland, and Malcolm, king of Scots, and two other kings, Mælbeth and Jehmarc, submitted to him.

Count Robert died on a pilgrimage, and King William [the Conqueror] succeeded him while still in his minority.

1032. Here in this year that lightning appeared the like of which no man remembered before, and it also did harm everywhere in many places. And in the same year Ælfsige, bishop of Winchester, died, and Ælfwine, the king's priest, succeeded him.

1033. Here in this year Merehwit, bishop of Somerset, died, and is buried in Glastonbury.

1034. Here Bishop Æthelric died.

1036 [1035].[177] Here King Canute died at Shaftesbury, and he is buried in the Old Minster at Winchester, and he was king of all England for very nearly twenty years. And immediately after his death there was a meeting of all the witan at Oxford, and Earl Leofric and almost all the thegns from north of the Thames and the [royal] sailors in London elected Harald to rule all England for himself and his brother, Hardecanute, who was in Denmark. And Earl Godwine and all the chief men in Wessex opposed it as long as they could, but they could not devise anything against it. And then they [Godwine and the Wessex party] agreed that Ælfgifu, Hardecanute's mother, should settle in Winchester with the house carls of her son the king, and hold all Wessex in trust for him; and Earl Godwine was their right-hand man. Some men said that Harald was the son of King Canute and of Ælfgifu, daughter of Alderman Ælfhelm, but that seemed quite incredible to many men; and he was nevertheless absolute king over England.

1037. Here Ælfgifu, King Canute's widow, was banished—she was King Hardecanute's mother. And then she sought the protection of Baldwin south of the sea [the Channel], and he gave her a residence in Bruges and he protected her and kept her while she was there.

1038. Here Archbishop Æthelnoth died on November 1, and

177 *CD* 1035; *E* has simply misplaced the vacant annal for 1036. The account of Earl Godwine's treatment of Alfred Atheling and his followers entered under 1036 by *CD* has been omitted by the pro-Godwinist *E*.

shortly after that Æthelric, bishop of Sussex, and then before Christmas Brihtheah, bishop of Worcestershire, and soon after Ælfric, bishop of East Anglia. And then Bishop Eadsige succeeded to the archbishopric, and Grimcytel to that of Sussex, and Bishop Lifing to Worcestershire and to Gloucestershire.

1039 [1040].[178] Here King Harald died at Oxford on March 17, and he was buried at Westminster; and he ruled England [as regent and king] four years and sixteen weeks; and in his days sixteen ships [the standing navy] were paid eight marks per man, exactly as had been done before in the days of King Canute. And in this same year King Hardecanute came to Sandwich seven days before midsummer [June 24], and he was at once received both by the English and by the Danes, although his counsellors paid for it very heavily when they decreed that sixty-two ships [Hardecanute's own navy] should be paid eight marks per man. And in this same year the sester of wheat went to fifty-five pence and even higher.

1040 [1041]. Here the Danegeld was paid—that was twenty-one thousand and ninety-nine pounds; and after that thirty-two ships [the enlarged standing navy] were paid eleven thousand and forty-eight pounds. And in the same year Edward, son of King Æthelred, came here to England from abroad [Normandy]. He was the brother of King Hardecanute—they were both sons of Ælfgifu, who was the daughter of Earl Richard.

1041 [1042]. Here King Hardecanute died at Lambeth on June 8, and he had been king over all England two years less ten days; and he is buried in the Old Minster at Winchester with King Canute, his father. And before he was buried, all the people elected Edward king in London. May he hold it while God shall grant it to him! And that whole year was a very grievous time in many and various respects, both as to storms and as to crops. And more cattle perished that year than anybody before remembered, both from various diseases and from the storms.

At this same time Ælfsige, abbot of Peterborough, died, and then the monk, Earnwig, was elected abbot because he was a very good and a very gentle man.

[178] C 1040. The failure to leave blank the annuary number for 1039 (no entry in D) and the repetition of 1043 and 1046 set the dating of E from one to three years off in the section 1040–1052. The omission of annals for 1049–51 brings E back into line with C which alone preserves the correct chronology during these dozen years.

1042 [1043]. Here Edward was consecrated king in Winchester on Easter Day with great honor—that year Easter was on April 3. Archbishop Eadsige consecrated him and in the presence of all the people instructed him well and gave him good advice in both his own interest and [that of] all the people. And the priest, Stigand, was consecrated bishop of East Anglia. And soon after that the king ordered all the lands seized which his mother owned, and he took from her all that she had in gold and silver and countless [other] objects, because she had dealt too harshly with him.

1043 [1044]. Here Archbishop Eadsige gave up the bishopric because of bad health and, by the leave and counsel of the king and of Earl Godwine, consecrated to it Siward, abbot of Abingdon, as bishop. This was known to few other men before it was done, because the archbishop thought that, if more men should know about it, some other man in whom he would have less trust and confidence would request or buy it. And in this [year] there was a very great famine all over England, and grain was dearer than any man before remembered, so that the sester of wheat went up to sixty pence and even higher. And in the same year the king went out to Sandwich with thirty-five ships; and Æthelstan, the sacristan, succeeded to the abbacy at Abingdon; and Stigand obtained his bishopric.

1043b [1045]. Here King Edward took Earl Godwine's daughter [Edith] as his queen. And in the same year Bishop Brihtwald died, and he had held the bishopric thirty-eight years; and Hereman, the king's priest, succeeded to the bishopric. And in this year Wulfric was consecrated abbot of St. Augustine's at Christmas time on St. Stephen's Day [Dec. 26], by leave of the king and of Abbot Ælfstan, because of his [Ælfstan's] very bad health.

1044 [1046]. Here Lifing, bishop of Devon, died, and Leofric, the king's priest, succeeded him. And in this same year Abbot Ælfstan died at St. Augustine's [Canterbury], on July 5. And in this same year Osgod Clapa was banished.

1045 [1047]. Here Grimcytel, bishop of Sussex, died, and Heca, the king's priest, succeeded him. And in this year Ælfwine, bishop of Winchester, died on August 29, and Stigand, bishop in the north,[179] succeeded him. And in the same year Earl Swegen went out to Bruges

---

[179] This is clearly written from a southern point of view (see also Eadnoth, 1046b ad fin.).

in Baldwin's country [Flanders] and stayed there all winter and then in the summer went out to sea.

1046 [1048]. *Battle at Val-des-Dunes.*

Here Æthelstan, abbot of Abingdon, died and Spearhafoc, a monk of Bury St. Edmunds, succeeded him.

And in this same year Lothen and Erling came to Sandwich with twenty-five ships and there took countless booty in men and in gold and in silver, so that no man knew how much it all was. And then they went around the Isle of Thanet and wanted to do the same there, but the natives stubbornly resisted them and prevented them both from landing and from [getting] water, and chased them away from there. And then they went from there to Essex and ravaged there and seized men and whatever they could find; and then they went east to Baldwin's country [Flanders] and there sold what they had plundered; and after that they went east to where they had previously come from [Denmark ?].

1046*b* [1049]. Here in this year there was the great synod at Rheims. Present there were Pope Leo and the archbishop of Burgundy and the archbishop of Besançon and the archbishop of Trier and the archbishop of Rheims and many men besides, both ordained and lay. And King Edward sent Bishop Duduc and Abbot Wulfric of St. Augustine's [Canterbury] and Abbot Ælfwine there so that they could inform the king what was decided there for Christendom.

And in this same year King Edward went out to Sandwich with a great fleet; and Earl Swegen with seven ships came in to Bosham and made a truce with the king; and he [Swegen] was promised that he would be [held] worthy of everything he had previously owned. But Earl Harold, his brother, and Earl Beorn objected, [saying] that he ought not be [held] worthy of any of the things which the king had granted him; but he was given four days' grace [to return] to his ships. Then about this time word came to the king that hostile ships lay to the west and were ravaging. Then Earl Godwine went west with two of the king's ships [of the standing navy]—Earl Harold commanded one, and Tostig, his brother, the other—and forty-two ships of the native sailors [of the national levy]. Then Earl Harold [*for* Beorn] was appointed captain of the King's ship which Earl Harold had previously commanded. Then they went west to Pevensey and lay there weather-bound. Within two days after that Earl Swegen came there and spoke with his father and with Earl Beorn and begged Beorn to go with him to the king at Sandwich and help him to [obtain] the king's friendship, and he agreed to it. Then they set out as though they were going to the king. While they were riding along, Swegen begged him to go with him to his ships—he said that his [own] sailors would desert him unless he went to them at once. Then they both went to where his ships lay. When they got there, Earl Swegen asked him to go to the ship with him. He stubbornly refused until his [Swegen's] sailors seized him and threw him into a boat and bound him and rowed to the ship and there put him on board. Then they hoisted their sails and ran west to Axmouth and kept him with them until they killed him; and they took the body and buried it in a church, and then his friends and his sailors came from London and exhumed him and carried him to Winchester to the Old Minster, and he is buried there with King Canute, his uncle. And Swegen then went east to Baldwin's country [Flanders] and stayed there all winter in Bruges under his full protection.

And in that same year Eadnoth, bishop in the north, died, and Ulf was appointed bishop.

1047 [1050]. Here in this year there was a great council in London at Mid-Lent; and nine crews [of the standing navy] were dismissed and five were kept.

And in this same year Earl Swegen came to England.

And in this same year there was the great synod at Rome, and King Edward sent Bishop Hereman and Bishop Ealdred there, and they arrived on Easter eve. And the pope again had a synod at Vercelli and Bishop Ulf attended it, and they say that his staff was almost broken [and would have been], if he had not given very great treasures, because he did not know the rites as well as he should. And in this year Archbishop Eadsige died on October 29.

1048 [1051]. Here in this year in the spring King Edward appointed Robert of London archbishop of Canterbury. And the same spring he went to Rome for his pallium, and the king gave the bishopric of London to Spearhafoc, abbot of Abingdon, and the king gave [the] abbacy to Bishop Rudolph, his kinsman. Then the archbishop came from Rome one day before the eve of St. Peter's Day and occupied his archbishop's chair at Christ Church [Canterbury] on St. Peter's Day [June 29] and soon after went to the king. Then Abbot

Spearhafoc came to him on the way with the king's writ and seal to have him consecrate him bishop of London. Then the archbishop refused and said that the pope had forbidden him [to do] it. Then the abbot again went to the archbishop for that purpose and there requested ordination as a bishop, and the archbishop resolutely refused it to him and said that the pope had forbidden him [to do] it. Then the abbot went to London and occupied the bishopric, which the king had previously granted him, all that summer and that autumn with his absolute permission.

And then Eustace came from overseas soon after the bishop and went to the king and discussed with him what he then wanted, and then set out for home. When he came east to Canterbury, he and his men ate there and went to Dover. When he was some miles or more this [the London] side of Dover, he put on his coat of mail, and all his companions [likewise], and they went to Dover. When they arrived there, they wanted to put up where it pleased them. Then one of his men came and wanted to put up in the dwelling of a householder against his will, and he wounded the householder, and the householder killed him. Then Eustace got on his horse, and his companions on theirs, and [they] went to the householder and killed him inside his own house, and then [they] went up to the town and killed more than twenty men both inside and outside. And the townsmen killed nineteen men on the other side and wounded they knew not how many. And Eustace escaped with a few men and went back to the king and partially informed him how it had gone with them; and the king became very angry with the townsmen; and the king summoned Earl Godwine and ordered him to go on a raid into Kent to Dover, for Eustace had informed the king that it had been more the guilt of the townsmen than his—but this was not so. And the earl would not consent to the raid because he did not want to do damage to his own district.

Then the king sent for all his witan and ordered them to come to Gloucester about the second Feast of the Virgin [Sept. 8]. At that time the foreigners [French] had built a castle in Herefordshire in Earl Swegen's district and inflicted every injury and insult that they could on the king's men in the region. Then Earl Godwine and Earl Swegen and Earl Harold came together at Beverstone, and many men with them, with the intention of going to their royal lord and to all the

witan who were assembled with him, that they might have the advice
and help of the king and of all the witan, how to avenge the insult to
the king and the whole nation. Then the foreigners were with the king
beforehand and accused the earls so that they might not come into
his presence, for they [the foreigners] said that they [Godwine *et al.*]
wanted to come there to betray the king. Then Earl Siward and Earl
Leofric and many people with them from the north came to the king,
and Earl Godwine and his sons were informed that the king and the
men who were with him were plotting against them; and they firmly
prepared themselves to meet them, though they did not want to stand
against their royal lord. Then the witan determined that all hostility
should cease on both sides, and the king gave God's truce and his
absolute friendship to both sides.

Then the king and his witan determined that an assembly of all the
witan should be held for the second time in London at the autumnal
equinox [Sept. 24], and the king ordered an army called out, both
to the south of the Thames and to the north—quite the best that ever
was. Then Earl Swegen was declared an outlaw, and Earl Godwine
and Earl Harold were summoned to [come to] the assembly as quickly
as they could get there. When they arrived, they were called to the
assembly. Then he [Godwine] asked for a truce and hostages so that
he could come unharmed into the meeting and out of the meeting.
The king then asked for all of the thegns whom the earls previously
had, and they gave them all into his hands.[180] Then the king again
sent to them and ordered them to come with twelve men into the king's
council. Then the earl again asked for a truce and hostages so that
he might clear himself of each of the things with which he was
charged. Then the hostages were refused him, and he was given five
days' grace to leave the country. And then Earl Godwine and Earl
Swegen went to Bosham and pushed out their ships and went over sea
and sought Baldwin's protection and stayed there [Flanders] all that
winter. And Earl Harold went west to Ireland and stayed there all
that winter under the protection of the king [Diarmaid, king of Lein-
ster]. And soon after this happened, the king abandoned the lady who
had been consecrated his queen [Edith], and he had her deprived of

---

180 This sentence may mean that the earls' followers simply were placed under the
king's protection or that they actually transferred their allegiance to him. (See
Jolliffe, *Constitutional History*, p. 107.)

all that she owned in land and in gold and in silver and in all things, and committed her to his sister at Wherwell.

And Abbot Spearhafoc was then driven out of the bishopric of London, and William, the king's priest, was consecrated to it. And then Odda was appointed earl over Devon and over Somerset and over Dorset and over Cornwall; and Ælfgar, Earl Leofric's son, was given the earldom which Harold had previously owned.

1052. Here in this year Ælfgifu Emma, mother of King Edward and of King Hardecanute, died; and in the same year the king and his witan decided that ships should be sent out to Sandwich, and they appointed Earl Ralph and Earl Odda to lead them. Then Earl Godwine went out from Bruges with his ships to the Yser and put to sea one day before Midsummer eve [June 23] [so] that he came to Dungeness, which is south of Romney. This came then to the knowledge of the earls out at Sandwich, and they went out after the other ships; and a land force was ordered out against the ships. Meanwhile Earl Godwine was warned, and he went then to Pevensey; and the weather became so very bad that the earls could not find out what had happened to Earl Godwine. And then Earl Godwine again went out to sea until he came again to Bruges, and the other ships turned back again to Sandwich. And then it was decided that the ships should return to London, and other earls and other rowers should be appointed to the ships. This was then delayed so long that the fleet was completely abandoned, and they all went home. Then Earl Godwine found that out, and he hoisted sail, and his fleet [did likewise], and went west directly to the Isle of Wight and landed there and ravaged there until the people paid them as much as they demanded from them. And then they went west until they came to Portland, and they landed there and did whatever damage they could do.

At that time Harold had left Ireland with nine ships, and he then landed at Porlock, and many people were assembled there against him, but he did not hesitate to procure himself food. He went inland and there killed a great many of the people and seized cattle and men and property as he pleased. Then he went east to his father, and they both went east until they came to the Isle of Wight, and there they took what they had previously left behind. And they went from there to Pevensey and took along with them as many of the ships there as were seaworthy, and so until he came to Dungeness and secured all the ships that were in Romney and in Hythe and in Folkestone. He then turned east to Dover and there landed and seized as many ships and hostages there as they wanted, and so he went to Sandwich and did just the same; and hostages and provisions were given them wherever they wished. And then they went to the north mouth [of the Stour] and so towards London; and some ships then went inside the Isle of Sheppey and there did a great deal of damage, and they went to Milton Royal and burned it all, and went to London after the earls. When they came to London, the king and all the earls were lying there against them with fifty ships. Then the earls sent to the king and asked him that they might be [held] worthy of all those things which had been wrongly taken from them, but the king then refused for some time—so long that the people who were with the earl became very much stirred up against the king and against his people, so that the earl himself had difficulty in pacifying the people. Then Bishop Stigand and the wise men both inside and outside the town intervened with God's help, and they decided that hostages should be fixed on either side; and so it was done.

When Archbishop Robert and the Frenchmen learned this, they took their horses, and some went west to Pentecost Castle, some north to Robert's Castle. And Archbishop Robert and Bishop Ulf and their companions went out at the East Gate [of London] and killed and in other ways injured many young men, and went straight to the Naze, and there [Robert] placed himself in an unseaworthy ship and went alone overseas and abandoned his pallium and all Christendom here in England, just as God willed it—for he had previously obtained the [archiepiscopal] dignity just as God had not willed it.

A great assembly was then summoned outside London, and all the earls and the best men who were in this country were in that assembly. There Earl Godwine carried out his defense and justified himself before King Edward, his lord, and before the whole nation, that he was innocent of what was charged to him and to Harold, his son, and to all his children. And the king granted the earl and his children his absolute friendship and [his] entire earldom and all that he had previously owned, and [the same] to all the men who were with him. And the king gave to the lady all that she had previously owned. And Archbishop Robert was declared a complete outlaw, and all the Frenchmen [too], because they were responsible for most of the hostility between

Earl Godwine and the king. And Bishop Stigand succeeded to the archbishopric of Canterbury.

And at this same time Earnwig, abbot of Peterborough, surrendered the abbacy [though] in good health and gave it to the monk Leofric by leave of the king and of the monks; and Abbot Earnwig lived eight years after that. And Abbot Leofric so endowed [181] the monastery with goods that it was called the "Golden Borough." Then it increased greatly in land and in gold and in silver.[182]

1053. Here in this year Earl Godwine died on April 15, and he is buried in the Old Minster at Winchester; and Earl Harold, his son, succeeded to the earldom and to all that his father had owned; and Earl Ælfgar succeeded to the earldom which Harold had previously owned.

1054. *Battle at Mortemer.*

Here in this year Leo, the holy pope, died in Rome; and in this year there was a greater cattle plague than any man recalled for many years before. And Victor was elected pope.

1055. Here in this year Earl Siward died; and then a full assembly of the witan was summoned seven days before Mid-Lent, and Earl Ælfgar was outlawed because he was charged with being a traitor to the king and the whole nation, and he confessed it before all the men who were assembled there, though the word escaped him against his will.

And the king gave Tostig, son of Earl Godwine, the earldom which Earl Siward had previously owned. And Earl Ælfgar sought the protection of Gruffydd in North Wales; and in this year Gruffydd and Ælfgar burned St. Æthelbert's Church and the whole town of Hereford.

1056. *Here Henry, emperor of the Romans, died. His son, Henry, succeeded him.*

1057. Here in this year Atheling Edward, son of King Edmund, came here to England and died soon after, and his body is buried in St. Paul's church in London. And Pope Victor died and Stephen was elected pope—he was abbot of Monte Cassino. And Earl Leofric died and Ælfgar, his son, succeeded to the earldom which his father had previously had.

---

[181] The MS ——*dede* may equally well be emended to *godede* "endowed" or *gildede* "gilded."
[182] The greater part of this interpolated notice of local affairs has been written in on the margin by the scribe who wrote the preceding part of the annal.

1058. Here in this year Pope Stephen died, and Benedict was consecrated pope—this same [Benedict] sent a pallium here to England to Archbishop Stigand. And in this year Heca, bishop of Sussex, died, and Archbishop Stigand consecrated Ægelric, a monk in Christ Church [Canterbury], bishop of Sussex, and Abbot Siward bishop of Rochester.

1059. Here in this year Nicholas, who was bishop at the town of Florence, was elected pope, and Benedict, who had previously been pope, was driven out.

1060. *Here Henry, king of the French, died. Philip, his son, succeeded him.*

In this year Cynesige, archbishop of York, died on December 22, and Bishop Ealdred succeeded him; and Walter succeeded to the bishopric of Hereford.

1061. Here in this year Duduc, bishop of Somerset, died, and Gisa succeeded him. And in the same year Godwine, bishop at St. Martin's [Canterbury], died on March 9. And in the same year Wulfric, abbot of St. Augustine's [Canterbury], died in Easter week, on April 18. When word came to the king that Abbot Wulfric had died, he appointed the monk, Æthelsige, of the Old Minster [Winchester] to it [the abbacy]—he indeed had followed Archbishop Stigand [to Winchester]—and he was consecrated abbot at Windsor on St. Augustine's Day [May 26].

1062. *In this year Maine was conquered by William, count of Normandy.*

1063. Here Earl Harold and his brother, Earl Tostig, went to Wales both with a land force and with a fleet, and they conquered the country, and the people gave hostages to them and submitted, and after that they went and killed their king, Gruffydd, and brought his head to Harold, and he appointed another king to it [Wales].

1064 [1065].[183] Here in this year the Northumbrians came together and outlawed their earl, Tostig, and killed all the men of his household whom they could get at, both English and Danish, and seized all his weapons in York and gold and silver and all his treasures which they could hear of anywhere, and sent for Morcar, son of Earl Ælfgar, and elected him their earl; and he went south with the whole shire [Yorkshire] and with Nottinghamshire and Derbyshire and Lin-

183 As in *CD.*

colnshire until he came to Northampton; and his brother, Edwin, came to meet him with the men who were in his earldom [Mercia], and many Welsh also came with him. Earl Harold came there to meet them, and they sent him on a mission to King Edward, and [they] also sent messengers with him, and asked to have Morcar [for] their earl; and the King granted that and again sent Harold [to] [184] them at Northampton on the eve of St. Simon's and St. Jude's Day [Oct. 28]; and he made this known to them and pledged himself to it; and he there renewed Canute's law. But the northerners did great harm around Northampton while he [Harold] was on their mission, for they killed men, and burned houses and grain, and seized all the cattle they could get at—that was many thousands. And they seized many hundred men and led [them] north with them so that the shire [Northamptonshire or Oxfordshire] and the other shires which are near there were the worse off for many years. And Earl Tostig and his wife [Judith] and all those who wanted what he wanted went south overseas with him to Earl Baldwin, and he received them all, and they stayed there [Flanders] the whole winter.

1066. In this year the church at Westminster was consecrated on Childermas [Dec. 28]. And King Edward died on Twelfth-night [Jan. 5], and he was buried on Twelfth-day in the recently consecrated church at Westminster. And Earl Harold succeeded to the throne of England just as the king had granted it to him, and men also elected him to it; and he was consecrated king on Twelfth-day [Jan. 6]. And the same year that he became king, he went out to sea with a fleet against William. And meanwhile Earl Tostig came into the Humber with sixty ships; Earl Edwin came with a land force and drove him out, and the butsecarls [185] deserted him; and he went to Scotland with twelve small vessels, and Harold, the Norwegian king, met him with three hundred ships, and Tostig submitted to him, and they both went into the Humber until they came to York. And Earl Morcar and Earl Edwin fought against them, and the Norwegian king won the victory. And King Harold was informed of what had been done and what had happened there, and he came with a great army of Englishmen and met him at Stamford Bridge and killed him and Earl Tostig and with [great] bravery overcame the whole army. And meanwhile Earl

[184] Cf. Plummer, II, 252.
[185] The mariners of the royal navy, as opposed to the national levy.

William landed at Hastings on Michaelmas [Sept. 29], and Harold came from the north and fought against him before his [Harold's] army had all come up; and he and his two brothers, Gyrth and Leofwine, fell there. And William conquered this country, and came to Westminster, and Archbishop Ealdred consecrated him king, and men paid him tribute and gave hostages and later redeemed their lands.[186]

And then Leofric, abbot of Peterborough, was on that same expedition, and fell sick there, and came home, and died, soon after on Halloween [Oct. 31]. God have mercy on his soul! In his day there was all joy and all good in Peterborough, and he was dear to all people so that the king gave to St. Peter and to him the abbacy of Burton-upon-Trent and that of Coventry, which Earl Leofric, who was his uncle, had formerly founded, and that of Crowland and that of Thorney. And he gave more property to the monastery of Peterborough, in gold and in silver and in vestments and in land, than anyone else had ever done before him or anyone after him. Then "Golden Borough" became "Wretched Borough." Then the monks elected the provost Brand abbot because he was a very good and a very wise man, and sent him to Atheling Edgar because the people of the country thought that he would become king, and the atheling gladly granted it to him. When King William heard of this, he was very angry and said that the abbot had offended him. Then good men intervened and reconciled them because the abbot was a good man. He then gave the king forty marks of gold in settlement, and he lived a short time after that—only three years. Afterwards all sorts of distress and evil came to the monastery. God have mercy on it!

1067.[187] Here the king went overseas and took hostages and treasures with him, and came back the next year on St. Nicholas' Day [Dec. 6], and on that day Christ Church in Canterbury was burned; and when he came back he gave away every man's land. And this summer Child Edgar and Mærleswegen and many men with him set out and went to Scotland; and King Malcolm received them all, and married the child's sister, Margaret.

1068. Here in this year King William gave Earl Robert the earldom of Northumberland. Then the natives of the region attacked him and killed him, and nine hundred men with him. And Atheling Edgar

---

[186] On the Norman Conquest and the reigns of the Norman kings, see E. A. Freeman, *The History of the Norman Conquest of England* (Oxford, 1876), 6 vols.; G. B. Adams, *History of England from the Norman Conquest to the Death of John* (London, 1905); H. W. C. Davis, *England under the Normans and Angevins* (New York, 1905).

[187] On the confused chronology of this and the following two annals as they appear in *D* and *E* (*C* ending with 1066), see Freeman, *op. cit.,* Vol. IV.

then came with all the Northumbrians to York, and the townsmen made peace with him. And King William came from the south with his whole fyrd and sacked the town [York] and killed many hundred men. And the atheling returned to Scotland.

1069. In this year Bishop Ægelric was charged at Peterborough and sent to Westminster, and his brother, Bishop Ægelwine, was outlawed. Then between the two festivals of the Virgin [Aug. 15–Sept. 8] the sons of King Svein and his brother, Jarl Asbjǫrn, came from the east from Denmark with three hundred ships. And then Earl Waltheof went out to sea and he and Atheling Edgar and many hundred men with him came and met the fleet in the Humber and went to York, and landed and conquered the castles and killed many hundred men and brought a great deal of treasure to this ship, and placed the chief men in bonds, and lay between the Ouse and the Trent all winter. And King William entered the shire [Yorkshire] and ravaged it all.

And in this same year Brand, abbot of Peterborough, died on November 27.

1070. Here Earl Waltheof made peace with the king. And in the following spring the king had all the monasteries sacked that were in England.

Then in the same year King Svein came from Denmark into the Humber, and the natives came to meet him and made peace with him, supposing that he would conquer the country. Then Christian, the Danish bishop, and Jarl Asbjǫrn and the Danish housecarls with them came to Ely, and the English people from the whole Fenland came to them, supposing that they would win the whole country. Then the monks of Peterborough heard that their own men wanted to plunder the monastery—namely, Hereward and his gang [outlaws, Danes, and monks]. That was because they had heard that the king had given the abbacy to a French abbot named Turold and that he was a very stern man; and [he] had at that time come to Stamford with all his Frenchmen. There was then a sacristan there named Yware. He took by night all that he could: gospels and vestments and copes and robes and such small articles, whatever he could, and he went at once before day to Abbot Turold and told him that he sought his protection and informed him how the outlaws planned to come to Peterborough—he did that entirely on the advice of the monks. Then at once in the morning all the outlaws came with many ships and wanted to get into the monastery, but the monks resisted so that they could not get in. Then they set [it on] fire and burned all the monks' houses and the whole town except one house. Then they came in through the fire at *Bolhiðe* gate, and the monks came towards them, praying for peace; but they paid no attention: they entered the monastery, climbed up to the holy crucifix, then took the crown, all of pure gold, from our Lord's head, then took the footrest which was beneath his foot—it was entirely of red gold. They climbed up to the steeple, brought down the crosier which was hidden there; it was entirely of gold and silver. They seized there two gold and nine silver reliquaries, and they seized fifteen large crucifixes both of gold and of silver. They there took so much gold and silver and so many treasures in money and in vestments and in books that no man can tell another —saying that they did it out of loyalty to the monastery. Afterwards they went on board ship and proceeded to Ely, where they committed all the treasures to safekeeping. The Danes thought that they would forestall the Frenchmen. They drove away all the monks, none remaining there except one monk who was called Tall Leofwine—he lay sick in the infirmary.

Then Abbot Turold came, and one hundred and sixty Frenchmen with him, and all fully armed. When he arrived, he found everything burned, inside and outside, except the church alone. By then the outlaws—knowing that he would come there—were all afloat. This was done on June 2. The two kings, William and Svein, came to an agreement. Then the Danes went out of Ely with all the above-mentioned treasure and took [it] with them. When they were well out to sea, a great storm arose and scattered all the ships in which the treasures were. Some went to Norway, some to Ireland, some to Denmark; and all that got there [i. e., to Denmark] was the crozier and some reliquaries and some crucifixes and many of the other treasures, and they brought them to a royal vill which was called . . . and placed them all in the church. But later through their carelessness and drunkenness the church and all that was in it was burned in one night.

The monastery of Peterborough was thus burned and sacked. May Almighty God take pity on it in his great mercy! And thus Abbot Turold came to Peterborough, and the monks then returned and did Christ's service in the church, which had stood the whole week before without service of any kind. When Bishop Ægelric heard about this, he excommunicated all the men who had committed that crime.

Then there was a great famine this year. And this summer the Scandinavian fleet came from the north out of the Humber into the Thames and lay there two nights and afterwards proceeded to Denmark. And Earl Baldwin died, and his son, Arnulf, succeeded to the throne; and Earl William [of Hereford] was to be his guardian, and also the king of France, but then Earl Robert came and killed his kinsman, Arnulf, and the earl and routed the king and killed many thousands of his men.

1071. Here Earl Edwin and Earl Morcar escaped and wandered about the forest and open country. Then Earl Morcar went to Ely in a ship; and Earl Edwin was treacherously killed by his own men. And Bishop Ægelwine and Siward Beorn and many hundred men with them came to Ely; and when King William learned this, he called out a fleet and a land force and surrounded that [is]land and built a bridge [over the Ouse] and went in [over the bridge to the island], and the fleet [remained] on the side toward the sea. And then all the outlaws surrendered—these were Bishop Ægelwine and Earl Morcar and all who were with them except Hereward alone and all those who wanted [to be] with him; and he boldly led them out. And the king seized ships and arms and many treasures; and he dealt with the men as he pleased; and he sent Bishop Ægelwine to Abingdon, and he died there soon after in the winter.

1072. Here King William led a fleet and a land force to Scotland and blockaded the country by sea with ships and led his land force in [to Scotland] at the Firth of Forth, and he found nothing there, for which he was the better off. And King Malcolm came and made peace with King William and gave hostages and became his man; and the king went home with his whole fyrd.

And Bishop Ægelric died—he had been ordained bishop of York, but it was unjustly taken from him and the bishopric of Durham given him, and he kept it as long as he wished and afterwards gave it up and went to St. Peter's monastery at Peterborough and there lived the life of a monk for twelve years. Then after King William had conquered England, he took him from Peterborough and sent him to Westminster; and he died on October 15, and he is buried there inside the monastery in St. Nicholas' chapel.

1073. In this year King William led an English and French army overseas and won the land of Maine, and the Englishmen severely despoiled it—they destroyed vineyards and burned towns and laid waste the country, and they forced it all to submit to William; and afterwards they returned home to England.

1074. In this year King William went overseas to Normandy, and Child Edgar came from Scotland to Normandy. And the king restored him and all his men to their full legal rights, and he stayed in the king's household and exercised such rights as the king granted him.

1075. In this year King William gave the daughter of William, son of Osbeorn, to Earl Ralph. The said Ralph was a Breton on his mother's side, and his father was an Englishman named Ralph and was born in Norfolk. For that reason the king had given the earldom of Norfolk and Suffolk to his son. He [Earl Ralph] then brought his wife to Norwich.

> There was the bride-ale
> To men as a bale.

Earl Roger and Earl Waltheof and bishops and abbots were there, and they there resolved to drive the king out of the kingdom of England. And what they had resolved was at once made known to the king in Normandy. It was Earl Roger and Earl Ralph who were the leaders of the plot. And they enticed the Bretons to their side and sent east to Denmark for a fleet to help them. And Roger went west to his earldom [Herefordshire] and assembled his people to the detriment of the king, but he was prevented. And Ralph in his earldom [Norfolk, Suffolk], too, wanted to take the field with his people, but the castlemen [Normans] who were in England and also the natives came against him and prevented him from doing anything; instead he went aboard ship at Norwich. And his wife stayed in the castle and held it until she was granted peace. And then she and all her men who wanted to go with her left England. And afterwards the king came to England and seized Earl Roger, his kinsman, and imprisoned him; and he also seized Earl Waltheof.

And soon after this two hundred ships came from the east from Denmark, and two chieftains, Canute, son of Svein, and Earl Hakon, were in them. And they did not dare engage in battle with King William, but proceeded overseas to Flanders.

And the Lady Edith died in Winchester a week before Christmas; and the king had her brought to Westminster with great honor and laid her with King Edward, her lord.

And he was in Westminster that Christmas; and all the Bretons who were at the bride-ale in Norwich were ruined:

> Some were blinded,
> And some driven from the country;
> So William's betrayers
> Were humbled.

1076. In this year Svein, king of Denmark, died, and Harald, his son, succeeded to the throne.

And the king gave Westminster to Abbot Vitalis, who was formerly abbot of Bernay. And Earl Waltheof was beheaded in Winchester and his body was carried to Crowland.

And the king went overseas and led his fyrd to Brittany and besieged the castle of Dol-de-Bretagne; and the Bretons held it until the king [of France] came from France. And William went away and lost there both men and horses and many of his treasures.

1077. Here in this year the king of France and King William of England came to an agreement; but it lasted only a short time.

And this year one night before the Assumption of the Virgin [Aug. 15] London was burned more completely than it had ever been since it was founded.

And in this year Ægelwig, abbot of Evesham, died on February 16; and Bishop Hereman also died, on February 20.

1079. In this year King Malcolm came from Scotland into England between the two festivals of the Virgin [Aug. 15–Sept. 8] with a large fyrd and ravaged Northumberland as far as the Tyne and killed many hundred men and carried home a great deal of money and treasure and prisoners.

And the same year King William fought against his son, Robert, beyond Normandy near a castle called Gerberoy. And King William was wounded there, and the horse on which he was riding killed; and his son William was also wounded there and many men killed.

1080.[188] In this year Bishop Walchere of Durham was killed at a council, and a hundred men with him, French and Flemish; and he himself had been born in Lorraine. The Northumbrians did this in the month of May.

1081. In this year the king led a fyrd into Wales and there freed many hundred men.

1082. Here the king arrested Bishop Odo. And here there was a great famine.

1083. In this year the dispute arose in Glastonbury between Abbot Thurstan and his monks. It was first caused by the abbot's lack of wisdom in mistreating his monks in many ways; and the monks complained politely to him and asked him to rule them justly and to love

[188] With the account of an incident entered fifty years too early, *D* here comes to an end and leaves *E* the only vernacular authority for the events of the next seventy-five years.

them, and they would be faithful and obedient to him. But the abbot would not [do] any of this, but treated them badly and threatened them with worse. One day the abbot went into the chapter house and spoke against the monks and wanted to mistreat them. And he sent for laymen, and they came fully armed upon the monks in the chapter house; and then the monks were very much afraid of them and did not know what there was for them to do; but they fled in all directions. Some ran into the church and locked the doors against them, and they [the laymen] went into the church after them and wanted to drag them out, since they [the monks] dared not come out [of their own accord]. But a grievous thing happened there on that day —the Frenchmen broke into the choir and threw missiles toward the altar where the monks were, and some of the retainers went up to the upper floor and with arrows shot downwards toward the sanctuary, so that many arrows stuck in the cross which stood above the altar; and the wretched monks lay around the altar and some crept under and earnestly cried to God, begging his mercy, since they could obtain no mercy from men. What can we say, but that they shot unceasingly, and others broke down the doors there and went in and killed some of the monks and wounded many there; so that the blood came from the altar upon the steps and from the steps to the floor. Three were beaten to death there and eighteen wounded.

And in the same year Matilda, King William's queen, died on the day after Allhallows' Day [Nov. 1].

And in the same year after Christmas the king had a large and heavy tax exacted over all England: it was seventy-two pence for every hide.

1084. Here in this year Wulfwald, abbot of Chertsey, died on April 19.

1085. In this year men declared and said for a fact that Canute, king of Denmark, son of King Svein, was bound for England and planned to conquer this country with the help of Earl Robert of Flanders, for Canute had Robert's daughter for his wife. When William, king of England, who was then staying in Normandy—for he had possession both of England and Normandy—heard of this, he went to England with a greater army of horse and foot from France and from Brittany than had ever before visited this country, so that men wondered how this country could feed the whole army. But the king had the army distributed throughout the entire country to his vassals, and they fed the army, each according to the extent of his land. And men suffered great affliction this year; and the king had the land along the coast laid waste so that, if his enemies landed, they should not find anything which they could readily seize. But when the king learned for a fact that his enemies were blocked and could not carry out their expedition, he let some of the army go to their own country and he kept some in this country over the winter.

Then at Christmas the king was in Gloucester with his witan and there held his court for five days; and afterwards the archbishop and the clergy held a synod for three days. There Maurice was elected bishop of London, William [bishop] of Norfolk, and Robert [bishop] of Cheshire—they were all clerics of the king. After this the king had a great council and spoke very earnestly with his witan about this country—how it was occupied or with what men. Then he sent his men over all England into every shire and had them reckon how many hundred hides there were in the shire or what land and cattle the king himself owned in this country or what annual taxes he ought to receive from the shire. He also had them write down how much land his archbishops owned, and his suffragan bishops and his abbots and his earls, and—though I make my story too long—what or how much land and cattle each man who was a landowner in England possessed, and how much money it was worth. He had it surveyed so very closely that there was not a single hide or rood of land, nor—it is a shame to tell, though it seemed to him no shame to do—was there even an ox or a cow or a pig left that was not set down in his writing; and all the writings were afterwards brought to him.[189]

1085*b* [1086].[190] Here the king wore his crown and held his court in Winchester at Easter, and he planned his trip so that he was at Westminster during Pentecost, and there he dubbed his son Henry knight. Afterwards he travelled so that he came to Old Sarum at Lammas [Aug. 1], and his witan came to him there, and all the landowners who were of importance in all England, no matter whose men they might be, and they all submitted to him and became his men and swore oaths of fealty to him that they would be faithful to him against

[189] On the Domesday Survey, see especially F. W. Maitland, *Domesday Book and Beyond* (Cambridge, 1897).

[190] The repetition of the annuary number 1085 throws off the chronology by one year up to 1089 where the correct dating is restored by the omission of the year 1088. This account is of the important Salisbury oath.

all other men. From there he went to the Isle of Wight because he wanted to go to Normandy; and he later did so. And yet he first did according to his habit—he obtained a great deal of money from his men wherever he could find a pretext, either justly or otherwise. Then afterwards he went to Normandy, and Atheling Edgar, King Edward's kinsman, revolted from him because he did not receive much honor from him; but may Almighty God give him honor in the future! And Christina, the atheling's sister, retired into the minster at Romsey and took the veil.

And the same year was a very grievous year and a very miserable and sorrowful year in England through cattle plague, and grain and fruits were backward, and [there was] such great misfortune in the weather as one cannot easily imagine—the thunder and lightning was so violent that it killed many men, and things grew steadily worse and worse with men. May Almighty God better it when such be his will!

1086 [1087]. One thousand and eighty-seven years after the birth of our Lord Savior Christ, in the twenty-first year since William ruled and controlled England, as God granted him, there was a very heavy and very pestilent year in this country. Such a plague came on men that almost every other man suffered the worst illness, that is, the fever, and that so violently that many died of the illness. Afterwards, on account of the bad weather, which came as we told above, so severe a famine swept over all England that many hundred men died a wretched death through that famine. Alas, how wretched and how sorrowful a time it was then, when the suffering men lay almost at the point of death, and then the sharp famine came and completely destroyed them.

Who cannot feel pity for such a time? Or who is so hardhearted that cannot lament such misfortune? But such things happen for a people's sins because they will not love God and righteousness; so it was in those days that there was little righteousness in this country with any man except with the monks wherever they fared well. The king and the chief men coveted gold and silver much too much and did not care how sinfully it was obtained so long as it came to them. The king gave his land out on the hardest terms he could; then another would come and offer more than the first had previously given, and the king would let it to the man who offered him more. Then a third would come and offer yet more, and the king would give it to him who offered most of all. And he did not care how sinfully the reeves obtained it [money] from poor men, nor how many illegal acts they performed, but the more that was said about the just law, the more illegal acts were performed. They levied unjust tolls and they did many other injustices which are difficult to tell about.

Also in the same year before autumn the holy church of St. Paul, the bishop's see in London, was burned, and many other churches and the largest and finest part of the whole town. So also at that same time almost every principal town in all England was burned. Alas, a sorrowful and lamentable time was this year which brought forth so many misfortunes.

Also in the same year before the Assumption of the Virgin [Aug. 15] King William went from Normandy into France with a fyrd and raided against his own lord, King Philip, and killed a large part of his men and burned the town of Mantes-Gassicourt and all the holy churches that were in the town; and two holy men who served God dwelling in an anchoret's cell, were burned there.

This being thus finished, King William returned to Normandy. A sorrowful thing he did, and a more sorrowful happened to him. How more sorrowful? He fell sick and was sorely afflicted. What can I say? Sharp death, which spares neither powerful nor humble men, seized him. He died in Normandy on the day after the Nativity of the Virgin [Sept. 8] and was buried at Caen in St. Stephen's church, which he had formerly built and then lavishly endowed.

Alas, how false and how unstable are this world's riches! He who had previously been a powerful king and lord of many a land, he had of the whole land but a seven-foot measure. And he who was once clothed with gold and with jewels, he lay then covered with earth.

He left behind him three sons. The eldest was named Robert, who was duke of Normandy after him. The second was named William, who wore the royal crown in England after him. The third was named Henry, to whom his father bequeathed innumerable treasures.

If anyone wishes to know what kind of man he was or what honor he had or how many countries he was lord of, we will write of him just as we knew him, we who have looked upon him and at one time lived in his court. King William, about whom we are speaking, was a very wise and very powerful man, and more distinguished and stronger than any of his predecessors were. He was mild to the good men who loved God and inordinately stern to the men who opposed his will. On the very site where God had granted him that he might conquer England, he built a splendid monastery [Battle Abbey, Sussex] and placed monks there and endowed it well. In his day the splendid church in Canterbury was built and also very many others over all England. This country was also plentifully filled with monks, and they lived their life according to the rule of St. Benedict; and Christendom was such in his day that every man who wished followed what fitted his rank. He was also very distinguished: three times each year he wore his royal crown, as often as he was in England. At Easter he wore it in Winchester, at Pentecost in Westminster, at Christmas in Gloucester, and then there were with him all the prominent men over all England, archbishops and suffragan bishops, abbots and earls, thegns and knights.

So, too, he was a very stern and fierce man, so that no one dared do anything against his will. Earls who had acted against his will he had in bonds; he deposed bishops from their bishoprics and abbots from their abbacies; and he put thegns in prison. And finally he did not spare his own brother, named Odo. The latter was a very powerful bishop in Normandy—his bishop's see was in Bayeux; and he was the most prominent man besides the king; and he had an earldom in England, and when the king [was] in Normandy, he was master in this country. And he [William] put him in prison. Among other things not to be forgotten is the good peace which he made in his country, so that a man who was of any importance could travel unmolested over his kingdom with his bosom full of gold; and no man dared kill another, even if he had done ever so great an injury to him; and if any man lay with a woman against her will, he immediately lost the members with which he had played.[191]

He reigned over England, and by his craft so surveyed it that there was not one hide of land in England but that he knew who owned it and what it was worth; and afterwards he set [it] down in his writing [Domesday Survey]. Wales was in his power, and he built castles there and completely controlled that people. So also he subjected Scotland to himself by his great strength. The country of Normandy was his by right of inheritance, and he reigned over the

[191] According to Anglo-Saxon usage; see Alfred's law code, chap. 25 (Liebermann, *Die Gesetze der Angelsachsen,* I, p. 64).

countship called Maine, and if he had lived two years more, he would
have conquered Ireland by his ingenuity,[192] and without any arms.
Truly in his time men suffered great hardship and very many wrongs.

> He caused castles to be built
> And poor men to be greatly oppressed.
> The king was very severe
> And took from his subjects many a mark
> Of gold and more hundreds of pounds of silver.
> He took this by weight and with great injustice
> From his people, for little need.
> He fell into covetousness,
> And he loved greediness very much.
> He set up many deer preserves and also enacted laws
> That whoever killed a hart or hind
> Should be blinded.
> He placed a ban on harts, also on boars.
> He loved the stags as much
> As if he were their father.
> He also made laws concerning hares that they should run free.
> His great men complained of it and the poor men bewailed it,
> But he [was] so stern that he did not care for all their hate.
> But they had to follow the king's will
> If they wanted to live or hold land,
> Land or property, or particularly his favor.
> Alas! that any man should be so proud,
> Should raise himself up and account himself above all men.
> May Almighty God show mercy to his soul
> And grant him forgiveness of his sins.

We have written these things about him, both good and bad, so that
good men may take to virtue and shun evil and go in the way that
leads us to the heavenly kingdom.

We can write of many things that happened in the same year. So
it was in Denmark that the Danes, who were formerly accounted the
most loyal of all peoples, turned to the greatest faithlessness and to the
greatest treachery that ever might be. They elected, and submitted
to, King Canute and swore oaths to him, and afterwards basely killed

---

[192] MS *werscipe* may be translated "prudence," "wariness," "cunning."

him in a church. It also happened in Spain that the heathen went and ravaged the Christians and subjected many to their power. But the Christian king, who was named Alphonso, sent to each country everywhere and asked for help, and help came to him from every country that was Christian; and they went and killed and drove away all the heathen people and won their country back through God's help.

Also in this same country in the same year many prominent men died: Stigand, bishop of Chichester, and the abbot of St. Augustine's [Canterbury] and the abbot of Bath and he of Pershore and then the lord of them all, William, king of England, of whom we spoke before. After his death his son, named William like his father, succeeded to the throne and was consecrated king by Archbishop Lanfranc in Westminster three days before Michaelmas [Sept. 26]; and all the men in England submitted to him and swore oaths to him. This being thus finished, the king went to Winchester and inspected the treasure house and the treasures which his father had previously gathered—no man could express how much was gathered there in gold and in silver and in vessels and in robes and in jewels and in many other precious things which are difficult to tell of. The king then did as his father had instructed him before he was dead—he distributed the treasures for his father's soul to every monastery that was in England: to one monastery ten marks of gold, to another six, and to every country church sixty pennies, and a hundred pounds of money was sent to every shire to be distributed among poor men for his soul; and before he died, he [William the Conqueror] had ordered that all the men who were in prison under his authority should be released. And the king was in London at Christmas.

1087 [1088]. In this year this country was very much stirred up and filled with great treason, so that the most powerful Frenchmen who were in this country wanted to betray their lord the king and wanted to have as king his brother, Robert, who was duke of Normandy. Foremost in this plot were Bishop Odo and Bishop Geoffrey and William, bishop of Durham. The king had done so well by the bishop [193] that all England went according to his counsel and as he wished; and he planned to do by him [the king] as Judas Iscariot did

[193] It is impossible to say with certainty whether these references to the traitorous bishop apply to Odo or to William.

by our Lord. And Earl Roger was also in the plot, and very many people with them, all Frenchmen; and this plot was formed in the spring. As soon as Easter came, they went and ravaged and burned and laid waste the king's farms, and destroyed the land of all the men who were loyal to the king. And each of them went to his castle and garrisoned it and provisioned it as best he could. Bishop Geoffrey and Robert of Mowbray went to Bristol and pillaged and brought the booty to the castle, and afterwards left the castle and ravaged Bath and all the adjacent country; and they laid waste the whole district of Berkeley. And the chief men of Hereford and all the shire with them and the men of Shropshire, together with many people from Wales, came and ravaged and burned in Worcestershire until they came to the town [Worcester]; and then they wanted to burn the town and loot the church and get possession of the king's castle. Seeing these things, the venerable Bishop Wulfstan was sorely troubled in his mind because the castle had been entrusted to his keeping. Nevertheless, the men of his household went out with a few men from the castle and by God's mercy and by the bishop's merit killed and captured five hundred men and routed all the others. The bishop of Durham did all the harm he could everywhere in the north. One of them was named Roger [Bigod], who surprised the castle at Norwich and did the worst of all over the whole country. Hugh was also one who did not improve things either in Leicestershire or in Northampton. Bishop Odo, who had started the affair, went into Kent to his earldom and completely destroyed it and laid waste the king's land and the archbishop's as well and carried all the property into his castle in Rochester.

When the king heard of all these things and how treacherously they were acting towards him, he was greatly troubled in his mind. He then sent for Englishmen and explained his exigency to them and asked their help and promised them the best laws that there had ever been before in this country, and he prohibited all unjust taxes and granted to men their forests and the right of hunting—but it did not stand any length of time. But, nevertheless, the Englishmen came to the aid of the king their lord. They then went towards Rochester and planned to get hold of Bishop Odo, thinking that if they had him who had previously been the leader of the plot, they might the better get hold of all the others. They came then to the castle at Tonbridge Urban; Bishop Odo's knights and many others who wanted to hold it against the king were in the castle. But the Englishmen went and destroyed the castle, and the men who were in it made peace with the king. The king with his army went towards Rochester, and they supposed that the bishop was there; but the king was informed that the bishop had gone out to the castle at Pevensey, and the king with his army followed and invested the castle with a very large army for fully six weeks.

Meanwhile the duke of Normandy, Robert, the king's brother, assembled a great many people and expected to conquer England with the help of the men in this country who were against the king; and he sent some of his men to this country and he himself planned to follow. But the Englishmen who guarded the sea[coast] seized some of the men and killed and drowned more than anyone could count.

After that food failed those in the castle. Then they asked for peace and gave it up to the king, and the bishop swore that he would leave England and not come again to this country unless the king should send for him, and that he would surrender the castle in Rochester. Just as the bishop was leaving and was supposed to surrender the castle, and the king had sent his men [as an escort] with him, the men who were in the castle rose up and seized the bishop and the king's men and put them in prison. Very good knights were inside the castle: Eustace the Younger and three sons of Earl Roger and all the best-born men who were in this country or in Normandy.

When the king heard of these things, he followed with the army which he had there and sent all over England and ordered that every law-abiding man should come to him, French and English, from town and from country. Many people then came to him, and he went to Rochester and besieged the castle until those who were in it made peace and surrendered the castle. Bishop Odo, with the men who were in the castle, went overseas, and so the bishop lost the position which he had in this country. After that the king sent an army to Durham and had the castle invested, and the bishop [William] made peace and surrendered the castle and left his bishopric and went to Normandy. Many Frenchmen also left their lands and went overseas, and the king gave their lands to the men who were loyal to him.

1089. In this year the venerable father and comfort of monks, Archbishop Lanfranc, departed from this life, but we trust that he went to the heavenly kingdom. A great earthquake also occurred over

all England on August 11. And it was a very backward year for grain
and fruits of every kind, so that many men reaped their grain about
Martinmas [Nov. 11] and even later.

1090. *In the thirteenth year of the Indiction.*[194]

This being thus finished, just as we previously related above about
the king and about his brother and about his men, the king considered
how he might punish his brother Robert [and] [195] harass him the
most and conquer Normandy from him. So by his cunning or by
treasures he secured the castle and the harbor at St. Valéry-en-Caux,
and he likewise secured the one at Aumâle, and he placed his knights
in them, and they did damage to the country by ravaging and burning. After this he secured more castles in the country and placed his
retainers in them.

After Robert, duke of Normandy, perceived that his sworn men
had failed him and had surrendered their castles to his detriment, he
sent to his lord Philip, king of France, and he [Philip] came to
Normandy with a large army, and the king and the duke with an immense fyrd besieged the castle in which the king of England's men
were. King William of England sent to Philip, king of France, and
he for love of him or for his great treasures abandoned his vassal,
Duke Robert, and his [Robert's] country [Normandy], and returned
to France and left them as they were. And during these events this
country was greatly oppressed by illegal taxes and by many other misfortunes.

1091. In this year King William held his court in Westminster at
Christmas, and after that at Candlemas [Feb. 2] he went out of
England into Normandy to injure his brother. While he was there,
their reconciliation took place on condition that the duke should give
him Fécamp and the countship of Eu and Cherbourg, and in addition [that] the king's men should remain unmolested in the castles
which they had secured against the duke's will. And the king promised that he would force into submission Maine which their father
had formerly won and which had revolted from the duke, and everything that his father had owned beyond there [in French territory]
except what he [Robert] had granted to the king [William], and
that all those who had previously lost their land in England on the

---

194 1090 is the thirteenth year of the fifty-first indiction reckoned from A. D. 312.
195 For this likely emendation, see Plummer, II, 278 f.

duke's account should have it back by this agreement; and the duke should have as much in England as stood in their agreement. And if the duke died without a son by lawful wedlock, the king would be heir to all of Normandy. By this same agreement, if the king died, the duke would be heir to all of England. Twelve of the best [men] on the king's side and twelve on the duke's swore to this agreement—yet it stood but for a short time afterward.

During the course of this reconciliation Atheling Edgar was deprived of the lands which the duke had formerly assigned to him; and he went out of Normandy to Scotland to the king [Malcolm III], his brother-in-law, and to his sister.

While King William was out of England, King Malcolm came from Scotland here to England and ravaged a great deal of it, until the good men who had charge of this country sent a fyrd against him and turned him back. When King William heard of this in Normandy, he made ready his departure and came to England, and his brother, Duke Robert, with him, and at once ordered a fyrd summoned out, both a fleet and a land force; but before he could get to Scotland, almost the entire fleet was miserably destroyed four days before Michaelmas [Sept. 29]. And the king and his brother went with the land force; but when King Malcolm heard that they wanted to seek him out with a fyrd, he went with his fyrd out of Scotland into Lothian in England and waited there. When King William approached with his fyrd, Duke Robert and Atheling Edgar intervened and so reconciled the kings that King Malcolm came to our king and became his man with quite the same obedience as he had previously done to his father and confirmed it with oath. And King William promised him, in land and in all [other] things, what he had previously had under his father.

In this treaty Atheling Edgar was also reconciled with the king, and the kings then parted in great peace—but it stood only a short time. And Duke Robert stayed here with the king almost until Christmas, and during that time found little honesty in their agreement, and two days before the feast [of Christmas] took ship in the Isle of Wight and went to Normandy, and Atheling Edgar with him.

1092. In this year King William went north to Carlisle with a great fyrd and restored the town and built the castle and drove out Dolfin, who had previously ruled the country there, and garrisoned the castle with his men and afterwards turned south here and sent a large number of peasants [196] with their wives and with their cattle to live there and to till the land.

1093. In this year in the spring King William was taken so ill at Gloucester that he was everywhere reported dead, and in his illness he made many vows to God: to lead his own life in righteousness, and to grant peace and protection to God's churches and never again to sell them for money, and to have all just laws among his people. And the archbishopric of Canterbury, which had up to this time remained in his own possession, he committed to Anselm, who had previously been abbot of Bec [at Le Bec-Hellouin], the bishopric of Lincoln to Robert, his chancellor, and granted land to many monasteries; but later, when he became well, he retracted this and renounced all the good laws which he had previously promised us.

Then after this the king of Scotland sent and demanded [fulfillment of the terms of] the agreement which had been promised him; and King William summoned him to Gloucester and sent hostages to him in Scotland, and later Atheling Edgar, and afterwards men to meet him who brought him with great honor to the king. But when he [Malcolm] came to the king, he could not be [held] worthy either of speech with our king or of [the terms of] the agreement that had been promised him; and consequently they parted in great hostility, and King Malcolm returned home to Scotland. But as soon as he came home, he assembled his fyrd and went into England, and ravaged with greater folly than became him, and Robert, earl of Northumbria, with his men trapped him unawares and killed him. He was killed by Morel of Bamborough, who was the earl's steward and King Malcolm's sponsor. With him was also killed his son, Edward, who should have been king after him if he had lived. When the good queen Margaret heard of this—her dearest lord and son thus betrayed— she was mortally afflicted in mind and went to church with her priests and received her [last] rites and prayed to God so that she gave up her ghost. And then the Scots elected as king Donald, Malcolm's brother, and drove out all the English who had previously been with King Malcolm. When Duncan, son of King Malcolm—he was in King William's court, for his father had formerly given him as a hostage

[196] MS *Eyrlisces folces*. Thorpe's emendation to *cyrlisces* "churlish" is borne out by the *multos uillanos* of the *Annals of Waverley,* ed. H. R. Luard, *Annales monastici,* "Rolls Series" (London, 1865), II, 202.

to our king's father and here he had afterwards remained—heard that all this had so happened, he came to the king and paid [him] such allegiance as the king wished to have from him, and so with his consent went to Scotland with the help that he could get of English and French, and deprived his kinsman [uncle], Donald, of the kingdom and was received as king. But some of the Scots gathered together again and killed almost all his men, and he himself escaped with a few. Afterwards they were reconciled on condition that he would never again introduce Englishmen or Frenchmen into that country.

1094. Here at Christmas King William held his court at Gloucester and messengers came to him there from his brother, Robert of Normandy. They declared that his brother would renounce all peace and compact unless the king would carry out everything they had previously [1091] settled in the agreement; and he then called him forsworn and faithless unless he held to the agreement or went there [to Normandy] and exculpated himself where the agreement had formerly been made and also sworn to.

Then the king went to Hastings at Candlemas [Feb. 2]; and while he was waiting there for favorable weather, he had the monastery at Battle consecrated, and he deprived Herbert Losang, bishop of Thetford, of his crosier, and after that at Mid-Lent he went overseas to Normandy. After he arrived there, he and his brother Robert, the duke, said that they should come together in peace, and they did so, and [yet] they could not be reconciled. After that they again came together with the same men who had formerly [1091] made the agreement and also sworn the oaths, and they imputed the entire breach [of the agreement] to the king; but he would neither admit this nor hold to the agreement, and consequently they parted in great hostility.

And afterwards the king won the castle at Bures and captured the duke's men in it, some of whom he sent here to England. On the other hand, the duke with the help of the king of France won the castle at Argentan and there captured Roger of Poitou and seven hundred of the king's knights with him, and later the one at Le Houlme. And each of them frequently burned towns against the other, and also seized men.

Then the king sent here to England and ordered twenty thousand Englishmen summoned out to help him in Normandy; but when they came to the sea, they were ordered to return and to give the money which they had received for the king's profit—that was half a pound [to] each man; and they did so.

And after this the duke of Normandy, with the king of France and with all whom they could gather, went towards Eu, where King William was, and intended to besiege him; and so they went until they came to Longueville. There the king of France was turned back by intrigue, and so later the whole expedition broke up. Here, meanwhile, King William sent for his brother, Henry, who was in the castle at Domfront, but because he could not go through Normandy in peace, he [William] sent ships and Hugh, earl of Chester, for him. But whereas they ought to have gone towards Eu where the king was, they went to England and landed at Southampton on Halloween [Oct. 31] and afterwards remained here, and at Christmas were in London.

Also in this same year the Welshmen assembled and began fighting against the French who were in Wales or in the vicinity and [who] had formerly deprived them of their lands, and destroyed many forts and castles, and killed men; and later, as their force increased, they divided themselves [into] more [bands]. Hugh, earl of Shropshire, fought against one of these [bands] and routed it. But nevertheless the whole year the others held back from no damage that they could inflict.

This year also the Scots tricked and killed their king, Duncan, and afterwards for the second time [197] took as their king his paternal uncle, Donald, by whose counsel and at whose instigation he had been betrayed to death.

1095. In this year King William was at Wissant during the first four days of Christmas-tide, and after the fourth day he came to this country and landed at Dover. And Henry, the king's brother, stayed here in England until spring and then went overseas to Normandy with much treasure [to be employed] in the name of the king against their brother, Duke Robert, and repeatedly fought against the duke and inflicted great injury on him both in land and in men.

And then at Easter the king held his court in Winchester and Robert, earl of Northumbria, refused to come to court; and therefore the king was greatly incensed against him and sent to him and sternly commanded him, if he wanted to be [held] worthy of peace, to come

[197] See 1093.

to court at Pentecost. In this year Easter was on March 25, and during Easter on the eve of St. Ambrose's Day, that is, April 4,[198] a great number of stars were seen falling from heaven over nearly this whole country for almost the entire night—not one or two at a time, but so thickly that no man could count them. After this, at Pentecost, the king was in Windsor, and all his witan with him except the earl of Northumbria, for the king would neither give him hostages nor grant by pledges that he might come and go in peace.

And the king therefore called out his fyrd and went to Northumbria against the earl and, as soon as he arrived there, he captured many —and nearly all of the best—of the earl's retinue in a fortress [Newcastle-upon-Tyne] and put them in prison, and besieged the castle at Tynemouth until he captured it and the earl's brother and all those who were in it with him, and afterwards went to Bamborough and there besieged the earl. But when the king saw that he could not overcome him, he ordered a castle built in front of Bamborough and called it in his tongue "Malveisin," that is in English, "Bad Neighbor," and garrisoned it heavily with his men, and after that went south. Then soon after the king had gone south, the earl one night went out of Bamborough towards Tynemouth, but those who were in the new castle [Malveisin] noticed him and followed and attacked him and wounded him and later captured him, and they killed some of those who were with him and took the others alive.

In the meantime the king was informed that the Welshmen had destroyed a certain castle in Wales called Montgomery and had killed Earl Hugh's men, who were supposed to hold it; and he therefore ordered another fyrd hastily summoned out, and after Michaelmas [Sept. 29] he went into Wales and divided his fyrd and traversed the whole country, so that the whole fyrd came together at Snowdon [Carnarvonshire, Wales] on All Saints' Day [Nov. 1]. But the Welsh in front kept withdrawing into the mountains and hills so that they could not get at them, and the king turned home because he saw that he could do no more there that winter.

When the king came back, he ordered Robert, earl of Northumbria, to be arrested and brought to Bamborough and both [his] eyes to be put out, unless those who were in it would give up the castle. His wife

[198] April 3 would be the *eve* of St. Ambrose's Day.

and Morel, who was the steward and also his kinsman, were holding it. By this means, the castle was given up, and Morel then stayed in the king's court; and through him many among both clergy and also laymen were discovered who in their designs were traitors to the king. Before this time the king had ordered some of them put in prison, and afterwards [had it] proclaimed very importunately over this whole country that all those who held land of the king, as they wished to be [held] worthy of his protection, were to be at court on time. And the king ordered Earl Robert brought to Windsor and confined there in the castle.

Also in this same year towards Easter the pope's emissary came here to England—that was Walter, bishop of the town of Albano, a man of very good life—and he gave Archbishop Anselm his pallium at Pentecost on behalf of Pope Urban; and he received it at his archbishop's see in Canterbury. And Bishop Walter remained here in England for a long time this year, and the Peter's Pence was afterwards sent along with him as it had not been done for many years previous.

This same year the weather was very unseasonable, and consequently the crops turned out but middling throughout this whole country.

1096. In this year King William held his court at Christmas in Windsor, and William, bishop of Durham, died there on New Year's day. And on the octave of the Epiphany [Jan. 13] the king and all his witan were at Old Sarum. There Geoffrey Bainard accused William of Eu, the king's kinsman, of having been traitor to the king, and fought it out with him and beat him in single combat; and after he was beaten, the king ordered his eyes put out and afterwards [ordered him] castrated; and the king ordered his steward, named William, who was his [William's] cousin on his mother's side, to be hanged on a cross. Count Odo of Champagne, the king's uncle, and many others were also blinded there, and some were brought to London and there mutilated.

This year, too, there was a very great disturbance at Easter among this entire people and many other peoples because of Urban, who was called pope though he did not have possession of the see in Rome; and countless men went with wives and children to fight against the heathen

[First Crusade]. On account of this expedition the king and his brother, Duke Robert, were reconciled so that the king went overseas and redeemed all Normandy from him for money, just as they had agreed; and afterwards the duke went [on the Crusade], and with him the count of Flanders and the count of Boulogne-sur-Mer and many other leaders as well. And Duke Robert and those who went with him stayed that winter in Apulia. But many thousands of the people who went by way of Hungary wretchedly perished there and on the way, and toward winter many turned home, wretched and hunger-bitten.

This was a very grievous year throughout all England both on account of many taxes and also on account of the very grievous famine which this year greatly afflicted this country.

Also in this year the chief men who governed this country again and again sent a fyrd into Wales and thereby greatly afflicted many a man—but nothing was gained there except loss of men and waste of money.

1097. Here in this year King William was in Normandy at Christmas, and then towards Easter came here to England because he planned to hold his court in Winchester, but he was delayed by bad weather until Easter eve, when he landed first at Arundel and consequently held his court at Windsor.

And after that he went with a large army [199] into Wales and thoroughly traversed the country with his fyrd with the help of several Welshmen who had come to him and were his guides, and he remained there from midsummer [June 24] until nearly August and suffered there great loss of men and of horses and also of many other things. Then the Welshmen, after they had revolted from the king, elected many chieftains from among themselves, one of whom was called Cadogan who was the most honored of them—he was the nephew of King Gruffydd. But when the king saw that he could carry out nothing of his purpose there, he returned to this country and soon after that had castles built along the borders.

Then at Michaelmas [time], on October 4, a strange star appeared shining in the evening and shortly setting. It was seen in the southwest, and the light which glowed from it seemed very long, shining

[199] The MS *here* would seem to signify an army composed of foreign mercenaries, as opposed to the native fyrd mentioned later in the same sentence.

southeast; and it appeared in this fashion almost all week. Many men supposed that it was a comet.

Soon after this Archbishop Anselm of Canterbury took leave of the king—though it was, as men surmised, displeasing to the king—and went overseas, because it seemed to him that little was done in this nation according to right and according to his order.

And after that, at Martinmas [Nov. 11], the king went overseas to Normandy, but while he was waiting for favorable weather, his court did the greatest damage in the shire where they were that court or army could ever do in a country at peace. This was a very grievous year in all respects, and especially troublesome in storms at the time when the soil was supposed to be tilled and again when the crops were to be gathered in, and in excessive taxes which never ceased. Many shires which belonged to London for [forced] labor were also severely oppressed by the wall which they built about the tower, and by the bridge which was almost completely carried away by a flood, and by the building of the king's hall which was erected in Westminster—and many a man was oppressed by these things.

Also in this same year, near Michaelmas [Sept. 29], Atheling Edgar went with a fyrd into Scotland with the help of the king and conquered the country after severe fighting and drove out King Donald and there appointed as king in King William's allegiance his kinsman Edgar, who was son of King Malcolm and of Margaret, the queen, and afterwards returned to England.

1098. In this year at Christmas King William was in Normandy, and Walcelin, bishop of Winchester, and Baldwin, abbot of Bury St. Edmunds, both died within the [Christmas] season.

And in this year Turold, abbot of Peterborough, also died.

In the summer of this year also a pool welled forth blood at Finchamstead in Berkshire, as many honest men said who were supposed to have seen it.

And Earl Hugh was killed in Anglesey [Wales] by vikings,[200] and his brother Robert became his heir, just as he obtained it from the king.

Before Michaelmas [Sept. 29] the sky appeared as if it were burn-

[200] The MS *utwikingas*, literally "out-" or "foreign vikings" is perhaps intended to distinguish the foreign, *i. e.*, Norwegian, vikings from the Irish, or local, vikings employed by the Welsh.

ing almost the whole night. This was a very disastrous year because of many excessive taxes and because of great rains which did not cease all year—nearly every crop in the Fenland was destroyed.

1099. Here at Christmas King William was in Normandy and at Easter came here to England and at Pentecost for the first time held his court in his new building at Westminster and there gave the bishopric of Durham to Ralph, his chaplain, who had previously instituted and superintended all his assembles over the whole of England, and soon after that he went overseas and drove Count Hélie out of Maine and afterwards brought it under his power, and so at Michaelmas [Sept. 29] again came here to England.

This year also on Martinmas [Nov. 11] the tide rose higher and did more harm than anyone remembered it ever to have done before; and there was a new moon that same day.

And Osmund, bishop of Old Sarum, died in Advent.

1100. In this year King William held his court at Christmas in Gloucester and at Easter in Winchester and at Pentecost in Westminster.

And at Pentecost blood was seen welling from the earth at a village in Berkshire, as many said who were supposed to have seen it. And after that, on the morning after Lammas [Aug. 1], King William, while hunting, was shot with an arrow by one of his men and was afterwards brought to Winchester and buried in the episcopal residence—that was the thirteenth year after he succeeded to the throne.

He was very strong and stern to his country and to his men and towards all his neighbors and very formidable, and he constantly oppressed this people with an army and with heavy taxes by the counsels of evil men that were always agreeable to him and by his own covetousness, because in his days all righteousness fell and all unrighteousness arose toward God and toward the world. He oppressed God's churches, and all the bishoprics and abbacies whose heads died in his days he either sold for money or kept in his own possession and rented out, because he wanted to be the heir of every man, ordained or lay, and so on the day when he fell he had in his own possession the archbishopric of Canterbury and the bishopric of Winchester, and that of Old Sarum, and eleven abbacies—he had rented them all out. And, though I delay my story longer, everything that was hateful to God and to honorable men—all this was customary in this country in his time; and therefore he was hateful to almost all his people and odious to God, just as his end displayed, for he departed in the midst of his unrighteousness without repentance or any amends.

He was killed on a Thursday, and buried the next morning; and after he was buried, those of the witan who were near at hand elected his brother Henry king, and he at once gave the bishopric of Winchester to William Giffard and then went to London, and on the following Sunday before the altar at Westminster promised God and all the people to abolish all the injustices which existed in his brother's time and to maintain the best laws that had stood in any king's day before him. And after that Maurice, the bishop of London, consecrated him king, and everyone in this country submitted to him and swore oaths and became his man.

And soon after that the king, by the advice of those who were about him, had Bishop Ralph of Durham arrested and brought into the tower in London and there imprisoned. Then before Michaelmas [Sept. 29] Archbishop Anselm of Canterbury came here to England, as King Henry, by the advice of his witan, had sent for him; for he had left this country on account of the great injustice which King William had done him.

And soon after this the king was betrothed to Matilda, daughter of King Malcolm of Scotland and of Margaret, the good queen, kinswoman of King Edward and of the true royal line of England; and on Martinmas [Nov. 11] she was given to him with great honor in Westminster, and Archbishop Anselm wedded her to him and afterwards consecrated her queen. And Archbishop Thomas of York died soon after this.

Also, in the autumn of this same year Duke Robert [of Normandy] and Count Robert of Flanders and Eustace, count of Boulogne-sur-Mer came home to Normandy from Jerusalem. And as soon as Duke Robert came to Normandy, he was joyfully received by all the people except the castles that were occupied by King Henry's men, against which he had had many campaigns [201] and battles.

1101. Here in this year at Christmas King Henry held his court in Westminster, and at Easter in Winchester.

And soon after that, the chief men here in England grew hostile to

[201] MS *gewealc* as "campaigns," according to Max Förster, "König Eadgars Tod," *Englische Studien,* LXXII (1937), 11.

the king, both on account of their own great faithlessness, and also on account of Duke Robert of Normandy, who planned to invade this country. And the king then sent ships out to sea to injure and hinder his brother, but some of them later failed in time of need and deserted the king and submitted to Duke Robert. Then at midsummer [June 24] the king went out to Pevensey with his whole fyrd against his brother and there awaited him, but in the meantime Duke Robert landed at Portsmouth twelve days before Lammas [Aug. 1], and the king with all his fyrd came against him. But the chief men intervened and reconciled the brothers, on condition that the king renounce everything in Normandy that he was keeping by force from the duke, and that all those in England who had previously lost their lands on account of the duke get them back again, and also [that] Count Eustace [have] all his father's land in this country, and that Duke Robert have three thousand marks of silver from England every year; and whichever of the brothers outlived the other be heir to all England and also to Normandy, unless the deceased had an heir by lawful wedlock. And then twelve of the highest [men] from either side confirmed this by oath, and the duke afterwards remained here in England until after Michaelmas [Sept. 29], and his men constantly did a great deal of damage as they went about, while the duke stayed here in England.

This year, too, at Candlemas [Feb. 2], Bishop Ralph escaped at night out of the tower in London where he was imprisoned and went to Normandy; [it was] mainly through his doing and egging-on [that] Duke Robert came to England with hostile intentions this year.

1102. In this year at Christmas King Henry was in Westminster and at Easter in Winchester.

And soon after that, discord arose between the king and Earl Robert of Bellême, who had the earldom of Shrewsbury here in England, which his father, Earl Roger, had formerly owned, and great power besides both on this side of the sea and on the other. And the king went and besieged the castle at Arundel, but when he could not win it quickly enough, he had castles built in front of it and garrisoned them with his men and later went to *Brigg* with his whole fyrd and stayed there until he got possession of the castle and deprived Earl Robert of his lands and confiscated everything he owned in England, and so the earl departed overseas, and the fyrd then returned home.

After that, at Michaelmas [Sept. 29] the king was at Westminster with all the chief men in this country, ordained and lay; and Archbishop Anselm held a synod of the clergy, and they there established many canons concerning Christendom. And many [bishops], both of French and English, there lost their crosiers and authorities which they had unjustly obtained or wickedly lived upon.

And in this same year in Pentecost week thieves came—some from Auvergne [Allemania?], some from France, and others from Flanders—and broke into the monastery of Peterborough and there seized a great deal of property in gold and in silver, that is, crucifixes and chalices and candlesticks.

1103. Here in this year at Christmas King Henry was at Westminster, and soon after that Bishop William Giffard left England, because he refused to receive his ordination illegally from Archbishop Gerard of York. And then at Easter the king held his court in Winchester; and after that Archbishop Anselm of Canterbury went to Rome, as he and the king had agreed.

This year also, Duke Robert of Normandy came to confer with the king here in England; and before he left, he renounced the three thousand marks which King Henry was supposed to give him each year according to the agreement [see 1101].

In this year also blood was seen [welling] from the earth at Finchamstead in Berkshire. This was a very grievous year here in England, on account of the many taxes and on account of the cattle plague and the ruin of crops, both of grain and also of all fruits. Also in the morning on St. Lawrence's Day [Aug. 10] the wind did greater damage here in England to all crops than anyone remembered that any wind had ever done before.

In this same year Matthias, abbot of Peterborough, died—he lived no longer than a year after he was made abbot. After Michaelmas, on October 21, he was received with a procession as abbot, and on the same day the following year he died in Gloucester and was buried there.

1104. Here in this year, at Christmas, King Henry held his court in Westminster, and at Easter in Winchester, and at Pentecost again in Westminster.

This year the first day of Pentecost was June 5; and on the following Tuesday at noon four circles of a white color appeared around the sun, each intertwined under the other as though they were painted. All who saw it wondered because they did not recall ever having seen such things before.

After this, Duke Robert of Normandy, and Robert of Bellême, whom King Henry had previously deprived of his lands and driven from England, were reconciled; and by their reconciliation the king of England and the duke of Normandy became hostile [to one another]. And the king sent his people overseas to Normandy, and the chief men there in Normandy received them and, in treason to their lord the duke, put them up in their castles, from which they inflicted many injuries on the duke in ravaging and in burning. Also this year William, earl of Mortain, left England for Normandy, but after he had departed he acted against the king. For this reason the king deprived him of his lands and everything he had here in England.

It is not easy to tell of the miseries which this country was sustaining at this time on account of many different injustices and taxes which never ceased nor failed. And constantly, as the king went about, there was much plundering upon his wretched people by his court, and in addition frequent burnings and killings.

> All this was to provoke God with,
> And to harass these poor people.

1105. In this year, at Christmas, King Henry held his court at Windsor. And after that, in the spring, he went overseas to Normandy against his brother, Duke Robert. And while he stayed there, he won from his brother Caen and Bayeux and nearly all the castles, and the chief men there in the country became subject to him, and later in the autumn he returned to England. And what he had won in Normandy remained afterwards in peace and in obedience to him, except those who lived anywhere near Earl William of Mortain, who repeatedly harassed him as much as he could because of the loss of his land here in England. And then before Christmas Robert of Bellême came here to England to the king.

This was a very grievous year in this country, on account of the ruin of crops and the many taxes which never ceased, before the king went over [to Normandy] and while he was there and again after he came back.

1106. Here in this year King Henry was in Westminster at Christmas and there held his court, and at that season Robert of Bellême departed from the king in hostility, from this country to Normandy.

After this, before spring, the king was at Northampton, and Duke Robert, his brother, came there to him from Normandy; and because the king would not give up what he had taken from him in Normandy, they parted in hostility, and the duke at once went back again overseas.

During the first week in Lent, on Friday, February 16, a strange star appeared in the evening, and for a long time after that was seen each evening shining for a while. The star appeared in the southwest— it seemed small and dark, but the light that came from it was very bright and appeared like an immense beam shining northeast; and one evening it seemed as if the beam were flashing back towards the star. Some men said that they saw more unknown stars at this time, but we do not state this more definitely because we did not see it ourself. On the eve of Good Friday, that is, the Thursday before Easter, two moons were seen in the sky before day, one in the east and the other in the west, both full, and that same day was the fourteenth day of the moon.

At Easter the king was at Bath and at Pentecost at Old Sarum, because he did not wish to hold a court on his departure overseas. After that before August the king went overseas to Normandy, and nearly everyone in the country submitted to his will except Robert of Bellême and the earl of Mortain and a few others of the chief men who still stood by the duke of Normandy; and therefore the king later went with a fyrd and besieged a castle of the earl of Mortain, named Tinchebray. While the king was besieging the castle, Duke Robert of Normandy came upon the king with his fyrd on Michaelmas eve [Sept. 28], and with him Robert of Bellême and William, earl of Mortain, and all those who wanted to be on his side. But the greater strength and the victory were the king's. There the duke of Normandy was captured, and the earl of Mortain and Robert of Estouteville-Ecalles, and afterwards they were sent to England and put in prison. Robert of Bellême was routed there, and William Crispin captured, and many with him. Atheling Edgar, who a short time before had deserted the king for the duke, was also captured there—the king later let him go free. Afterwards the king conquered everything that was in Normandy and established it under his will and power.

This year also there was a very serious and wicked war between the emperor of Saxony [Henry IV] and his son, and during this war the father died, and the son succeeded to the throne.

1107. In this year, at Christmas, King Henry was in Normandy and organized and established that country under his power, and after that, in the spring, he came here to England, and at Easter held his court in Windsor, and at Pentecost in Westminster, and later, at the beginning of August, he was again in Westminster and there gave and assigned bishoprics and abbacies which [were] without a head or guardian in England or in Normandy. There were so many of these that no one recalled that an equal number had ever before been given out at one time.

And at this same time, among the others who received abbacies, Ernulf, who had previously been abbot in Canterbury, succeeded to the abbacy of Peterborough. This was just seven years after King Henry succeeded to the throne and was the forty-first year since the French conquered this country. Many said that they saw various signs in the moon this year, and its light waxing and waning contrary to its nature.

This year Bishop Maurice of London died, and Robert, abbot of Bury St. Edmunds, and Richard, abbot of Ely. This year also King Edgar of Scotland died on January 13, and Alexander, his brother, succeeded to the throne, as King Henry granted him.

1108. Here in this year, at Christmas, King Henry was in Westminster, and at Easter in Winchester, and at Pentecost again in Westminster, and after that, before August, he went to Normandy.

And Philip, the king of France, died on August 5, and his son, Louis, succeeded to the throne; and later there were many battles between the king of France and the king of England while he [Henry] stayed in Normandy.

In this year also Archbishop Gérard of York died before Pentecost, and afterwards Thomas was appointed to the archbishopric.

1109. Here in this year King Henry was in Normandy at Christmas and at Easter, and before Pentecost he came here to England and held his court in Westminster. There the agreements were concluded and the oaths sworn for the marriage of his daughter [Adelaide] to the emperor [Henry V].

This year there were very many thunderstorms, and those very terrible; and Archbishop Anselm of Canterbury died on March 22; [202] and the first day of Easter [week] was on the Greater Litany [April 25].

[202] Actually April 21, the eleventh of the kalends of May, not of April as in the MS.

1110. In this year, at Christmas, King Henry held his court in Westminster, and at Easter he was at Marlborough, and at Pentecost for the first time held his court at the new Windsor.

This year before spring the king sent his daughter [Adelaide] with many treasures overseas and gave her [in marriage] to the Emperor [Henry V].

On the fifth night in the month of May the moon appeared shining brightly in the evening, and later its light waned little by little, so that it soon was so completely extinguished that neither light nor sphere nor any part of it at all was visible. And it continued so almost until day and then appeared shining full and bright—it was on that same day a fortnight old. All that night the air was very clear, and the stars over the whole sky shining very brightly; and that night fruits were severely damaged by frost. After that in the month of June a star appeared in the northeast, and its light gleamed in front of it to the southwest, and it was seen like that many nights; and later in the night, when it rose higher, it was seen going back to the northwest.

This year Philip of Briouze-St.-Gervaise and William Mallet and William Bainart were deprived of their lands.

Also in this year Count Hélie died who held Maine of King Henry and acknowledged [203] [him], and after his death the count of Anjou [Fulk] succeeded to it and held it against the king.

This was a very grievous year here in England, on account of the taxes which the king exacted for his daughter's marriage, and on account of the bad weather by which the crops were greatly damaged and the fruits over the entire country almost completely destroyed.

This year work was first begun on the new monastery in Chertsey.

1111. In this year King Henry did not wear his crown at Christmas nor at Easter nor at Pentecost, and in August he went overseas to Normandy because of the hostility which some [people] on the borders of France had against him, and especially because of the count of Anjou, who held Maine against him. And after he arrived there, they carried on many raids and burnings and ravagings between them.

In this year Count Robert of Flanders died, and his son, Baldwin, succeeded him.

[203] Reading the MS *oncweow* as *oncneow* (with Earle, *Two of the Saxon Chronicles Parallel,* p. 362).

This year there was a very long and grievous and severe winter, and the crops were greatly damaged by it, and there was the most severe cattle plague that any man could remember.

1112. All this year King Henry remained in Normandy on account of the quarrel which he had with France and with the count of Anjou, who held Maine against him. And while he was there, he deprived the earl of Évreux and William Crispin of their lands, and drove them out of Normandy, and he gave his land back to Philip of Briouze-St.-Gervaise, who had previously been deprived of it; and he had Robert of Bellême seized and put in prison.

This was a very good and very productive year in forest and field, but it was very severe and distressing on account of a great pestilence.

1113. Here in this year King Henry was in Normandy at Christmas and at Easter and at Pentecost, and after that, in the summer, he sent Robert of Bellême here to England to the castle at Wareham, and soon after came himself here to England.

1114. In this year King Henry held his court at Christmas in Windsor, and afterwards he held no court again this year.

And at midsummer [June 24] he went with a fyrd into Wales, and the Welsh came and made a truce with the king, and he had castles built there, and after that, in September, he went overseas to Normandy.

Late in May this year a strange star with a long beam was seen shining many nights. Also one day in this same year there was a greater ebb tide everywhere than anyone before remembered, so that men went riding and walking over the Thames east of the bridge in London. This year there were very strong winds in the month of October, but it [the wind] was excessively strong on the night of the Octave of St. Martin [Nov. 18], and that was apparent everywhere in woods and villages.

Also in this year the king gave the archbishopric of Canterbury to Ralph, who had previously been bishop of Rochester; and Thomas, archbishop of York, died, and Thurstan, who had previously been the king's chaplain, succeeded him.

In this same time the king went to the sea and wished to cross, but bad weather stopped him. Meanwhile he sent his summonses for Abbot Ernulf of Peterborough and ordered him to come to him speedily, because he wished to speak with him in secret. When he came to him, he forced upon him the bishopric of Rochester, and the archbishops and bishops and the nobility who were in England supported the king, and he [Ernulf] long resisted them, but it was of no use. And the king then ordered the archbishop to lead him to Canterbury and consecrate him bishop, whether he wished or not. This took place in the village called Eastbourne—that was on September 15. When the monks of Peterborough heard about this, they were sorrier than they had ever been before, because he was a very good and mild man and had done much good inside and outside [the monastery] while he lived there. May God Almighty abide with him always!

Then soon after that, at the request of the archbishop of Canterbury, the king gave the abbacy to a monk of Sées named John; and soon after that the king and the archbishop of Canterbury sent him to Rome for the archbishop's pallium, and a monk with him who was named Warner,[204] and Archdeacon John, the archbishop's nephew; and things went well with them there. This took place on September 21 in the village called Rowner.

And the same year the king went aboard ship at Portsmouth.

1115. Here at Christmas King Henry was in Normandy; and while he was there, he had all the chief men in Normandy give homage and oaths of allegiance to his son, William, whom he had by his queen, and after that, in the month of July, he came here to England.

This year there was a more severe winter with snow and frost than anyone who was then living ever remembered before, and as a result there was a great mortality of cattle.

In this year Pope Paschal sent a pallium here to England to Ralph, archbishop of Canterbury, and he received it with great honor at his archbishop's see in Canterbury. Anselm, abbot of Rome, who was Archbishop Anselm's nephew, and Abbot John of Peterborough,[205] brought it.

1116. In this year at Christmas King Henry was at St. Albans, and there had the monastery consecrated, and at Easter [was] at Odiham. And this year, too, there was a very grievous and severe and long winter for cattle and all things. And after Easter the king at once went overseas to Normandy, and there were many raids and plunderings and castles taken between France and Normandy. This hostility existed mainly because King Henry supported his nephew, Count Theobald of Blois, who was then at war with his lord, Louis, king of France.

[204] The words "for the archbishop's pallium" and "monk" are inserted by a later hand which also changed "is" to "was" in the last phrase.
[205] "And Abbot John of Peterborough" supplied by a later hand.

This was a very oppressive and disastrous year for crops, on account of the excessive rains which came just before August and caused much trouble and distress until Candlemas [Feb. 2] came. This year, too, was so barren in mast that none was heard spoken of in this whole country or in Wales. This country and this people were in addition often sorely oppressed this year by the tax which the king levied on both town and country.

In this year the entire monastery of Peterborough was burned, and all the houses except the chapter house and the dormitory, and in addition to that the greater part of the village was burned. All this happened on a Friday—that was August 4.

1117. All this year King Henry stayed in Normandy because of [his] quarrel with the king of France and his other neighbors. And then in the summer the king of France and the count of Flanders with him came with a fyrd to Normandy and stayed there one night and on the next day went back without a fight. And Normandy was greatly oppressed both by taxes and by a fyrd which King Henry assembled against them. This nation was also sorely afflicted by these same multiple taxes.

This year, too, on the night of December 1, there were most terrific storms with thunder and lightning and rain and hail; and on the night of December 11 the moon remained for a long time in the night as if it were all bloody, and later was eclipsed. Also, on the night of December 16 the sky seemed very red, as if it were burning. And on the Octave of St. John the Evangelist [Jan. 3] there was a great earthquake in Lombardy, in which many churches and towers and houses fell and did a great deal of damage to men. This was a very barren year for grain, on account of the rains, which did not stop for nearly the whole year.

And Abbot Gilbert of Westminster died on December 6, and Faricius, abbot of Abingdon, on February 23; and in this same year. . . .[206]

1118. Here all this year King Henry stayed in Normandy, on account of the war of the king of France and the count of Anjou and the count of Flanders; and the count of Flanders was wounded in Normandy and, so wounded, went to Flanders. The king was greatly afflicted by their quarreling and lost a great deal both of money and

[206] About a line and a half has been left blank.

also of land; and he was troubled most by his own men, who frequently revolted from him and betrayed him and submitted to his enemies and surrendered their castles, to the detriment and betrayal of the king. England paid dearly for all this with the many taxes which did not cease this whole year.

In this year, on one evening in the week of Epiphany [Jan. 6], there was very great lightning followed by a tremendous thunder-clap.

And Queen Matilda died in Westminster on May 1 and was buried there; and Count Robert of Meulan also died this year.

Also in this year on St. Thomas' Day [Dec. 21] there was a more violent wind than anyone who was then living could remember, and that was apparent everywhere both on houses and also on trees.

This year, too, Pope Paschal died, and John of Gaeta, whose other name was Gelasius, succeeded to the papacy.

1119. All this year King Henry stayed in Normandy and was often greatly afflicted by the war with the king of France and also with his own men, who treacherously revolted from him, until the two kings came together in Normandy with their people. There the king of France was routed and all his best men captured; and afterwards many of King Henry's men who had previously opposed him with their castles submitted to him and made terms with him, and he took some of the castles by storm.

This year William, son of King Henry and Queen Matilda, went to Normandy to his father, and there the daughter of the count of Anjou was given to him and wedded [to him] as [his] wife.

On Michaelmas eve [Sept. 28] there was a great earthquake in some places here in England, though particularly in Gloucestershire and in Worcestershire.

In this same year Pope Gelasius died on this side of the Alps and was buried in Cluny, and after him the archbishop of Vienne, named Calixtus, was elected pope. Later, on St. Luke the Evangelist's Day [Oct. 18], he came to France to Rheims and there held a council, and Archbishop Thurstan of York went there. And because he received his ordination from the Pope illegally and in opposition to the archiepiscopal see of Canterbury and against the king's will, the king refused him [permission to] return to England; and so he lost his archbishopric and went with the pope to Rome.

Also in this year Count Baldwin of Flanders died of the wound which he had received in Normandy, and Charles, his cousin, succeeded him to the rule—he was son of Canute, the holy king of Denmark.

1120. This year the king of England and the king of France were reconciled; and after their reconciliation all of King Henry's own men in Normandy and the count of Flanders and the count of Ponthieu made terms with him. After this King Henry occupied his castles and his land in Normandy according to his will, and so before Advent he came here to England.

And on that journey the king's two sons, William and Richard, were drowned, and also Richard, earl of Chester, and Ottuel, his brother, and very many of the king's court—stewards and chamberlains and cupbearers and various other officers and a countless number of very fine people with them. Their death was a double grief to their friends: first, that they were so suddenly deprived of this life; second, that few of their bodies were later found anywhere.

This year the light came twice to the Sepulchre of Our Lord in Jerusalem, once at Easter and a second time on the Assumption of the Virgin [Aug. 15], as trustworthy people said who came from there.

And Archbishop Thurstan of York was reconciled to the king by the pope and came here to England and received his bishopric, though it was displeasing to the archbishop of Canterbury.

1121. Here at Christmas King Henry was in Brampton, and after that before Candlemas [Feb. 2] Adelaide was married to him at Windsor and afterwards consecrated queen—she was the daughter of the duke of Louvain [Godfrey VII].

And the moon was eclipsed on the eve of April 5, and it was fourteen days old.

And the king was in Berkeley at Easter, and afterwards at Pentecost he held a great court in Westminster and then in the summer went into Wales with a fyrd, and the Welsh came to meet him, and they made terms with him according to the king's will.

This year the count of Anjou came from Jerusalem to his country and afterwards sent here to England and had his daughter brought back who had previously been given to William, the king's son.

And on the night of Christmas Eve there was a very great wind over this whole country, and that was clearly seen in many things.

1122. In this year King Henry was in Norwich at Christmas, and at Easter he was in Northampton.

And in the spring before that the town of Gloucester was burned while the monks were singing the mass and the deacon had begun the gospel, *Preteriens Jesus*. Then the fire came into the upper part of the steeple and destroyed the whole church and all the treasures that were in it except a few books and three vestments. That was on March 8.

And afterwards, on March 22, the Tuesday after Palm Sunday, there was a very strong wind. After that many signs came far and wide over England, and many prodigies were seen and heard. And on the night of July 25 there was a very great earthquake over all Somerset and in Gloucestershire. And afterwards on September 8—that was the Nativity of the Virgin—there was a very great wind from nine in the morning until dark night.

This same year Ralph, the archbishop of Canterbury, died—that was on October 20. After that there were many sailors on the sea and on [fresh] water who said that they saw near the earth in the northeast a great and broad fire which grew in length up to the sky, and the sky divided into four parts and fought against it as if it were bound to extinguish it, and the fire then stopped growing upward toward the heavens. They saw that fire at daybreak, and it lasted until it was light everywhere. That was on December 7.

1123. In this year at Christmas King Henry was at Dunstable, and ambassadors from the count of Anjou came there to meet him; and from there he went to Woodstock, and his bishops and all his court with him. Then it happened on a Wednesday—that was on January 10 —that the king was riding in his park with Bishop Roger of Old Sarum on one side of him and Bishop Robert Bloet of Lincoln on the other, and they rode there conversing. Then the bishop of Lincoln sank down and said to the king, "Lord King, I'm dying," and the king got down from his horse and caught him in his arms and had him carried home to his lodging; and in a short time he was dead. And he was carried to Lincoln with great honor and buried in front of St. Mary's altar, and the bishop of Chester, named Robert Pecceth, buried him.

Soon after that the king sent his summonses over all England and ordered all his bishops and his abbots and his thegns to come to meet him at Gloucester at the assembly of his witan on Candlemas Day [Feb. 2]—and they did so. When they were assembled there, the king asked them to elect an archbishop to Canterbury, whomever they wished, and he would grant it to them. Then the bishops spoke among themselves and said that they never again wanted to have a man in monastic orders for archbishop over them, but all went in a body to the king and asked that they be allowed to elect a secular cleric for archbishop, whomever they wished; and the king granted it to them. All this had previously been done through the bishop of Old Sarum and through the bishop of Lincoln before he died, because they had never loved the rule of monks, but had always been against monks and their rule; and the prior and the monks of Canterbury and all the others who were men in monastic orders there opposed it fully two days. But it was of no use, for the bishop of Old Sarum was powerful and controlled all England and was opposed to it as much as he could [be] and knew [how to]. Then they elected a cleric named William of Corbeil—he was a canon of a monastery named *Cicc* [now St. Osyth]—and brought him before the king, and the king gave him the archbishopric, and all the bishops received him. Almost all the monks and earls and thegns who were there opposed him.

At the same time there came a legate of Rome whose name was Henry—he was abbot of the monastery of St. Jean d'Angely—and he came for the Peter's Pence. And he said to the king that it was unjust for a cleric to be set over monks—and [especially] seeing that previously they had legally elected an archbishop in their chapter—but the king refused to annul it [William's election] for love of the bishop of Old Sarum. Then the archbishop went to Canterbury soon after that and was received there, though it was against their will, and was at once consecrated [arch]bishop there by the bishop of London and Bishop Ernulf of Rochester and Bishop William Giffard of Winchester and Bishop Bernard of Wales and Bishop Roger of Old Sarum. Then in the spring the archbishop went at once to Rome for his pallium, and with him went Bishop Bernard of Wales and Sigefrith, abbot of Glastonbury, and Anselm, abbot of Bury St. Edmunds, and John, archdeacon of Canterbury, and Giffard, who was the king's court chaplain.

At the same time Archbishop Thurstan of York went to Rome at the pope's command and arrived there three days before the archbishop of Canterbury came, and was received there with great honor. Then the archbishop of Canterbury came and was there a full week before he could get audience with the pope—that was because the pope had been given to understand that he had received the archbishopric illegally and in opposition to the monks of the cathedral [Christ Church, Canterbury]. But that overcame Rome which overcomes the whole world—that is, gold and silver; and the pope was appeased and gave him his pallium, and the archbishop swore, on the heads of St. Peter and St. Paul, obedience to him in all things which the pope imposed on him, and [the pope] then sent him home with his blessing.

While the archbishop was away from England, the king gave the bishopric of Bath to the queen's chancellor, named Godfrey—he was born in Louvain. That was at Woodstock, on the day of the Annunciation of the Virgin [March 25]. Soon after that the king went to Winchester and stayed there the whole Easter season, and while he was there, he gave the bishopric of Lincoln to a cleric named Alexander—he was the nephew of the bishop of Old Sarum. He did this all for love of the bishop.

Then the king went from there to Portsmouth and stayed there all through Pentecost week. As soon as he had a favorable wind, he crossed to Normandy and entrusted all England to the administration and to the power of Bishop Roger of Old Sarum. Then the king stayed in Normandy this whole year, and great hostility arose between him and his thegns, so that Count Waleran of Meulan, and Amaury, and Hugh of Montfort-sur-Risle and William of Roumare and many others revolted from him and held their castles against him. And the king resolutely opposed them, and this same year he won from Waleran his castle, Pont-Audemer, and from Hugh [the castle of] Montfort-sur-Risle, and after that his success became steadily greater.

This same year, before the bishop of Lincoln came to his bishopric, nearly the whole town of Lincoln was burned, and a countless number of people, men and women, were burned; and more damage was done there than one person could tell another. That was on May 19.

1124. All this year King Henry was in Normandy; that was on account of the great hostility which he had with King Louis of France and with the count of Anjou and, most of all, with his own men.

Then it happened on the day of the Annunciation of the Virgin [March 25] that count Waleran of Meulan went from one of his castles, called Beaumont-le-Roger, to another of his castles, Vatteville—with him went Amaury, the steward of the king of France, and Hugh, son of Gervais, and Hugh of Montfort-sur-Risle, and many other good knights. Then the king's knights from all the castles that were in the vicinity came against them and fought against them and routed them and captured Count Waleran and Hugh, son of Gervais, and Hugh of Montfort-sur-Risle, and twenty-five other knights, and brought them to the king; and the king had Count Waleran and Hugh, son of Gervais, imprisoned in the castle at Rouen, and he sent Hugh of Montfort-sur-Risle to England and had him placed in cruel bonds in the castle at Gloucester. And he sent as many of the others as seemed good to him north and south to his castles into confinement. The king then went afterwards and won all the castles of Count Waleran that were in Normandy and all the others which his enemies held against him.

All this hostility was on account of the son of Duke Robert of Normandy, named William. This same William had married the younger daughter of Count Fulk of Anjou, and therefore the king of France and all the earls and all the powerful men sided with him and said that the king was wrongly keeping his brother, Robert, in confinement, and had unjustly driven his son, William, out of Normandy.

This same year there was in England much bad weather for grain and for all fruit, so that between Christmas and Candlemas [Feb. 2] seed wheat for an acre—that is, two seedlips—was sold for six shillings, and seed barley—that is, three seedlips—for six shillings, and seed oats for an acre—that is, four seedlips—for four shillings. That was because there was little grain, and the penny was so debased that the man who had one pound at a market could by no means get the value of twelve pennies for it.

In this same year the blessed Bishop Ernulf of Rochester died; he had previously been abbot of Peterborough—that was on March 15. And after that King Alexander of Scotland died on April 23, and David, his brother, who was earl of Northamptonshire, succeeded to the throne, and held both the kingdom in Scotland and the earldom in England at one time. And on December 14 the pope in Rome, named Calixtus, died, and Honorius succeeded to the papacy.

This same year after St. Andrew's Day [Nov. 30] before Christmas Ralph Basset and the king's thegns held a council of the witan at

Hundehog in Leicestershire and hanged more thieves there than had
ever been [hanged] before—that was altogether forty-four men in
that short time; and six men were deprived of their eyes and testicles.
Many trustworthy men said that many were there punished with
great injustice; but our Lord God Almighty, who sees and knows all
secret things, sees that the poor people are treated with complete injustice—first they are robbed of their possessions and then they are
killed. It was a very grievous year—the man who had any goods was
robbed of them by heavy taxes and an oppressive court; those who had
no [goods] died of hunger.

1125. In this year before Christmas King Henry sent from Normandy to England and ordered all the moneyers who were in England
to be deprived of their members: that was the right hand of each of
them and their testicles below. That was because the man who had a
pound could not get the value of a penny [for it] at a market. And
Bishop Roger of Old Sarum sent over all England and ordered them
[the moneyers] all to come to Winchester at Christmas. When they
got there, they were taken one by one and each deprived of the right
hand and the testicles below. All this was done during Twelve Nights;
and that was all [done] with great injustice, because they had ruined
the whole country with their great counterfeitings. They all paid for it.

In this year the pope of Rome sent a cardinal named John of Crema
to England. He came first to the king in Normandy, and the king received him with great honor, then entrusted him to Archbishop William of Canterbury; and he conducted him to Canterbury, and he was
received there with great honor and with a great procession, and he
sang the high mass on Easter Day at Christ's altar. And afterwards
he went over all England to all the bishoprics and abbacies that were
in this country, and he was received with honor everywhere, and all
gave him great and splendid gifts. And afterwards he held his council
in London for fully three days on the Nativity of the Virgin in September [Sept. 8] with archbishops and with suffragan bishops and abbots
and clergy and laity, and there proclaimed the same laws which Archbishop Anselm had formerly proclaimed and many more—though it
was of little use. And from there he went overseas soon after Michaelmas [Sept. 29] and so to Rome, and [with him] Archbishop William
of Canterbury and Archbishop Thurstan of York and Bishop Alex-

ander of Lincoln and John, bishop of Lothian, and Geoffrey, abbot of St. Albans, and [they] were there received by Pope Honorius with great honor and stayed there the whole winter.

In this same year there was so great a flood on St. Lawrence's Day [Aug. 10] that many villages were inundated and many men were drowned and bridges broken and grain and meadowland completely ruined, and famine and disease [raged] among men and cattle, and for all crops [it was] a worse season than there had been for many years before.

And this same year Abbot John of Peterborough died on October 14.

1126. All this year King Henry was in Normandy until after harvest time; then he came to England between the Nativity of the Virgin [Sept. 8] and Michaelmas [Sept. 29]. With him came the queen and his daughter whom he had previously given to Emperor Henry of Lorraine for his wife; and he brought with him Count Waleran and Hugh, son of Gervais, and he sent the count to *Brigg* into confinement, and from there he later sent him to Wallingford, and Hugh to Windsor and had him placed in heavy bonds.

And after Michaelmas [Sept. 29] David, king of the Scots, came from Scotland here to England, and King Henry received him with great honor, and he stayed in this country the whole year.

In this same year the king had his brother, Robert, taken from Bishop Roger of Old Sarum and committed him to his son, Robert, earl of Gloucester, and had him brought to Bristol and there placed in the castle. This was all done by the advice of his daughter and of her uncle, David, king of Scots.

1127. This year King Henry held his court at Christmas in Windsor. David, king of Scots, was there, and all the chief clergy and laity that were in England. And there he caused the archbishops and bishops and abbots and earls and all the thegns who were there to swear [to place] England and Normandy after his day in the hands of his daughter Adelaide, who had formerly been the wife of the emperor of Saxony; and afterwards he sent her to Normandy—with her went her brother, Robert, earl of Gloucester, and Brian, son of Duke Alan Fergant—and had her married to the son of the count of Anjou, whose name was Geoffrey Martel. Nonetheless [207] it displeased all

207 MS *naþema* "none the more."

the French and English; but the king did it in order to have peace from the count of Anjou and to have help against his nephew, William.

This same year in the spring Count Charles of Flanders was killed by his own men in a church where he was lying and praying to God in front of the altar during the mass. And the king of France brought the son of Duke William of Normandy and gave him the countship [of Flanders], and the natives accepted him. This same William had previously married the daughter of the count of Anjou, but they were subsequently divorced on account of consanguinity—that was all through the agency of King Henry of England. Afterwards he married the sister-in-law of the king of France [Joan, daughter of the marquis of Montferrat], and therefore the king gave him the countship of Flanders.

This same year he gave the abbacy of Peterborough to an abbot named Henry of Poitou, who had in his possession the abbacy of St. Jean d'Angely, and all the archbishops and bishops said that it was unjust and that he ought not have two abbacies in his possession. But this same Henry led the king to understand that he had left his abbacy on account of the great hostility that existed in the country and that he acted by the advice and leave of the pope of Rome and of the abbot of Cluny and because he was legate for the Peter's Pence. But that did not make it any the truer—he simply wanted to have possession of both, and did have as long as it was God's will. While a member of the secular clergy, he was bishop of Soissons; later he became a monk in Cluny and then prior in the same monastery; and afterwards he became prior in Savigny-le-Vieux; after that, because he was the kinsman of the king of England and of the count of Poitou, the count gave him the abbacy of St. Jean d'Angely. Afterwards by his great trickeries he obtained the archbishopric of Besançon and kept it for three days; then he rightly lost it, because he had previously obtained it wrongly. Later he obtained the bishopric of Saintes, which was five miles from his abbey—he kept that almost a week. The abbot of Cluny took him from there as he previously had from Besançon.

Then he reflected that if he could get firmly established in England he could have what he wanted. He then begged the king and said to him that he was an old and broken-down man and that he could not endure the great injustice and the great hostility that were in their country, and then asked particularly for the abbacy of Peterborough through him and through all his friends; and the king granted it to him because he [Henry] was his kinsman and because he was a principal in swearing oath and bearing witness when the son of the duke of Normandy and the daughter of the count of Anjou were divorced on account of their consanguinity. The abbacy was thus miserably granted between Christmas and Candlemas [Feb. 2] at London. And so he [Henry] went with the king to Winchester and from there he came to Peterborough, and there he lived exactly as drones do in a hive—all that the bees drag toward them the drones devour and drag away. So did he—all that he could take, inside and outside, from the clergy and from the laity, he sent overseas, and did no good there nor left any good there. Let no one think it strange what we say for a fact, for it was well known over the whole country, that immediately after he arrived—that was on the Sunday when *Exurge quare, O Domine* is sung—many men saw and heard many hunters hunting. The hunters were black and large and hideous and their hounds all black and broad-eyed and hideous, and they rode on black horses and on black bucks.[208] This was seen in the park itself in the village of Peterborough and in all the woods that stretched from the same village to Stamford, and the monks heard the horns blowing that they blew in the night. Trustworthy men, who noticed them at night, said from the way it seemed to them that there were probably about twenty or thirty horn-blowers. This was seen and heard from the time he arrived there all spring up to Easter. This was his entry. Of his exit we cannot yet say anything. May God provide!

1128. All this year King Henry was in Normandy on account of the hostility which existed between him and his nephew, the count of Flanders; but the count was wounded at a fight by a young man and, so wounded, he went to St. Bertin's monastery [at St. Omer] and at once became a monk there and lived five days after that. And then he died and was buried there. May God have mercy on his soul! That was on July 27.

This same year Bishop Ralph Flambard of Durham died and was buried there on September 5.

And this same year the above-mentioned Abbot Henry went to his own monastery in Poitou by the king's leave. He gave the king to

[208] On this fine version of the "Wild Hunt," see H. Flasdieck, "Harlekin," *Anglia*, LXI (1937), 329 and nn.

understand that he would completely abandon that monastery and that country and live with him there in England and in the monastery of Peterborough; but this did not make it any the truer. He did it because he wanted to stay there [at Peterborough], by his great tricks, were it a year or more, and then come back. May God Almighty have compassion on that wretched place!

This same year Hugh of the Knights Templars came from Jerusalem to the king in Normandy, and the king received him with great honor and gave him many treasures of gold and of silver. And afterwards he sent him to England, and he was received there by all good men, and all gave him treasures, and similarly in Scotland, and by him [they] sent much property all in gold and in silver to Jerusalem. And he called people [to go] out to Jerusalem, and there went with him and after him more people than ever before since the first expedition took place in the day of Pope Urban—though it was of little use. He said that a great war was preparing between the Christians and the heathen; when they arrived there, it was nothing but lying. All the people were thus miserably afflicted.

1129. In this year the king sent to England for Count Waleran and for Hugh, son of Gervais, and they there gave hostages for themselves, and Hugh went home to his own country to France and Waleran stayed with the king, and the king gave him all his land except for one of his castles. Afterwards the king came to England in the autumn and the count came with him, and they then became as good friends as they had previously been enemies.

Then by the king's advice and by his leave Archbishop William of Canterbury at once sent all over England and ordered the bishops and abbots and archdeacons and all the priors, monks, and canons that were in all the [monastic] cells in England, and then all those who had to preserve and protect Christendom, that they should all come to London at Michaelmas [Sept. 29] and there discuss all God's laws. When they had arrived, the council began on Monday and continued till Friday. When it all came out, the whole matter was about archdeacons' wives and priests' wives—that they were to abandon them by St. Andrew's Day [Nov. 30], and he who refused to do so should lose his church and his house and his home and have no further claim to them. Archbishop William of Canterbury and all the suffragan bishops who were in England made this order. And the king gave them all leave to go home; and so they went home; and all the decrees were of no use—they all held on to their wives by the king's leave, as they had previously done.

This same year Bishop William Giffard of Winchester died and was buried there on January 25; and after Michaelmas [Sept. 29] King Henry gave the bishopric to his nephew, Abbot Henry of Glastonbury. And he was consecrated bishop by Archbishop William of Canterbury on November 17.

This same year Pope Honorius died. He was hardly dead before two popes were elected there: the one was named Peter, he was a monk of Cluny and was born of the richest man of Rome—those of Rome and the duke of Sicily [Roger II] sided with him; the other was named Gregory, he was a cleric and was driven out of Rome by the other pope and his kinsmen—the emperor of Saxony [Lothaire II] and the king of France and King Henry of England and everyone on this side of the Alps sided with him. Now there was more heresy in Christendom than there had ever been before. May Christ provide a remedy for His wretched people!

This same year, on the eve of St. Nicholas' Day [Dec. 5], shortly before dawn, there was a great earthquake.

1130. This year the church of Canterbury was consecrated by Archbishop William on May 4. Present there were Bishops John of Rochester, Gilbert Universal of London, Henry of Winchester, Alexander of Lincoln, Roger of Old Sarum, Simon of Worcester, Roger of Coventry, Godfrey of Bath, Everard of Norwich, Sigefrith of Chichester, Bernard of St. David's [Pembrokeshire, Wales], Audoenus of Evreux from Normandy, John of Sées.

The fourth day after that King Henry was in Rochester, and the town was almost completely destroyed by fire; and Archbishop William and the above-mentioned bishops with him consecrated St. Andrew's Church [at Rochester]; and King Henry went overseas to Normandy in the autumn.

This same year after Easter Henry, abbot of St. Jean d'Angely, came to Peterborough and said that he had completely abandoned the monastery [of St. Jean d'Angely]. After him the abbot [of] Cluny, named Peter, came to England by the king's leave and was received with great honor wherever he came. He came to Peterborough, and Abbot Henry there promised him to get the monastery of Peterborough to be subject to Cluny for him; but it is said as a proverb: the hedge abides that which divides fields.[209] May God Almighty blot out evil counsels! And soon after that the abbot of Cluny went home to his country.

1131. This year after Christmas on a Sunday evening at the first sleep, the northern sky appeared as if it were burning fire, so that all who saw it were more terrified than they had ever been before—that was on January 11. This same year there was a worse cattle plague all over England than there had ever been before in the memory of man; it was of cattle and of pigs, so that in the villages where there had been ten or twelve ploughs going, not one was left there, and the man who had had two hundred or three hundred pigs, not one was left to him. After that the hens died. Then meat and cheese and butter ran short. May God amend it when it is His will!

And King Henry came home to England before autumn after the first feast of St. Peter [Aug. 1].

This same year, before Easter, Abbot Henry went from Peterborough overseas to Normandy and there spoke with the king and told him that the abbot of Cluny had ordered him to come to him and commit to him the abbacy of St. Jean d'Angely; and afterwards he would come home by his leave. And so he went home to his own monastery and stayed there until Midsummer Day [June 24]. And the second day after St. John's Day [June 24] the monks elected an abbot from among themselves, and brought him into church with a procession, sang *Te Deum laudamus,* rang the bells, set him on the abbot's seat, did him every obedience which they ought to do to their abbot; and the earl and all the chief men and the monks of the monastery drove the other abbot, Henry, out of the monastery. They had to—in twenty-five years they had never enjoyed one good day. Here all his great tricks failed him; now he had to creep into every corner of his big bag [to see] if there might be at least one feeble trick by which he could once more deceive Christ and all Christian people. Then he went to Cluny, and he was kept there so that he could not go either east or west. The abbot of Cluny said that they had lost the monastery of St. Jean d'Angely through him and through his great folly. Then he

---

[209] This obscure proverb, which renders literally the MS *hæge sitteð þa aceres dæleth,* does not appear in Liebermann's collection of OE proverbs and proverbial sayings (*Die Gesetze der Angelsachsen,* II, 200, 657–58), nor does it seem to have survived into later times.

could think of no better reparation for himself, but promised them and swore oaths on relics that if he were allowed to visit England, he would get the monastery of Peterborough for them, so that he would place there a prior from Cluny and a sacristan and a treasurer and a keeper of the wardrobe, and he would commit to them all the things that were inside and outside the monastery. Thus he went to France and stayed there all year. May Christ provide for the wretched monks of Peterborough and for the wretched place! Now they need the help of Christ and of all Christian people.

1132. This year King Henry came to England. Then Abbot Henry came and accused the monks of Peterborough to the king, because he wanted to subject the monastery to Cluny, so that the king was nearly fooled and sent for the monks; and through the mercy of God and through the bishop of Old Sarum and the bishop of Lincoln and the other powerful men who were there, the king then knew that he was acting treacherously. When he could [do] no more, he wanted his nephew to be abbot of Peterborough; but Christ did not will it. It was not very long after that that the king sent for him and had him give up the abbacy of Peterborough and leave the country; and the king gave the abbacy to a prior of St. Neots named Martin. He came into the monastery on St. Peter's Day [June 29] with great honor.

1135. In this year King Henry went overseas at Lammas [Aug. 1], and the second day as he lay asleep aboard ship, the day darkened over all countries, and the sun became as though it were a three-nights-old moon, and the stars [shone] around it at midday.

Men were greatly amazed and frightened and said that a great event would come after this. So it did, for the same year the king died the day after St. Andrew's Day [Nov. 30] in Normandy. Then these lands at once grew dark,[210] for everyone that could at once robbed another. Then his son and his friends took his body and brought [it] to England and buried it at Reading. He was a good man and there was great fear of him. No man dared wrong another in his time. He made peace for man and beast. Whoever carried his load of gold and silver, no man dared say anything but good to him.

In the meantime his nephew, Stephen of Blois, had come to England,

---

[210] On the emended MS reading, *þa þestre[den] sona þas landes,* see H. Bradley, "'Trẹson,' in the Anglo-Saxon Chronicle," *Modern Language Review,* XII (1917), 72–74; N. R. Ker, "Some Notes on the Peterborough Chronicle," *Medium Aevum,* III (1934), 136 f.

and he went to London, and the people of London received him and
sent for Archbishop William of Corbeil and consecrated him king on
Christmas Day. In this king's time there was nothing but discord and
evil and robbery, for the powerful men who were traitors soon rose
against him—first and foremost, Baldwin of Réviers, and he held
Exeter against him; and the king besieged it, and afterwards Baldwin
came to terms. Then the others went and held their castles against him,
and David, king of Scotland, began fighting against him. In spite of
that, their ambassadors then intervened and they came together and
were reconciled—though it was of little use.

1137. This year King Stephen went overseas to Normandy and
was received there, because they supposed that he would be as his
uncle had been and because he had obtained his treasure; but he distributed it and scattered it foolishly. King Henry had gathered much gold
and silver, and no good was done for his soul with it.

When King Stephen came to England, he held his assembly at Oxford, and there he arrested Bishop Roger of Old Sarum and his
nephews, Alexander, bishop of Lincoln, and Chancellor Roger, and
put them all in prison until they surrendered their castles. When the
traitors realized that he was a mild and soft and good man and did not
enforce justice, they all committed terrible crimes.[211] They had done
him homage and sworn oaths, but they did not keep faith. All of them
were forsworn and their pledges abandoned, for every powerful man
built his castles and held them against him—and they filled the country
full of castles. They severely oppressed the wretched men of the country with work on castles; when the castles were built, they filled them
with devils and evil men. Then they seized those men who they
thought had any property—men and women, both by night and by day
—and put them in prison to get their gold and silver and tortured
them with indescribable torture, for never were there any martyrs so
tortured as they were. They were hung up by the feet and smoked with
foul smoke. They were hung by the thumbs or by the head, and coats
of mail were hung on their feet. Knotted string was placed about their
heads and twisted until it went to the brain. They put them in a prison
in which there were serpents and snakes and toads, and killed them

[211] "Terrible crimes" for the MS *wunder* (generally translated "wonder") follows
J. S. P. Tatlock, "The 'Chronicle' Misunderstood," *American Historical Review*,
XLI (1935-36), 703.

that way. They put some into a torture house, that is, in a chest that was short and narrow and shallow, and put sharp stones in it and pressed the man inside so that they broke all his limbs. In many of the castles there were fillets and snares—these were chain fetters one of which was all that two or three men could carry. It was adjusted in this way, namely, fastened to a beam, and they placed a sharp iron around the man's throat and his neck so that he could not [move] in any direction—neither sit nor lie nor sleep, but [had to] support the whole [weight of the] iron. They killed many thousands by starvation.

I neither know how to, nor can I, recount all the horrors and all the tortures that they did to the wretched men in this country. And it lasted the nineteen years that Stephen was king, and it kept getting worse and worse. They regularly levied taxes on the villages and called it tallage.[212] When the wretched men had nothing more to give, they robbed and burned all the villages so that you might easily go a whole day's journey [and] you would never find a man settled in a village or land tilled. Then grain was dear, also meat and cheese and butter, because there was none in the country. Wretched men died of starvation; some went begging alms who at one time were rich men; others fled the country.

Never before had there been greater wretchedness in the country; never had heathen men done worse than they did; for over and over again they failed to spare either church or churchyard, but seized all the valuables that were there and afterwards burned the church and everything with it. Nor did they spare the land of bishop or abbot or priest, but robbed monks and clerics, and every man [robbed] another anywhere he could. If two or three men came riding to a village, all the villagers fled before them—they supposed that they were robbers. The bishops and clergy cursed them constantly, but that was nothing to them, for they were all accursed and forsworn and lost.

Wherever men tilled, the earth bore no grain, for the land was totally ruined by such acts; and they openly said that Christ and his saints slept. Such and more than we can relate we endured nineteen years for our sins.

In all this evil time Abbot Martin held his abbacy [of Peterborough] twenty and a half years and eight days with great labor and provided

212 In the original, *tenserie*.

the monks and the guests with everything they needed and exercised much charity in the house; and nevertheless he worked on the church and added lands and income to it and richly endowed it and had it roofed and on St. Peter's Day [June 29] brought them [the monks] into the new minster with much honor—that was *the year 1140 from the incarnation of the Lord, twenty-three from the burning of the monastery.* And he went to Rome and there was well received by Pope Eugenius and there obtained privileges: one for all the lands of the abbacy and another for the lands which belong to the office of sacristan, and, if he had lived longer, he had intended to do the same for the office of treasurer. And he got back the lands which powerful men held by force: from William Malduit, who held the castle of Rockingham, he got Cottingham and Easton Maudit, and from Hugh of *Waltevile* he got Irthlingborough and Stanwick, and from Aldwinkle sixty shillings each year. And he created many monks and planted vineyards and made many improvements and made the village better than it had previously been, and was a good monk and a good man, and therefore God and good men loved him.

Now we will tell something of what happened in King Stephen's time. In his time [213] the Jews of Norwich bought a Christian child before Easter and tortured him with all the same tortures with which our Lord was tortured, and on Good Friday hanged him on a cross in hatred [214] of our Lord and afterwards buried him. They supposed that this would stay hidden, but our Lord revealed that he was a holy martyr, and the monks took him and solemnly buried him in the church, and through our Lord he performed wonderful and various miracles, and he was called St. William.

1138. In this year David, king of Scotland, came with an immense fyrd to England—he wanted to conquer this country. And against him came Earl William of Aumâle, to whom the king had committed York, and the other loyal men with a few followers, and fought against them [the Scots] and routed the king at the Standard [near Northallerton] and killed a great many of his troops.

1140.[215] In this year King Stephen wanted to seize Robert, earl

[213] Probably about 1145.
[214] MS *luue* "love."
[215] This long entry is simply a collection of isolated items covering most of Stephen's reign and arranged with no regard for chronology. The correct or probably correct dates of the individual events have been inserted in square brackets; see Plum-

of Gloucester, son of King Henry, but he was unable to, for he [Robert] became aware of it [April, 1137].

After that in the spring the sun and the day darkened about noontime as men were eating; then candles were lit to eat by; and that was on March 20 [1140]—men were greatly amazed.

After that William, archbishop of Canterbury, died [Nov. 21, 1136], and the king made Theobald archbishop who had been abbot of Bec [at Le Bec-Hellouin].

After that a very great war developed between the king and Randolph, earl of Chester [Dec., 1140], because he [Stephen] did not give him all that he [Randolph] demanded of him as he [Stephen] did to everyone else; but always, the more he [Stephen] gave to them, the worse they were to him. The earl held Lincoln against the king and took from him all that he was supposed to have, and the king went there and besieged him and his brother, William of Roumare, in the castle, and the earl stole out and went for Robert, earl of Gloucester, and brought him there with a large fyrd, and they fought violently on Candlemas [Feb. 2, 1141] against their lord and captured him—for his men betrayed him and fled—and they led him to Bristol and there put him in prison and fetters. Then all England was more disturbed than it had been before, and nothing but evil was in the country.

After that came [Sept., 1139] King Henry's daughter, who had been empress in Germany and was now countess of Anjou, and she came to London and the people of London wanted to seize her, and she fled [June, 1141] and lost a great deal there.

After that Henry, bishop of Winchester, King Stephen's brother, spoke with Earl Robert and with the empress and swore oaths to them that he would never again side with the king his brother and he cursed all the men who held with him, and told them that he would give up Winchester to them [March, 1141]; and he induced them to come there. When they were there, the king's queen came with all her force and besieged them [Aug., 1141]; there was great famine inside. When they could hold out no longer, they stole out and fled; and those outside became aware of it and followed them and captured

mer, II, 313–14, where the authorities are quoted, and further, J. H. Round, *Geoffrey de Mandeville* (London, 1892), and the surveys of Norman history listed in the note to 1066.

Robert, earl of Gloucester [Sept. 14, 1141], and led him to Rochester and there put him in prison; and the empress fled into a monastery [probably Gloucester]. Then the wise men went between the king's friends and the earl's friends and arranged such terms that the king should be let out of prison for the earl and the earl for the king, and they did so [Nov., 1141].

Then after that the king and Earl Randolph came to terms at Stamford [1142] and swore oaths and confirmed pledges that neither would betray the other; but it was of no use, for the king later arrested him in Northampton through wicked counsel, and put him in prison, and through worse counsel again let him out, on condition that he swear on relics and provide hostages that he would surrender all his castles. He surrendered some, and others he did not, and then he did more harm here than he should have [1146].

Then England was completely split up: some sided with the king and others with the empress; for, when the king was in prison, the earls and the powerful men supposed that he would never get out again, and they came to an agreement with the empress and brought her to Oxford and gave her the town [March or May, 1141]. When the king got out, he heard about this, and he took his fyrd and besieged her in the tower, and she was let down at night from the tower with ropes and stole out and so fled and went on foot to Wallingford [Dec., 1142].

After that she went overseas [1147]. And the men of Normandy all turned from the king to the count of Anjou, some voluntarily and others under compulsion, for he besieged them till they surrendered their castles, and they got no help from the king [1141-44].

Then Eustace, the king's son, went to France and married the sister [Constance] of the king of France [Feb., 1140], expecting thereby to get hold of Normandy, but he had little success, and justly, for he was a bad man. For wherever he came, he did more harm than good —he robbed the lands and levied heavy taxes. He brought his wife to England and placed her in the castle at Canterbury. She was a good woman, but she had little happiness with him, and Christ did not will that he should long rule, and he died [Aug., 1153] and his mother also [May 3, 1152].

And the count of Anjou died [Sept. 7, 1151], and his son, Henry, succeeded to the countship. And the queen of France was divorced from the king [March, 1152] and she came to young Count Henry, and he took her for his wife [May, 1152] and all Poitou with her. Then he went with a large fyrd to England [Jan., 1153] and won castles, and the king went against him with a much larger fyrd; and nevertheless they did not fight, but the archbishop and the wise men intervened and made the agreement [Nov. 6, 1153] that the king should be lord and king while he lived, and after his day Henry should be king. And he [Henry] held him for father, and he [Stephen] him for son, and peace and concord was to exist between them and in all England. This and the other agreements that they made the king and the count swore to hold, and the bishops and the earls and all the powerful men. Then the count was received at Winchester and at London with great honor, and everyone did him homage and swore to keep the peace; and it soon became a much better peace than there had ever been here. Then the king was stronger than he had ever been before; and the count went overseas and all the people loved him because he exercised good justice and made peace.

1154. In this year King Stephen died and was buried where his wife and his son were buried at Faversham, the monastery they had founded. When the king died, the count was overseas and no one dared do anything but good on account of the great fear of him. When he came to England, he was received with great honor and consecrated king in London on the Saturday before Christmas; and he held a great court there.

The same day that Martin, abbot of Peterborough, was to go there, he took sick and died on January 2, and the monks within a day elected another from among themselves who was named William of *Walte-vile,* a good cleric and a good man and well loved of the king and of all good men; and they solemnly buried the abbot in a church. And the abbot-elect and the monks with him went at once to the king at Oxford; and he gave him the abbacy. And he went at once to Lincoln and was there consecrated abbot before he came home, and afterwards he was received with great honor at Peterborough with a great procession; and so he was also at Ramsey and at Thorney and at . . . . and Spalding and at . . . . and . . . . and he now is abbot and has started off well. Christ grant him a good end! [216]

[216] The mutilated state of the end of the MS makes several readings in the final lines conjectural. On the end of the MS, see the Introduction.

APPENDIX A

NOTES ON CERTAIN PLACES IN THE CHRONICLE

The years in which the places are mentioned in the Chronicle are here given in parentheses. Where the original name is lost or the site is unknown or dubious, the Old English form is used and the name is printed in italics. The locations of a few of the charter sites on the one-inch maps of the Ordinance Survey (*OS*) have been recorded. The abbreviation *PN* followed by a county name refers to the volumes of the English Place-Name Society publications. *DEPN* denotes E. Ekwall, *Concise Oxford Dictionary of English Place-Names,* 2d ed. (Oxford, 1940). Magoun, I, refers to F. P. Magoun, Jr., "Territorial, Place-, and River-Names in the Old-English Chronicle, *A*-Text (Parker Ms.)," *Harvard Studies and Notes in Philology and Literature,* XVIII (1935), 69–111. Magoun, II, refers to the same author's "Territorial, Place-, and River-Names in the Old-English Annals, *D*-Text (Ms. Cotton Tiberius B. IV)," *ibid.,* XX (1938), 147–80.

Aclea (782, 789, 851). Whether or not these three occurrences refer to the same place is dubious. Oakley Farm, Dorset, near Woodyates, has been suggested for the site of the synods of 782 and 789 (see Magoun, II), while the battle site of 851 is apparently in Surrey, though the identification with Ockley, Surrey, is probably incorrect (Magoun, I).

Æþelhuniglond (675). A lost site; on the name itself, see S. Karlström, *Old English Compound Place-Names in-ING* (Uppsala, 1927), p. 117.

Allemanic territory (788). A district centering on the present Baden.

Ancarig (656). Apparently "hermit island" and evidently a locality north of Peterborough in the Crowland district. There seems to be no reason to identify it with the old and well-established name of Thorney, Cambridgeshire (see Thorpe, *The Anglo-Saxon Chronicle,* I, 393; Plummer, II, 27; but cf. *PN Cambridge,* pp. 280, lx).

Angle (449). The traditional home of the Angles in East Schleswig.

Armenia, error for Armorica (Preface). Bede (HE I. 1) has (*de tractu*) *armoricano*. The error may have crept in either through a further corruption of the incorrect *armonicano* in some Bede MSS or through the reading of *Armenia* a few lines above in Bede.

Arwe, River (1016.) The identification with the River Orwell, Suffolk, is not certain, but some river in East Anglia is apparently meant.

Asen Dike, Northamptonshire (656). *OS* 158 A5–6.

Ashdown, Berkshire (648, 661, 871, 1006). Originally an extensive section of the Berkshire downs (Stevenson, *Asser's Life,* pp. 235–37). The name survives in Ashdown Park in Ashbury, Berkshire (A. Mawer, "Some Place-Name Identifications in the Anglo-Saxon Chronicle," in *Anglia* [Berlin, 1925], I, 44).

Ashingdon, Essex (1016, 1020). In 1016 the place name is in the making (*Assandun*, "Assa's hill").

Ashton, Northamptonshire (963). Either *OS* 157 D9 or *OS* 171 C8.

Assa's hill (1016). See Ashingdon; identification with Ashdon, Essex (M. Christy, "The Battle of 'Assandun'; Where Was It Fought?," *Journal of the British Archeological Association*, n. s., XXXI [1925], 168-90) is not likely.

Austrasia (892). Eastern kingdom of the Franks.

Auvergne, district of (1102). This may be an error for Alemannia, "Alemannic territory."

Aylesford, Kent (455, 1016). The battle site of 455 appears as *Ægelesþreþ* in *E* and *D*, *Agælesþreþ* in *A*, and *Ægelesford* in *G*. On Mawer's objection (*op. cit.*, p. 44) to the identification with Aylesford, see J. K. Wallenberg, *Kentish Place-Names* (Uppsala, 1931), pp. 286 f., n. 1.

Beandun (614). If the *Beamdun*-form of *B* and *C* is correct, this might formally be identified with Bampton, Oxfordshire.

Bedanheafod (675). A lost site.

Beorgford (752). Possibly one of the Mercian Barfords.

Berkeley, district of, Gloucestershire (1087). The district name, *Beorclea hyrnesse*, survives as the name of a manor, Berkeley Harness, in Berkeley.

Bernicia, English kingdom of (634, 678). Later the northern portion of Northumbria.

Biedcanford (571). Probably not to be confused with *Bedanford* = Bedford (see Magoun, I, under *Bedcanford*).

Bolhiðe, gate of (1070). One of the gates of the monastery of Peterborough.

Bradanœ, Cambridgeshire (656). "Broad River," an old course of the Nene, whose name is preserved in Bradney Farm (*OS* 172 A8) and Bradney House (*OS* 172 B8).

Breedon-on-the-Hill, Leicestershire, (675, 731). The *Breodun* of the MS in 731 has also been identified with Bredon Hill, Worcestershire (see Magoun, II).

Brigg (1102, 1126). A short form for the *Cwatbrycg* of the *A*-text, and accordingly not to be identified with Bridgnorth, Shropshire, but with Quatt and Quatford, near Bridgnorth, or with a lost site in the vicinity (see Magoun, I, under *Cwatbrycg*).

Brunanburh (937). An unidentified site. For the many discussions of this battle site, see Magoun, I; Hoffman-Hirtz, *Une Chronique anglo-saxonne*, p. 115, n. 1; A. Campbell, *The Battle of Brunanburh* (London, 1938), pp. 57-80; most recently, A. H. Smith, in *London Medieval Studies*, Vol. I, Part 1 (1937), 56-58, urges an identification with Bromborough, Wirral (Cheshire), on the Mersey River.

Burh, see Peterborough.

Cære (710). Possibly River Carron, Stirlingshire, Scotland (see Magoun, II).

Caninganmersc (1010). Identifications with several Southampton, Wiltshire, and Hampshire sites have been suggested (see Magoun, II, under *Cane<n>ganmersc*).

Carhampton, Somerset (833, 840). A parish near Dunster.

Carisbrooke, Isle of Wight (530, 544). A village on Lukely Brook.

Cealchyð (785). Chelsea, Middlesex, and Chalkhythe, Kent, have been suggested (Magoun, I; see most recently *PN Middlesex,* pp. 85–86).

Cedenac (675). Possibly a site in Charnwood Forest, Leicestershire, as first suggested by Wm. Stubbs, in *Archæological Journal,* XVIII (1861), 202 f.

Cerdicesora (495, 514). An unidentified site, apparently in Hampshire (see Magoun, I).

Chiltern Hills (1009). In Oxfordshire, Buckinghamshire, Bedfordshire, Hertfordshire.

Cicc (1123). Now St. Osyth, Essex.

Clofesho (822). Possibly Cliffe at Hoo, Kent (Magoun, I; see also Plummer, II, 69–70).

Corfe Castle, Dorset (979). The actual phrase of the MS, *Corfes geat,* survives in Coryates, many miles west of Corfe Castle.

Costesford (675). An unidentified site.

Crecganford (456). Probably Crayford, Kent; but see Magoun, I, and *DEPN.*

Cuckhamsley Barrow, Berkshire (1006). A popular distortion of this name appears in the by-form, Skutchamfly.

Cuggedic (656). A lost site.

Cymenesora (477). Probably in Sussex, near, but not identical with, Keynor (see Magoun, I).

Dægsanstan (603). Probably Dawstane in Liddesdale, Roxburghshire, Scotland (see Magoun, I).

Deira, English kingdom of (634, 643, 678). Later the southern portion of Northumbria.

Dereuorð (656). MS *Dereuord,* "deer enclosure." A lost site.

Eadwinesclif (761). An unidentified site, perhaps in the Eildon Hills, Roxburghshire, Scotland (see Magoun, II).

Eahte hundred (963). Once the field district around Oundle, Northamptonshire.

Ecgbrihtesstan (878). A lost site, perhaps near West Knoyle village, Wiltshire (see Magoun, I; Stevenson, *Asser's Life,* pp. 267–69).

Ellandun (823). In Wiltshire—possibly the down west of Swindon (see Oman, *England,* p. 392).

Elvet Hall, Durham (762). Now a ward of the city of Durham.

Eðandun (878). Probably Edington, Wiltshire, but Edington, Somerset, has also been suggested.

Exe River, mouth of, Devon (1001). The town Exmouth is of later origin.

Eye, Northamptonshire (963). *OS* 158 D4.

Fenland, the (1080, 1098). In Huntingdonshire, Norfolk, Cambridgeshire, Lincolnshire.

Feþanleah (584). Faddiley, Cheshire, is unlikely, and Fretherne, Gloucestershire, is impossible.

Feðermuð (656). MS -*mud*. A lost "junction of four streams."

Five Boroughs (1013, 1015). The five towns, Leicester, Lincoln, Nottingham, Stamford (Lincolnshire), and Derby, federated under the Danes.

Flanders (1075, 1085, 1096, 1100, 1102, 1117, 1118, 1119, 1120, 1127, 1128). In the eleventh century Flanders extended from Ghent to the littoral between Calais and the Escaut.

Folies (656). Cf. Folly River in the parish of Peakirk, Northamptonshire.

Freoricburna (777). A lost brook-site.

Gerberoy, dép. Oise (1079). For this identification of the *Gerborneð* of the text, see E. A. Freeman, *History of the Norman Conquest,* IV (Oxford, 1871), 439, n. 1.

Golden Borough, the (1052, 1066). An occasional designation for Peterborough. Cf. Wretched Borough.

Grætecros (656). A lost Northamptonshire site.

Hæfe (710). The River Avon, Stirlingshire, Scotland, or the Firth of Forth.

Hamoaze, the, Devon and Cornwall (997). The estuary of the Tamar.

Hardanger, district of, Norway (787). The area about Hardanger Fjord in the southwest of Norway.

Heabureahg, island of (686). The island no longer exists, but the name probably survives in Avery Farm, Kent, situated at the extremity of the Hoo Allhallows promontory.

Heanbyrig (675). An unidentified site.

Helaþyrna (778). An unidentified site near High Coniscliffe, Durham.

Helge å (1025). River in Skåne province, formerly Denmark, now Sweden.

Heopwinesfleot (449). Probably Ebbsfleet, Kent, but see Erik Tengstrand, *Genitival Composition in Old English Place-Names* (Uppsala, 1940), pp. 314–17.

Hoge (686). Probably Hoo Allhallows, Kent.

Hrepingas (675). Probably the Rippingale (Leicestershire) district, though not necessarily Rippingale itself.

Hundehog (1124). Plummer's identification with Hundcot, *rectior* Huncote, Leicestershire, is not likely on formal grounds (see *DEPN*).

Icanho (653). A lost site probably at or near Boston, Lincolnshire.

Iglea (878). A lost site, Iley Oak, Wiltshire, probably identical with the present Southleigh Wood.

Ipswich, Suffolk (991). MS *G . . . wic.*

King's Cliff, Northamptonshire (656). *OS* 157 F6.

King's Delph, Cambridgeshire (963). *OS* 172 A4–5.

Lindisfarne, island of, Northumberland (779, 780, 782, 793, 803). Now more usually Holy Island.

Lindsey, district of, Leicestershire (627, 768, 874, 993, 1013, 1014). The district covering formerly the present county of Lincolnshire, now only the northern part.

Lodeshac (675). An unidentified site.

Lothian, Scotland (1091, 1125). The northern district of Northumbria (see W. J. Watson, *The History of the Celtic Place-Names of Scotland* [Edinburgh, 1926], p. 101).

Lufgeard (675). An unidentified site.

Lympne River, mouth of (892). Lympne Harbor, Kent.

Mæredun (871). Marden, Wiltshire, is unlikely (A. Mawer, "Some Place-Name Identications in the Anglo-Saxon Chronicles," in *Anglica* [Berlin, 1925], I, 49–50) ; cf. Magoun, I, under *Mere-tun*).

Maldon, Essex (991). See E. D. Laborde, "The Site of the Battle of Maldon," *EHR*, XL (1925), 161–73.

Maserfeld (641). On the suggested identification with Oswestry, Shropshire, see Plummer's *Bede*, II, 152; cf. Hodgkin, *History*, p. 284*n*; Oman, *England*, pp. 280 f.

Mearcredesburnansteð (485). Apparently in Sussex.

Medeshamsted (654, 656, 963). Early name of Peterborough, *q.v.*

Medeswæl (654). The well from which Peterborough is said to derive its first name, *Medeshamsted*.

Merantun (755). The identification with Merton, Surrey, is dubious.

Merelad (963.) An old channel running between Whittlesey Mere, Huntingdonshire, and the Nene, Northamptonshire and Lincolnshire.

Mowbray (1087). Montbray, dép. Manche.

Must (963). Formerly an arm of the Nene, Northamptonshire and Lincolnshire, running into the Ouse, Northamptonshire and Norfolk— now called Cat's Water, Northamptonshire. See *PN Northamptonshire*, p. 2, where Cat's Water is not, however, identified with the earlier Must. See *Map of Britain in the Dark Ages* (Southampton, 1935), south sheet D7.

Natanleag, district of (508). (Miswritten *Nazanleog; Natanleag* in *ABC*.) The old district name appears in Nately Scures, Hampshire.

Naze, the, Essex (1052). A headland south of Hamford Water.

Neustria (885, 887). Western kingdom of the Franks.

Olanig (1016). Probably Alney Island, Gloucestershire, in the River Severn (see Magoun, II).

Ouse River (1010). The Great Ouse; through Northamptonshire, Buckinghamshire, Bedfordshire, Huntingdonshire, Cambridgeshire, and Norfolk.

Paccelad (656). A lost channel in the vicinity of Whittlesey Mere, Huntingdonshire.

Pentecost Castle (1052). Apparently the famous Richard's Castle, Herefordshire, built by Richard, son of Scrob, under Edward the Confessor.

Peterborough. The earliest name of Peterborough was *Medeshamsted,* followed by *Burh,* "borough," in the tenth century (see 963), which was extended to Peterborough only in the fourteenth century.

Pincanhealh (788). Probably Finchale, Durham, but see Magoun, II.

Quentavic, dép. Pas-de-Calais (839). A once-important harbor, no longer existing, at the mouth of the Canche, 2 km. south of Etaples.

Raggewith (656). An unidentified site.

Robert's Castle (1052). An unidentified place.

Romney Marsh, Kent (796). Formerly a large fen-district in southern Kent.

Saxony (778, 1106, 1127, 1129). A district in northwestern Germany centering about the Elbe-Weser region.

Scælfremere (656). A lost fen-site south of Peterborough.

Scuffenhalch (675). An unidentified site.

Seletun (779). Either Selby, Yorkshire West Riding, or Salton, Yorkshire North Riding (see Magoun, II).

Seven Boroughs, the (1015). The Five Boroughs (*q.v.*), with, perhaps, York and Chester.

Snowdon, Carnavonshire, Wales (1095). Here some place in the Snowdonia district is meant.

Thorp (963). Longthorpe or Thorpe Hall, Northamptonshire, in Peterborough parish.

Throckenholt, Cambridgeshire (656). *OS* 158 B8.

Wættleburne (675). An unidentified brook.

Wagele (664). See Plummer's *Bede,* II, 195–96, for the obscure site of the burial place of Tuda, bishop of Lindisfarne.

Waltevile (1137, 1154). The identification with the modern Thorp Waterville, Northamptonshire, seems dubious in the light of the later spellings, all with *Water-*. See *PN Northamptonshire,* p. 219.

Warmington, Northamptonshire (963). *OS* 171 B8.

Watling Street (1013). In its fullest extension, the Roman road from the east coast of Kent through London and westwards to Wroxeter, Shropshire.

Weald, the (477, 755, 892). In Kent, Surrey, Sussex, Hampshire.

Whittlesey Mere, Huntingdonshire (656, 963). *OS* 172 B4.

Wibbandun (568). The old identification with Wimbledon, Surrey, is impossible—see *PN Surrey,* p. 38, n. 1.

Wigborough, Somerset (851). The name now belongs to a farm near South Petherton.

Winwidfeld (654). The river Uinuaed (Bede III. 24) near which this battle was fought was apparently in the vicinity of Leeds, Yorkshire

West Riding; but see Oman, *England,* p. 284, n. 3. There exists near Leeds a Win moor (Hodgkin, *History,* I, 382 f., n. 1a).

Wippedesfleot (465). An unidentified site.

Wodnesbeorh (592, 715). Probably Adam's Grave, a rise near Alton Priors, Wiltshire.

Wretched Borough, the (1066). An occasional designation for Peterborough. Cf. Golden Borough.

APPENDIX B

NOTES ON CERTAIN PERSONS IN THE CHRONICLE

The years in which the persons are mentioned in the Chronicle are here given in parentheses.

Abba, alderman (656). MS *Abon*.

Ælfmær (1011). Possibly identical with Ælfmær, abbot of St. Augustine's. Canterbury, appearing in the same year.

Aidan, king of the Scots of Dalriada (603). MS *Ægðan*.

Bachsecg, Danish king (871). ON *Bakskiki* (?).

Condidan, British king (577). Some have seen in this name the Cynddylan of the well-known Llywarch Hen poetry (Plummer, II, 17; cf. Oman, *England,* p. 246, n. 1).

Crida (593). This name may possibly stand for *Creoda,* an early king of Mercia (Plummer, II, 18).

Cutha (568, 571). On the difficulty of placing this and the Cutha of 584 in the West Saxon pedigree—the shortened name can stand for Cuthwulf, Cuthwine, etc.—see Plummer, II, 16; Oman, *England,* p. 248, n. 2.

Cwichelm (593). A person of doubtful identity.

Cynfael, British king (577). MS *Coinmail,* probably error for *Commail = Conmail.*

Dalriadi (Preface, 603). The inhabitants of the Irish kingdom Dalriada (Argyllshire, Scotland) colonized from Dalriada, county Antrim, Ireland.

Donald, brother of Malcolm III (1093, 1094, 1097). MS *Dufenal.*

East Angles (906). Here refers to the Scandinavians settled in East Anglia.

Ecglaf (1025). Possibly the brother-in-law of Earl Godwine.

Farinmail, British king (577). Possibly identical with Nennius' Fernmail (Ffyrnfael).

Geraint, king of Cornwall (710). MS *Gerente.*

Godwine, archbishop of Lyon (693). MS *Godune.*

Gruffydd, king of North Wales (1055, 1063, 1097). MS *Griffin.*

Heardbert (778). Perhaps identical with the Heardbert of 798.

Hereward (1070, 1071). The familiar by-name, "the Wake," is unhistorical and was attached by a Peterborough chronicler in the fourteenth century who took the name from the Wake family of Bourne, Leicestershire; whence Kingsley's title.

Hwicce (800). A tribe occupying Gloucestershire, Worcestershire, and the southwest part of Warwickshire.

Jehmarc, a Scottish prince (1031). This corrupted name is possibly to be equated with Imeirgi, Celtic king of Argyll.

Lothen, Danish viking (1046). ON *Loðinn.*

Mægla, son of Port (501). The name appears to be of British origin.

Mælbeth, Scottish prince (1031). This name is commonly, but erroneously, identified with the famous Macbeth—see Plummer, II, 207.

Merewald, brother of King Wulfhere (656). MS *Merwala.*

Myranheafod, a nickname of Thurcytel's (1010). The name can be glossed "mare's head" or "ant's head."

Nunna, king of Sussex (710). MS *Nun.*

Oisc, son of Hengest (455, 456, 465, 473, 488). A late equivalent, through popular, non-etymological association, is Æsc.

Sidrac, Danish jarl (871). ON *Sigtryggr* (?).

Sigebald (710). MS *H-* for *S-.*

Sigeric, archbishop of Canterbury (989, 991, 995). MS *Siric.*

Spearhafoc, abbot of Abingdon (1046, 1048). A nickname: sparhawk, *i. e.,* "sparrowhawk."

Thored, son of Gunner (966). Possibly identical with the Earl Thored of 992—see Plummer, II, 159-60.

Thurcytel Myranheafod, Danish leader (1010). ON *þorkell merhofði.*

Ulf (1025). Possibly brother-in-law of King Canute.

Webhard, joint king in Kent (692). Bede v. 8: *Suæbhard.*

BIBLIOGRAPHY

BIBLIOGRAPHICAL NOTICES

Gross, Charles. Sources and Literature of English History. 2d ed. London, 1915. Pp. 233–37.

Hoffman-Hirtz, Marie. Une Chronique anglo-saxonne. Strasbourg, 1933. Pp. 133–43.

Hoops, Johannes. "Sachsenchronik," in *Reallexikon der germanischen Altertumskunde* (Strasbourg, 1911 ff.).

Kennedy, A. G. A Bibliography of Writings on the English Language. Cambridge, Mass., 1927. Nos. 3443–50, 4546–48.

Plummer, Charles. Two of the Saxon Chronicles Parallel. 2 vols. Oxford, 1892–99. Vol. II, pp. xxiii–cxxxvii *passim*.

PARTIAL AND COMPLETE EDITIONS OF E [1]

Gibson, Edmund. Chronicon Saxonicum ex MSS codicibus nunc primum integrum edidit ac Latinum fecit Edmundus Gibson. Oxford, 1692. Based on E with extracts and collations from *A, B, F, G*. Contains also an annotated list of place-name elements and an *explicatio* of place names in the chronicles.

Ingram, James. The Saxon Chronicle, with an English Translation, and Notes, Critical and Explanatory. London, 1823; London and New York, Everyman's Library, 1912.
The early part in the main follows Gibson; the remainder is a conflation of all seven manuscripts.

Petrie, Henry. "The Anglo-Saxon Chronicle." In *Monumenta Historica Britannica,* I (1948), 291–466.
A reconstructed text based on *A* to 975 with passages from other texts placed in brackets, and the remainder to 1066 from *A, C, D, E, F, G,* the source being noted for each annal.

Thorpe, Benjamin. The Anglo-Saxon Chronicle, According to the Several Original Authorities. Vol. I. London, 1861.
The six manuscripts parallel, but with a certain amount of emendation, conflation, rearrangement, and omission.

Earle, John. Two of the Saxon Chronicles Parallel. Oxford, 1865.
A faithful reprint of *A* and *E* with supplementary extracts from the other manuscripts.

Plummer, Charles. Two of the Saxon Chronicles Parallel. 2 vols. Oxford, 1892–99.
A revision of Earle with some extracts omitted and others added. Excellent text, introduction, notes, and index.

[1] Listed in chronological order.

PARTIAL TRANSLATIONS OF *E* [2]

Gibson, above.

[Gurney, Anna]. A Literal Translation of the Anglo-Saxon Chronicle. Norwich, 1819 (for private circulation).
An independent, unannotated translation to 1066 from Gibson's text.

Ingram, above.

Giles, J. A. The Venerable Bede's Ecclesiastical History of England. Also the Anglo-Saxon Chronicle. London, 1847.
Based on Anna Gurney's translation collated with Ingram's. Giles mentions also Petrie's translation (to 1066), then unpublished.

Petrie, above.

Stevenson, Joseph. "The Anglo-Saxon Chronicle," *Church Historians of England*. London, 1853. Vol. II, Part I, pp. 1–168.
An almost exact reprint of Petrie up to 1066, the remainder independently translated from Ingram's text occasionally collated with the Laud MS.

Thorpe, above.
Apparently translated from Petrie's text of the original for the pre-Conquest section.

Gomme, E. E. C. The Anglo-Saxon Chronicle. London, 1909.
The translation follows Plummer's text and arrangement.

Viglione, Francesco. Studio critico-filologica sul' "Anglo-Saxon Chronicle." Pavia, 1922.
Translation of extracts, mainly from *A* and *E*.

Dahl, Torsten. Den oldengelske Krønike i Udvalg, oversat med Indledning og Noter. Copenhagen, 1936.
The extracts are mainly concerned with Anglo-Scandinavian affairs.

SOURCES OF *E* AND RELATIONSHIP TO THE OTHER
CHRONICLES

Birch, W. de Gray. Cartularium Saxonicum. 3 vols. London, 1885–93.

[English, H. S.] Ancient History, English and French. London, 1830.
Principally on the authorship of the chronicles.

Grubitz, Ernst. Kritische Untersuchung über die angelsächsischen Annalen bis zum Jahre 893. Göttingen, 1868.

Howorth, H. H. "The Anglo-Saxon Chronicle, Its Origin and History, Part I. The So-Called 'Peterborough Chronicle' or MS. E.," *Archæological Journal*, LXV (1908), 141-204.
Mainly an examination of the Peterborough interpolations.

—— "The Anglo-Saxon Chronicle, Its Origin and History, Part III. The Lost MS. EE and its relation to MS. D, the Waverly Annals, the History of Henry of Huntingdon and the poem of Gaimar," *Archæological Journal*, LXIX (1912), 312–70.

[2] Listed in chronological order.

Jolliffe, J. E. A. The Constitutional History of Medieval England. London, 1937.

Kemble, J. M. Codex diplomaticus aevi Saxonici. 6 vols. London, English Historical Society, 1839–48.

Liebermann, F. Die Gesetze der Angelsachsen. 3 vols. Halle, 1903–16.

Plummer, Charles. Two of the Saxon Chronicles Parallel. 2 vols. Oxford, 1892–99. Vol. II, §§ 4–64, 116, and *passim*.

—— ed. Venerabilis Baedae opera historica. 2 vols. Oxford, 1896.

Smith, A. H. The Parker Chronicle (832–900). London, 1935.

Theopold, Ludwig. Kritische Untersuchungen über die Quellen zur angelsæchsischen Geschichte des achten Jahrhunderts. Lemgo, 1872.

THE LANGUAGE OF E

Bachman, Walter. Lautlehre des älteren Teiles der Chronik von Peterborough. Weida, 1927.

Behm, O. P. The Language of the Later Part of the Peterborough Chronicle. Uppsala, 1884.

Einarsson, Stefán. "Two Scandinavianisms in the Peterborough Chronicle," *Journal of English and Germanic Philology*, XXXVII (1938), 18–20.

Meyer, Heinrich. Zur Sprache der jüngeren Teile der Chronik von Peterborough. Freiburg im Breisgau, 1889.

Robertson, W. A. Tempus und Modus in der ae. Chronik, hss. A und E. Marburg, 1906.

Roth, Wilhelm. Die Wortstellung im Aussagehauptsatz angelsächsischer Originalprosa (Annalen 800–900, 1066–1154), Kapitel A-E. Berlin, 1914.

Rothstein, Ewald. Wortstellung in der Peterborough Chronicle. "Studien zur englischen Philologie," Vol. LXIV. Halle, 1922.

PLACE NAMES IN E

For a list of investigations on English place names, see the bibliography by F. P. Magoun, Jr., in L. J. Paetow, *A Guide to the Study of Medieval History*, rev. ed. (New York, 1931), pp. 46–53. The survey of the English Place-Name Society has dealt to date with the following counties: Bedfordshire, Buckinghamshire, Cambridgeshire, Devon, Essex, Hertfordshire, Huntingdonshire, Middlesex, Northamptonshire, Nottinghamshire, Surrey, Sussex, Warwickshire, Wiltshire, Worcestershire, Yorkshire (North Riding, East Riding). Special investigations of Chronicle place names are confined to the following works.

Magoun, F. P., Jr. "Territorial, Place-, and River-Names in the Old-English Chronicle, *A*-Text (Parker Ms.), *Harvard Studies and Notes in Philology and Literature*, XVIII (1935), 69–111. (Cited as Magoun, I.)

Magoun, F. P., Jr. "Territorial, Place-, and River-Names in the Old-English Annals, *D*-Text (Ms. Cotton Tiberius B. IV)," *Harvard Studies and Notes in Philology and Literature,* XX (1938), 147–80. (Cited as Magoun, II.)

Mawer, A. "Some Place-Name Identifications in the Anglo-Saxon Chronicles." In *Anglica* (Berlin, 1925), I, 41–54.

HISTORICAL STUDIES

Collingwood, R. G., and J. N. L. Myres. Roman Britain and the English Settlements. 2d ed. Oxford, 1937.

Hodgkin, R. H. History of the Anglo-Saxons. 2d ed. 2 vols. London, 1939. The notes supply a comprehensive modern bibliography of general and detailed studies on various aspects of Old English history up to the death of Alfred.

Oman, Charles. England before the Norman Conquest. 8th ed. London, 1938.

Stevenson, W. H. Asser's Life of King Alfred. Oxford, 1904.

INDEX

The abbreviations abp., bp., bro., dau., used after names designate archbishop, bishop, brother, daughter.